LOVE AND DEPTH IN THE AMERICAN NOVEL

Love and Depth in the American Novel

FROM STOWE TO JAMES

ASHLEY C. BARNES

University of Virginia Press · Charlottesville and London

University of Virginia Press
© 2020 by the Rector and Visitors of the University of Virginia
All rights reserved
Printed in the United States of America on acid-free paper

First published 2020

9 8 7 6 5 4 3 2 1

Library of Congress Cataloging-in-Publication Data

Names: Barnes, Ashley C., author.
Title: Love and depth in the American novel / Ashley C. Barnes.
Description: Charlottesville ; London : University of Virginia Press, 2020. | Includes
    bibliographical references and index.
Identifiers: LCCN 2019034811 (print) | LCCN 2019034812 (ebook) |
    ISBN 9780813944180 (hardcover) | ISBN 9780813944197 (paperback) |
    ISBN 9780813944203 (epub)
Subjects: LCSH: American fiction—19th century—History and criticism. | Love in
    literature—History and criticism. | Criticism—Moral and ethical aspects. | Ethics in
    literature. | Canon (Literature)
Classification: LCC PS374.L6 B37 2020 (print) | LCC PS374.L6 (ebook) |
    DDC 813/.3093543—dc23
LC record available at https://lccn.loc.gov/2019034811
LC ebook record available at https://lccn.loc.gov/2019034812

Cover art: Tom and Eva from *Uncle Tom's Cabin,* 1855 (Harry Ransom Center,
University of Texas at Austin); iStock/bernie_photo

CONTENTS

Acknowledgments   vii

Introduction   1

ONE   Love and Depth Canonized: Anti-Catholicism
and the Shaping of American Literary Standards   27

TWO   Sentimental Communion: Protestant Reading
Meets Catholic Worship in *Uncle Tom's Cabin*
and *The Gates Ajar*   53

THREE   Romantic Spectatorship: Self-Portrait as
a Stranger's Head in *The Blithedale Romance*
and *Pierre*   88

FOUR   Realistic Intercourse: Arranging Oneself
for Another in *The Morgesons* and
The Golden Bowl   123

FIVE   Love and Depth Revisited: History and
the Ethics of Reading American Literature Now   162

Notes   191

Bibliography   203

Index   219

ACKNOWLEDGMENTS

I am no longer sure there was a time when I was not writing this book, but there must have been a beginning, and it is fortunate for me that Dorothy Hale was there to superintend this project at the start. She taught me how to think and argue about literary texts. If any readers of this book find it convincing, they should attribute that to the years she dedicated to helping me learn to make sense. Dorri Beam has been equally crucial to this book's development; she taught me how to think and argue about nineteenth-century American literature. Over the years she has helped me navigate the discipline, intellectually and professionally. Finally, I am grateful for the exemplary intelligence and patience brought to bear on my early work on this book by Samuel Otter and by Robert Alter.

Huge thanks to the English Department at Williams College for harboring me for so long and for providing such an encouraging place to write and teach and talk about books. The solidarity I found there with my fellow visiting assistant professors, especially with Margaux Cowden, kept me going.

It was a generous destiny that landed me at the University of Texas at Dallas, where I have been aided and abetted by my colleagues in the School of Arts and Humanities. I am especially grateful to Charles Hatfield, Annelise Heinz, Natalie Ring, Eric Schlereth, Shilyh Warren, Dan Wickberg, and Ben Wright for reading so many thousands of the words I wrote. The Texas branch of the Society for the Study of American Women Writers, where Desiree Henderson and Claudia Stokes have been especially supportive interlocutors, has been a vital source of conversation and camaraderie.

I am also indebted to farther-flung readers who have offered feedback at various stages of this project: Alex Benson, Anjuli Fatima Raza Kolb,

Ashley Reed, John Carlos Rowe, Cindy Weinstein, and two anonymous readers at *Legacy: A Journal of American Women Writers*. I am available to read anything any of you have written, anytime.

I thank the journals that have published versions of this work for allowing it to reappear in these pages. An early version of chapter 2 was published as "The Word Made Exhibition: Protestant Reading Meets Catholic Worship in *Uncle Tom's Cabin* and *The Gates Ajar*" in *Legacy*, vol. 29, no. 2 (2012): 179–200. Material now included in chapter 4 was published as "Fanny and Bob Forever: The Collage Aesthetic and the Love Story in *The Golden Bowl*" in the *Henry James Review*, vol. 35, no. 2 (2014): 95–115, and also appeared in *Henry James Today*, edited by John Carlos Rowe (Cambridge Scholars Publishing, 2014). An essay containing some of the material from chapter 3 was published as "Variations on a Melodrama: Imagining the Author in *Pierre* and *Of One Blood*" in *Arizona Quarterly*, vol. 73, no. 3 (2017): 23–47.

The staff at the Winterthur Library, who helped me investigate nineteenth-century interior decoration, were generous to a fault, as was Michael Gilmore at the Harry Ransom Center (HRC) in Austin. He spent more time and energy than I could reasonably ask for in helping me make use of their Uncle Tom's Cabin Collection. Both the HRC and Winterthur are full of wonderful things, and I wish I could write about them all.

I am grateful to Eric Brandt at the University of Virginia Press, whose enthusiasm for publishing this book gave me the very best reason to finish writing it. I appreciate his support, and Helen Marie Chandler's help, as the manuscript assumed its final shape. The anonymous readers for UVA Press responded to my work with a judiciousness and insight that helped me to see it anew and, I hope, to strengthen it.

Finally, it is my parents, Rudy and Jeanette Barnes, who taught me to read and write, period, and who taught me half of what I know about love in real life. The other half I learned from my husband, Jon Malesic, who is my favorite twenty-first-century writer, the best of readers, and a joy to inhabit the world with. This one goes out to you.

LOVE AND DEPTH IN THE AMERICAN NOVEL

Introduction

IN 1910, THE POPULAR NOVELIST Elizabeth Stuart Phelps published an essay, "The Great Hope," in a collection gathered by the influential editor of the *Atlantic Monthly*, William Dean Howells. Titled *In After Days*, the volume brought together notable writers in their sunset years who had been asked (tactfully, one hopes) to consider life after death. Phelps takes the occasion to argue that love is the engine of eternal life. But while "young lovers believe in the eternity of love—their own, and that of others," Phelps does not put full faith in married love, a fallible "attempt to fix" our "affectional errancy."[1] A more likely candidate for heavenly love is friendship, a bond whose "firmer qualities" nonetheless allow the unfolding of the "serial story" that is love (38, 40). What might await us in heaven is less a rapturous fulfillment than an intimacy that allows for change and growth. This is a fitting view for a writer who plotted character arcs for three novels about the afterlife.

Henry James also contributed an essay to *In After Days*. To the question he poses in his title—"Is There a Life after Death?"—he eventually answers yes. For James the chance of eternal life grows "in proportion as we do curiously and lovingly . . . try and test and explore, our general productive and, as we like conveniently to say, creative awareness of things."[2] The force that might last beyond death is this creative relation between the artist's "exquisite curiosity" and the universe's boundless stimuli, a circuit of desire that James sees as endlessly "fed and fed, rewarded and rewarded" (222). The artist needs the universe to feed his loving curiosity; the universe needs the artist to share its wealth. James, a writer for whom the adventure of consciousness is all the adventure a novel needs, proposes that this shared mental productivity is ceaseless.

Phelps's and James's responses appear to match the expected contrast between a bestselling sentimentalist and the man who invented prestige fiction. Phelps imagines love between persons; James imagines an affair between artist and universe. Where Phelps is concrete, James is abstract; where she is therapeutic, he is analytic. Likewise, the contrast between Phelps's confident references to God and James's hints that theology is "built on" "splendid illusion[s]" (233) accords with our sense that Phelps belongs to a presecular age, James to a modern demystified one.

But both were writing about the possibility of heaven at the start of the twentieth century. Both express faith in a kind of love that transcends the mortal self. Both Phelps's friendship and James's creative awareness name a desire that is mutable but enduring as the guarantor of immortality. And, crucially for the argument of this book, neither imagines that transcendent love as the full and final union of souls or as the definitive revelation of cosmic truth. What they describe is different from the ecstatic vision Herman Melville recorded in a letter to Nathaniel Hawthorne, recalling his sense that "your heart beat in my ribs and mine in yours, and both in God's."[3] Melville's is an image of revelatory love, consummated. Phelps and James imagine a love both less erotic and more persistent: the seemingly endless desire of friendship and shared curiosity.

That kind of love fits the model I call "communion." Communion, as I use the term, stands as an alternative to the apparently deeper love of mutual revelation that might be figured by the heart-swapping merge Melville imagines. Both Melville and Hawthorne do portray versions of communion in their fiction, and Phelps and James develop a more complex picture of communion in their own novels. Portrayals of love in fiction are what ground my argument in this book. But the two essays from *In After Days* serve to point out that both Phelps and James could be found in the same early twentieth-century volume proposing a self-other relation that would last forever. Each describes a nonrevelatory, non- (though not anti) climactic desire that pushes the self beyond itself and joins it to an other, perhaps for eternity.

The likeness between Phelps's and James's visions of desire has been all but invisible in American literary history, and this book aims to explain why. That explanation bears on a current critical impasse. For literary studies in general, the proverbial claim that "to know X is to love X" seldom applies; literary scholars seem bound to know a text or love it, but not both. That separation plays out as a false choice between historical perception versus ethical engagement. The critic may knowingly pin a text to a web of discourses so as to expose its role in cultural history, the handling often accorded to sentimental novels like those by Phelps. Or he may lovingly set it free from temporal contexts so as to appreciate its otherness, as has frequently been done with James's work. The ethicist cannot imagine real love attaching to what is historically localized; the historicist cannot imagine real knowledge affirming what it sees as the myth of timeless intimacy. These polarized positions are united, however, by a shared faith that the aim of reading is to reveal a deep truth, whether that truth is the mystery of otherness or the hard facts of history. The difference is that ethicist lovers tend to avert their eyes from the revelation while historicist knowers boldly present it.

Understanding how literary scholars came to live with this forced choice is one task of this book. I will argue that the choice either to love a book or to know it is the result of a methodological allegiance to an ideal of revelation. Another task of this book is to propose communion as an alternative model of interpretive intimacy, a model that encompasses historicist and ethicist aims. I locate this alternative in later nineteenth-century fictional portrayals of love and in the Christian debates about how to know and love God that undergird such fictions.

By juxtaposing fictional with religious discourses, this book shows that depth is a literary ideal with roots in a theological ideal: a claim for private, unmediated revelation as the right way to access the divine. By reading this theological history in tandem with literary representations of love, we can see the ideal of revelatory love as the product of a Protestant reaction against Catholic practice in mid-to-late nineteenth-century American culture. Communion, on the other hand, emerges as a resistant, Catholic-inflected model of knowing and loving. The result of this analysis is a sectarian genealogy of the competing versions of love that take form in American fiction. This book uses that account to argue for an ethics of historically contextualized reading. It thus aims to revise both how we think of the American love story and how we imagine the love of literature.

By reading theological history in tandem with literary representations of love, *Love and Depth in the American Novel* helps build a postsecular account of the American novel and how it has been read. I will say more below about the rationale and payoffs of that postsecular approach, and chapter 1 offers a more detailed account of that transition from religious to literary standards. But, in brief, how did an anti-Catholic argument for the best way to access God become an argument for the best American fiction and the right way to read it? Broadly speaking, a Protestant ideal of revelation took shape as a work of self-definition and self-defense against a growing Catholic population across the nineteenth century. Protestant clergy asserted the potential for revelation in the private encounter between a reader and the God he found in the Bible over against a Catholic model of loving and knowing God that was deemed impoverished because it was mediated through public ritual and historical institutions.

This self-defense generated a protocol both affective and interpretive because, for Protestants, reading the Bible taught a believer what transcendent love looked like and how it should feel to read about it. When the Bible is understood to be the message of God's love, a reader's true feeling can validate her true understanding of the text. And to claim to be closer to God than your competitor by virtue of the deeper feeling with which you read God's word is to occupy the final court of appeal. That claim grants one side legitimacy as the arbiter of broad questions of truth and value—theological, moral, political, and cultural. Social pressures in the nineteenth century gave Protestant leaders a motive to make such claims more emphatic. Losing the demographic battle to immigrant Catholics, Protestant elites asserted their more immediate and intense love of God, attained through personal reading, against the cheap intimacy offered by the mediated rituals of the Roman Catholic Church.

The terms of these theological arguments circulated throughout the nineteenth century in both popular and academic channels. The logic of those arguments framed wider discussions of visual and material culture that continued over the turn of the century. We can see the ideal of revelation, which I also call the "Protestant depth drive," migrating to American literary studies in the Melville revival in the 1920s, when critics enshrined authors whose writing provoked the feeling of a mysterious revelation withheld. This depth drive shaped the reading practices that supported both the construction and the deconstruction of the American literary canon. And a Protestant ideal of revelatory love continues to shape the possibilities for literary ethics, a rubric under which I include postcritique, new formalism, affect theory, and surface and reparative reading. The love story of communion resists the Protestant ideal of revelation. The novels that tell this story selectively co-opt Catholic practice to imagine a love that is mediated and public but still claims access to an otherness beyond the self. Phelps and James are both elite Protestants, but their fiction suggests their reach toward a Catholic-inflected ideal of communion rather than the Protestant ideal of deep revelation. All of the novels in this study manifest a Protestant co-opting of Catholic practices that is aimed at deflecting the depth drive. Harriet Beecher Stowe's *Uncle Tom's Cabin* and Phelps's *The Gates Ajar,* Hawthorne's *The Blithedale Romance* and Melville's *Pierre,* and Elizabeth Stoddard's *The Morgesons* and James's *The Golden Bowl* all imagine how characters might love each other without revelation. Both formally and thematically—and despite their genre distinctions as evangelical sentimentalism, gothic romance, or psychological realism—these novels incorporate aspects of Catholicism to present a love that is genuine and enduring, but not deeply revelatory.

The full significance and the shared vision of these love stories only emerge in the context of contemporaneous Christian debates over how to know and love God. I analyze the novels through the lens of historical archives that show how Protestant-Catholic conflict, and the contest between revelation and communion, defined interpretive and emotional protocols for American culture in and out of church. These archives include guides to Bible reading, debates over whether Jesus's portrait should be painted, and advice on decorating a spiritually vibrant home. Those contexts provide examples of how communion and revelation framed either/or choices both for theological interpretation and for everyday interpretive problems.

Seen in such contexts, what does communion look like in these novels? It appears in Stowe's Eva and Tom bonding over their free-associative Bible reading; in the pleasure Hawthorne's Miles Coverdale takes in watching Zenobia perform; in the understanding that Stoddard's Cassandra and Veronica Morgeson achieve by admiring each other's clothes. The great American love story that was canonized by Leslie Fiedler's *Love and Death in the American Novel* is a tale built on the frustrated longing for revelatory union. But characters like Stowe's Eva and Tom or James's Fanny and Bob Assingham do not gaze into each other's souls or plumb each other's depths. The world does not disappear when they are together. Instead they interpret the world of discourse—the Bible, the ongoing story of their friends' affairs—they inhabit together. These couples love each other by cocreating something new out of that shared context. It may seem a stretch to identify all of these relationships as love. But in each case we are presented with a relationship that allows the self to apprehend real otherness in a potentially endless intimacy.

Love and Depth aims to answer a literary-ethical question—what does it mean to know and love a text?—by using literary-historical methods. Under the rubric of ethicist criticism, I group scholars who see the "reading experience as a scene of virtual interpersonality," to use the characterization Lawrence Buell applied in 1999 when literary ethics was emerging as a distinct approach.[4] Martha Nussbaum had already made the case for reading as falling in love in her 1990 book *Love's Knowledge,* as Wayne Booth had made the case for reading as friendship in 1988's *The Company We Keep.* But the interpersonal reading approach need not be so explicitly humanist. The ideal of reading for intimacy with the text-as-other is equally available to poststructural and posthumanist treatments, as scholars from Gayatri Spivak to Judith Butler to J. Hillis Miller have demonstrated. Such interpretations, I argue, project a love story between the reader and the text, a story that may end in satisfaction or in yearning, depending on whether the text's otherness gets revealed or remains veiled.

Chapter 5 offers a more detailed analysis of literary-ethical approaches, but I want to clarify my investments here at the outset. The value of literary ethics lies in its articulation of how reading activates our desires for community and our moral imaginations. I count myself a sympathizer with Rita Felski's argument for a reading that attends to "the coconstitution of texts and readers" without "divorcing intellectual rigor from affective attachment."[5] I share the urge of surface and reparative readers to resist a hermeneutic that makes depth the only valid object of knowledge or of desire. I believe we need literary ethics to keep reminding us of the affective dimension of reading, of the social imagination that literature engages, and of the moral consequences of that engagement. But ethicists would do that work better if they read a wider range of texts that offer a wider range of intimacies.

The literary critics who pursue the ethics of reading, whether Nussbaum or Hillis Miller, Booth or Butler, have constructed a narrow canon. They valorize the likes of Henry James, Toni Morrison, and J. M. Coetzee, but they ignore the overtly ethical sentimental novel. Their preference testifies to an emotional elitism that loves only texts that adhere to a modernist aesthetic of restraint and opacity. Critics in the ethicist camp often privilege reading that requires what Dorothy Hale calls "self-binding," to discipline the desire for a revelation of otherness that never arrives.[6] This withholding of revelation grants the reader the most potent sense of the almost-thereness of transcendent difference, a reading experience that is simultaneously elevating and humbling. For a literary ethicist who wants to avoid the bad interpretation of colonizing sympathy or of ideological unveiling, this unconsummated desire is what true intimacy feels like. The result is a prescription for critical humility in the face of mystery. This ethicist prescription seems designed to assuage a widespread suspicion that English professors are guilty of producing an "affective deformation" in their vulnerable students, as Deidre Lynch puts it, by hardening those students' hearts against literary appeals.[7] But self-binding in the face of possible revelation is not the only way to feel close to the otherness of literature.

Love and Depth argues for widening the range of emotional attachments that count for ethical reading of a text. In pursuing that broad agenda, this book can be seen as joining a reform from within the ethicist camp. It answers Felski's call to "expand our repertoire of critical moods while embracing a richer array of critical methods" (13). It also joins C. Namwali Serpell's effort to move beyond literary ethics' allegiance to "an undifferentiated Otherness" that produces "a species of humble-bragging" on the part of the ethical critic.[8] Her own work applies an "Empsonian formalism" (23) to account for an eclectic emotional range of reader-text experiences, including vacuity and flippancy. For Serpell, "A literary text affords aesthetic, affective, and ethical experiences as we read over time" (22). My claim is that one such experience afforded by literature is historical. It is not that a text offers a window onto, or a mirror of, the past. Rather, a text's idiosyncratic engagement with the discourses of its moment calls us to reenvision the world inhabited by the text then, and, by extension, the one we inhabit now. In practice, a literary-ethical historicism resembles the hybrid of historicism and formalism that Marjorie Levinson describes as appreciating a text's unique power by examining how that text's "design" rearranges elements of the historical reality it inhabits.[9]

That is my intervention into the ethics of reading. I argue that literary ethics must accept—and, even more important, demonstrate—that historical contextualizing can forge real intimacy with literature. Too often the ethicist argument for loving literature has made historicist contextualizing at worst an enemy, or at best irrelevant, to critical intimacy. Too often it privileges a variety of love that isolates the text in an eternal present. There are better ways to defend the love of literature than ethicists have yet availed themselves of. They have turned to abstractions like surface and depth in order to distinguish reading for pleasure from reading for mastery. Such spatial metaphors are useful for provoking conversation about reading methods, as we saw from the debate that followed Stephen Best and Sharon Marcus's essay on surface reading in *Representations* in 2009. Even more useful, because it names an attitude toward the text and not a metaphorical geometry, is Eve Sedgwick's argument for reparative reading. But by applying the lens of Protestant-Catholic conflict, this book trades the inexact metaphors of surface and depth, and the ahistorical attitudes of reparation and suspicion, for terms rooted in a specific history with specific cultural politics.

It is worth clarifying that my argument focuses not on the full range of worship practices but on two idealized modes of contact with the divine: Protestant Bible reading and Catholic mass-going. This book is not an account of Protestant theology as such. It focuses on the Protestant-inflected approach to reading that gained clout in the northeastern United States in the latter half of the nineteenth century. And I focus less on Catholicism as such than I do on Catholicism as it existed in the Protestant imagination. The versions of communion that I identify in the half-dozen novels I read and in the cultural contexts informing those novels project, from within Protestantism, a partial reconciliation with the Catholic faith. The aim of understanding how nineteenth-century anti-Catholicism naturalized an ideal of revelatory love is to help current literary ethicists move beyond critiques that judge historicism as unloving and to think through different, historically grounded ways of approaching the radical otherness of a text.

Communion is one such alternative. It follows contextualist and historicist reading methods. Communion need not claim a definitive unpacking of the text itself. Reading as a relationship of communion looks more like collaboration with the text; it is motivated by something similar to the friendly curiosity that James and Phelps speak of. Such an approach wants to generate a broader interpretation of that text in its world, reading the text in concert with other discursive and material artifacts that belong to its time and place. From either of the extreme versions of revelatory reading, such interpretive communion looks faulty. Ethicist critics lump such contextual historicism with ideology critique and accuse it of being hardhearted. Historicist critics devoted to exposure accuse contextual historicism of softheadedness and narcissism. These criticisms may well be justified by the faults of any given interpretation. And revelatory reading of either persuasion is both necessary and valuable. But the extremes have for too long claimed theirs as the only defensible positions.

The ethical intervention made by *Love and Depth* has consequences for American literary studies. For example, it challenges the history of the American canon. We have long understood that the principles of exclusion that built the initial canon were based on race and gender and class. We have not seen so clearly that those principles were also sectarian. The critics who assembled the initial canon could credit themselves with eliminating the overt religiosity of sentimental novels. Later critics who dismantled that initial canon could credit themselves with eliminating the covert religiosity of claims for Hawthorne's or Melville's sublimity. But often, in practice, the reaction of historicism served to replace the old reverence for the timeless paradoxes of art with a new reverence for a deep ideological truth. Whether it guides the historicist critic who exposes sentimentality's bad faith, or the ethical critic who submits to a veiled Jamesian otherness, the idea that the text's deep power must be either exposed or submitted to continues to divide American literary studies.

Chapter 1 offers an account of how the anti-Catholic interpretive model of the Protestant depth drive shaped American literary history in its formative years. Two basic crux points will suggest how I see the revelatory ideal in action. Early on, Perry Miller or F. O. Matthiessen ventured to identify the guiding American spirit that vivified a historical text. Later, Richard Brodhead or Donald Pease aimed to show the historical motor that animated a spiritualized text. Either way the structuring assumptions of revelation remained in place. Early or late, critics sought the emotional payoff of revelation as a proof of real intimacy with the textual other. The later affair, however, has gone sour: the critic has shifted from a good lover to a bad one, from reverentially attentive to suspiciously prying. Felski describes this will-to-expose as the emotional appetite of critique (9). Sedgwick recognizes that "paranoia is a form of love."[10] But whether the critic jealously rummages the text to find its sins, or patiently waits for the text to reveal itself, love is provoked only by depth, and love's payoff—even if it never quite arrives—is understood as revelation. There are plenty of historicist critics who do not aim at such exposure. These are model readers, in my view. Yet literary ethics of the twenty-first century has not recognized such historicist intimacy, but instead has resumed the role of protecting the revelatory power of a text against the exposure that it sees as the aim of historicism.

The term "transcendence," as I use it in this book, functions within literary-ethical discussions of what constitutes a true understanding of true otherness. When I refer to communion as transcendent, or call communion a form of relationship with transcendence, I mean that communion achieves an intimacy with genuine otherness that is experienced as ongoing and inexhaustible. As in the essays by Phelps and James, "transcendence" signifies a relation that pushes decisively beyond the self and its moment-by-moment existence. That is an expansive definition, but it is consistent with the breadth of understandings I find in the love stories that are my textual focus and in the theologically inflected discourses that those stories engage.

Love and Depth does not make a theological argument. It does argue that theology has significantly shaped literary scholars' answers to the questions of what it means to know and love a text. My point that communion and revelation offer comparable access to literary and ethical transcendence is based on these two models' history as competing routes to the same theological transcendence—that is, to union with God. I want to specify the ways our vocabulary for talking about the ethics of reading has been shaped by this particular intra-Christian debate. To expunge the language of transcendence would be untrue to both the archival and the fictional texts I have assembled. I retain the term "transcendence," finally, to challenge the Protestant protocol that suspects that any interpretation aimed at something less than revelation must be solipsistic. That Protestant standard does not comprehend all the possibilities of transcendence.

Unlike the Protestant ideal of revelation, a Catholic-inflected practice of communion can imagine transcendence as embedded in the world, materializable and visible, hence its potential as a resource for denaturing the split between literary ethics and literary historicism. To overcome that split requires reimagining the love of literature such that one thing we might love about a text—one thing that could make a text feel transcendently other—is its historical agency.

I am aware that transcendence is a term with an "ideological function," as Carolyn Porter reminds us.[11] The idea of transcendence has served to extract a text from history, the better both to call it beautiful and to deny its political agency. Indeed, this ideology of transcendence finds its emotional justification in the Protestant standard of revelation. When the truly other is defined as beyond, not within, history, then an encounter with otherness that is mediated through historical context counts as bad intimacy. By that standard, to attain true love or true knowledge requires an encounter that makes the self tremble at near-contact with the timeless other. That hierarchy of true versus false love enables the interiorization of religious or aesthetic experience to register as an emotional gain.

To call a text transcendent in that ideological sense, as Porter argues, obfuscates the text's real power, which is to act in its own time and place. To advance a historicist literary ethics, I argue that we should reconceive transcendence as the literary power that Porter says inheres in a text's "active force within the discursive field" of its time and place (263). That active force is what I mean by the transcendent power of textual otherness. On this model of literary ethics, transcendent alterity can only be contacted when a reader engages a text in its discursive field. To put it another way, I am trying in this book to strip transcendence of its familiar ideological function and to sustain its ethical function as signifying a text's otherness, defined here as its unique power to act in history.

One final reason to maintain and to redefine the term "transcendence" is the postsecular approach of this study. My motive is not to remystify literature—nor, for that matter, am I trying to demystify it by historicizing the religious sources of the particular version of transcendence that became the gold standard for the objects and methods of literary study. A postsecular approach does not treat religion as an isolatable, stable phenomenon, but studies how and why the designation "religious" slips from one phenomenon to another. Indeed, as Charles LaPorte and Sebastian Lecourt write, "the idea of religion as a distinct sphere of beliefs and practices regarding transcendent values is largely an invention of modern Europe and therefore, as much as anything else, an effect of secularization."[12] Postsecular studies assumes that religion has not vanished with modernity but has translated into unexpected forms. And it assumes that in the modern world, as Charles Taylor has argued, multiple equivalent forms of transcendence coexist.[13]

Not all of those forms of transcendence enjoy an equivalent degree of cultural power. I single out this particular pair—the nineteenth-century American versions of Protestant and Catholic transcendence—to show how the winning Protestant version left its stamp on the interpretive and emotional ideals of American literary study. The Protestant defense against Catholic practice is arguably the motive force for secularization in American, if not European, modernity. As Tracy Fessenden puts it, "Protestantism's emancipation from Catholicism both provides the blueprint for, and sets the limits of, secularism's emancipation from 'religion' itself."[14] In studying American culture generally, a postsecular approach helps us "recognize," as Ashley Reed puts it, "how the American public sphere is structured by a set of assumptions about human experience that are drawn directly from Protestant doctrine and practice," a "de facto Protestant bias" that "obscures other modes of religious experience."[15] My point in working through this episode of American Christian intellectual history is to show how anti-Catholicism, as it influenced literary aesthetics, obscured alternative models of accessing transcendent otherness like the one I am identifying as communion. Reading through this religious history will help scholars of American literature recognize ways to love literature, and ways to conceive literary value, that escape residual forms of anti-Catholic anxiety.

It is true that the field of American literary studies has long recognized the Protestantism embedded in its own origin story. But the emotional and interpretive consequences of that Protestant allegiance have not been carefully enough examined. As Sarah Rivett recounts, the Perry Miller-inspired view of an American mind that was essentially Puritan lost traction in the 1980s as scholars turned against accounts that had made American Protestantism into a justification for American exceptionalism.[16] That turn did succeed in critiquing the Protestant-inflected claims to transcendence that undergirded the origins thesis and the original canon. New Historicists and New Americanists, however, were not interested in exploring, or owning, alternate versions of the relation to transcendence that might have served as ideals for literary study. For some of the most influential critics, the motive was to expose what they saw as false claims for literary transcendence by revealing what was really real: the historical unconscious or Foucauldian power networks. Such critics maintained the faith that truth lay behind a mediating screen.

If we have given up the idea that religion must fade in the bright light of modernity, American literary criticism would do better to examine than to disavow its debts to Christian debates and practices. A starting place would be a reexamination of the familiar genres of the sentimental, the romantic, and the realist—categories that serve to reinforce the secularization thesis. They adhere to a timeline whereby the Civil War marks a before-and-after pivot between a more religious and a more skeptical American literature. The overlap I proposed at the outset of this introduction—between Phelps's and James's ideas about the desire that generates immortality—already suggests the faultiness of any theory of a smooth trajectory toward modern unbelief. The love story of communion challenges that march toward demystification. It shows how evangelical sentimentalists, conflicted romantics, and sharp-eyed realists all share a vision of interpersonal connection that resists the ideal of revelation without abandoning a claim to intimacy with genuine alterity. That continuity has gone unremarked upon because the Protestant ideal of revelation continues to define what counts as depth or transcendence, whether depth or transcendence is a quality a given critic wishes to debunk or to defend.

This postsecular approach is valuable for literary studies more broadly. To recognize the Protestantism that has influenced critical methodology is to acknowledge what Deidre Lynch calls the "productive confusions" between sacred and secular reading in establishing paradigms for literary studies.[17] We may have heard the news that literary studies is not as secular as we once thought it was. Yet, as Michael Kaufmann observes, "professional histories" of literary studies still tend to rely on the "conviction that religion has long ago been left behind" to safeguard "the boundaries of a . . . secular academic discipline."[18] It is also common to hear claims like Franco Moretti's, that close reading is a "theological exercise."[19] Heather Love observes that critics' tendency to focus on "the singularity and richness of individual texts" reproduces the "encounter with a divine and inscrutable message" that she sees as the mark of Christian reading.[20] Arguments like Moretti's and Love's suggest the illegitimacy of close reading by aligning it with religiosity. I understand their objections to critical sanctimony, but such critiques overgeneralize the religious sources of reading and obscure the development of particular models of divine encounter in American culture. The result is a facile identification of close reading with pious Bible study. What Love and Moretti have described is something like the revelatory ideal established by a specifically conservative Protestantism. And, in fact, seemingly irreligious literary historicism has theological precedents in biblical historicism, a point I take up in chapter 1. In general, the effort to purify literary study of its religious antecedents has been more wishful than productive.

This book's effort to develop a more complex religious genealogy of the emotional protocols of reading shows how postsecularism serves both deconstructive and reconstructive purposes. Postsecularism may be said to deconstruct, for instance, when it argues that claims for secularity serve as professional hygiene or that Protestant values organize our basic methodological options. This argument also challenges the idea that the distinctions between sentimental, romantic, and realistic modes are strictly aesthetic. To see the religious history built into those categories is to understand that what is at stake in these generic distinctions is an argument over how to access transcendence. But postsecularism also serves reconstructive purposes. By considering how Catholic-Protestant tensions have shaped literary methods and categories, we gain access to a model of the love of literature that recognizes the desirability of works based on their embeddedness in a time and place, not just on their withholding revelation. The authors examined in Love and Depth all share a vision of mediated love that resists the Protestant ideal of revelation. That shared vision stands as a distinct claim to a transcendent intimacy that could go on forever.

I find perhaps the strongest reconstructive purpose for postsecular study articulated by Jenny Franchot's 1995 accounting of the faults in American literary scholarship. In an observation that still feels relevant, Franchot writes that American literary scholars did a disservice to their field by uncritically embracing a historical-materialist account of the subject and avoiding "a working familiarity with the competing ontological view, represented not by the subject but by the person—that is, a created individual who possesses varying amounts of free will, an immortal soul, and a guiding sense of an eternal destination."[21] She abjures Americanists not to dismiss such a concept of the person as naïve without examining it seriously. Franchot is discouraged by accounts that explain away religious commitment as effects of race and gender, analytic categories "deemed safer" (837) or more "interesting" (840) than religion. She finds that "to avoid being seen in the wrong light," "scholars are everywhere quietly ex- pected to perform" the "colonizing move" that "resituate[s] a particular sacred or an individual's interior life"—particularly individuals who are not white men—"into an understanding of culture that denies transcen- dence" (840). As she writes, "In our negation of mystery and conscience as categories of experience that disrupt deterministic, particularizing accounts of human identity . . . we disqualify ourselves from authoring profound scholarship" (836).

Sustaining the concept of transcendence does not require ignoring historical conflict, as Franchot herself pointed out. I hope to avoid the mistake Tracy Fessenden has more recently identified with postsecular studies: "Their subordination of particular histories, content, and contexts to some essential sacred something."[22] Such studies have the effect of reaf- firming that religion is a primitive stage by framing as a "laudable change" the shift "from a religious past . . . to a 'spiritual' present in which 'belief without content' prevails."[23] I do want to historicize revelatory reading as the product of an anti-Catholic argument that "my god is more transcen- dent than yours, because my love for him is deeper." My aim, though, is not to explain away the possibility of transcendence, but to show the value of the alternative account of transcendence that lost the contest. Readers will decide whether I succeed at striking that balance, but I want to affirm here that it is a balance worth striking.

In taking a postsecular approach, *Love and Depth* aims to intervene in the deadlock between ethicist versus historicist approaches. That in- tervention accounts for my focus on novels. *Love and Depth* joins a line of ethicist studies of novels including Nussbaum's *Love's Knowledge* to Serpell's *Seven Modes of Uncertainty* and others. Victorian novelists like George Eliot and Charles Dickens claim the novel as the incubator of sympathy; twentieth-century critics claiming an ethical value for novels can turn to the theory of heteroglossia developed by Mikhail Bakhtin, for whom the novel at its best represents the multivocal social world, and for whom poetry tends toward univocal expression.[24] For twenty-first century ethicist critics, as Dorothy Hale explains, the novel is a privileged genre because it so compellingly presents a world of deep subjectivity and then undercuts that depth with uncertainty. The novel's character development invites us to identify with and judge a fictional other, but the text itself (if it does its job right) refuses the reader the satisfaction of closure or certainty. Novels thus teach us the impossibility of the identifications and judgments we want to make (197).

But I also want to offer an alternative view of American literary history, one that proposes a different lineage from that found in, for example, Matthiessen's *American Renaissance.* So it might seem necessary to contend with the nonfiction and poetry of Henry David Thoreau, Ralph Waldo Emerson, and Walt Whitman. Thoreau is a potent spokesman for the revelatory ideal; when he reads a book by an author who "raised a corner of the veil from the statue of the divinity," in that reading Thoreau can "gaze upon as fresh a glory" as the author did; it is as if "no time has elapsed since that divinity was revealed."[25] Emerson is important to the development of the Protestant depth drive, too, and I will discuss his heterodox theology in chapter 1. Whitman is perhaps the most exuberant lover known to nineteenth-century American literature. And Whitman's poetry, insofar as it enables "the reader's discovery of what was never hidden" and does not hide but "releases erotic potentialities into every register of social life," as Peter Coviello puts it, does an exemplary job of resisting the Protestant depth drive.[26]

But the categories that most broadly define nineteenth-century American literature—evangelical sentimentalism, gothic romance, and psychological realism—are grounded in works of fiction. That is why this literary history requires arguing that versions of the same distinct desire manifest across those familiar boundaries. I want to claim the love story of communion as a viable narrative by which to reframe the American great-books list. That is why I focus on major works by major authors. These writers' work has been pivotal in both the construction and deconstruction of the American literary canon.

Love stories, in particular, have long figured as an important genre in histories of the novel because they allegorize the act of reading. Like detective stories, but with a more vigorous head-versus-heart conflict, love stories train readers in the protocols of interpretation. Writing about the realist novel in Britain, Leo Bersani notes that "the happy marriages" that conclude courtship plots "are the just consequences and rewards of just perceptions of character."[27] Deidre Lynch points out that in *Pride and Prejudice,* Jane Austen "celebrates the activity of interpretation" in order to "celebrate true love."[28] Perception is a tool for arriving at love, and love is both the reward and proof of a successful reading of another person. The same lesson can be taught by counterexample. Seduction novels reinforce the knowing-as-loving equation by telling the unhappy version of the story, where faulty reading of a meretricious suitor dooms a heroine to death. Extending that logic, Tony Tanner finds in the novel of adultery an allegory of the breakdown of the reader-text relationship.[29]

If novels about love are primers for how to read both books and people, the novel form itself has also been cast as a primer for how to read oneself, specifically as a deep psychological subject. Histories of the novel see it as a technology that produced the modern liberal subject. As Lynch argues, scenes like that of Elizabeth rereading Darcy's letter "present novel readers with instructions in fashioning an individualized interiority" (131). For Georg Lukacs, the novel's form indicates the "process of the problematic individual's journeying toward himself,"[30] and for Ian Watt, the novel furthers "not just the primacy of individual experience but the uniqueness of individual perception."[31] This is an individual constituted by private, not public, desires. Nancy Armstrong's *Desire and Domestic Fiction* argues that the novel of love in eighteenth- and nineteenth-century Britain shifted the locus of social control from a "collective body" to the individual and her "psychological motives."[32] Samuel Richardson's heroine Pamela is exemplary in making the letters she hides in her dress the source of her desirability, and thereby in helping us picture the human interior as a text to be deciphered. In these accounts, the novel form in general, and the love story in particular, teach us to privilege revelation. I make the case for a countertradition of novels of love that resisted the formation of the private liberal subject.

The accounts I have cited focus on British literature. But the novel of love matters to the American literary tradition too. In 2003 Ross Posnock would propose that Fiedler's 1948 "Come Back to the Raft Ag'in, Huck Honey," the essay that taught us to see Huck and Jim as lovers and introduced the thesis that *Love and Death* would develop, is "the most influential single essay ever written about American literature."³³ Fiedler's account means to puncture nationalist pieties about our literary greatness by showing the racialized desire that drove the American Adam into the wild. For many of Fiedler's colleagues, American novels are great because they abandoned the realist marriage plots of the British novel for a romance of self-invention.³⁴ Fiedler shows that there is a love plot in American fiction, too: a pattern of same-sex cross-race desire running through our best work. Such desire has to be veiled. But telling that love story enables American authors to achieve what Fiedler sees as the novel's work of carrying the torch to the back of the mental cave.³⁵

Fielder's work thus shows that revelation is also the ideal for knowing and loving in an antisocial, gothic fiction. In his account, the great American love story is the ever-baffled quest to access the depth of another soul. *Love and Death* also recognizes Protestant anti-Catholicism as a key driver of the literary ideal of revelation withheld. Fiedler begins his history of the novel in Europe, where he finds the bourgeois Protestant mind riven by commingled disgust with and longing for the Catholic faith. Having rejected the pagan figure of the great mother—a figure, Fiedler says, that Catholicism wisely retains as the Virgin Mary—the Protestant mind finds itself compelled to read and write novels. Novels exist, Fiedler says, in order to "satisfy the secret hunger of the puritanical bourgeoisie" with "bootlegged madonnas."³⁶ The gothic novel in particular, the form that American authors would adopt as their own, "feeds on what its principles abhor, the ritual and glitter, the politics and pageantry of the Roman Church" (138). In the American novel, those madonnas transform into the dark-skinned men who are most sinned against and thus most impossibly desirable. Fiedler argues for the dominant tradition of American love stories as a white man's imagined reconciliation between black and white. I argue for a different tradition of the love story that stands as a Protestant's imagined reconciliation between Catholic and Protestant faith.

According to Fiedler, it is only white male American authors who succeed at telling the tale of revelatory desire suppressed. As Robyn Wiegman observes, Fiedler's argument ultimately erases both the dark-skinned object of desire and the queerness of the desire itself, absorbing them into a drama of awakening white male genius.³⁷ Though he was a self-styled maverick and a Jewish intellectual in a WASP-y academy, Fiedler's

devotion to the aesthetic value of withheld revelation reinforces a conservative Protestant reading style. *Love and Death* reaffirms the value of
the same novelists Matthiessen anoints in his *American Renaissance*. And
though Fiedler justifiably sees himself taking sociohistorical conditions
into account more than his New Critical colleagues do, he is a historicist only on the grand scale. He does not concern himself with the local
development of tastes and perceptual habits that manifest in the anti-
Catholic discourse of the nineteenth century. To account for the attrac-
tion/repulsion of anti-Catholicism in American writing in a way that is
both psychologically and politically astute takes a historicist eye—like
that of a Jenny Franchot, Elizabeth Fenton, or Tracy Fessenden—reading
a wider range of texts.

That is why, in its effort to reframe the love of American literature, this
book adopts the basic historicist strategy of juxtaposing archival and contextual material with the text of the novels. My argument shares with affect
theory and psychoanalytic approaches an urge to take seriously the feeling
of reading. And, as those approaches often do, my work here depends on
the close analysis of idealized visions of reading. My key evidence is a selection of love stories, read in light of contemporaneous Christian debates.
This book is not an empirical study of actual nineteenth-century readers,
and it does not make claims for the experience of such readers. My claims
concern the tradition of the American novel and the modes of literary
practice prevailing today.

Like Gillian Silverman's account of nineteenth-century reading in *Bodies and Books,* for example, I examine how "fantasies of communion . . .
precipitate[d]" by "book reading" are portrayed."[38] Unlike Silverman,
though, I define "communion" through its use in religious discourse of
the time, rather than applying the frameworks of Freudian theory or phe-
nomenology. If the structures of feeling I call "revelation" and "communion" are persistent, they are not transhistorical. By contextualizing those
novelistic images of interpretive intimacy, and by tracking them diachronically with the codevelopment of religious and literary standards, I build
a genealogy of reading ideals that have shaped American literary studies.

In its wish to historicize forms of reader-text intimacy, *Love and Depth*
resembles Deidre Lynch's 2015 *Loving Literature,* which shows how literary
studies came to be identified with emotional labor during its disciplinary

genesis in eighteenth- and nineteenth-century Britain. Lynch tracks competing varieties of intimate experience with texts—"grateful love," "possessive love," "habitual" love, and "elegiac love" (15)—as a way to examine the development of modern subjectivity and the reading practices that sustain that subjectivity. My work aims to show how American literary scholars' critical affections have been guided by religious ideals, and I use this history to advocate for reintroducing a rival form of readerly intimacy into a field dominated by the depth drive. That advocacy follows from my investment in literary ethics, which seeks a model for the love of literature. That aim sets my work apart from the more thoroughgoing historicism of Lynch or of, say, Peter Coviello.[39] Their studies treat readers' and texts' accounts of intimacy not as potential models for our current practice but as signifiers in a broader political and cultural history. *Love and Depth* constructs a cultural history of reading to support an argument for an alternative mode of critical practice.

Reading the novels in a context suggested by the novels' own preoccupations—with Bible reading, with portraiture, with home decoration—was how I began this project. Only over time did I begin to see in those archival materials a pattern of Catholic-Protestant conflict that could help account for the novels' portrayals of love. In other words, *Love and Depth* did not begin with the question of how Catholic-Protestant tensions shaped the nineteenth-century novel. It began with my interest in the love stories these novels tell, and it developed through the ordinary historicist program of close reading literary texts alongside extraliterary contexts.

When this project began, though—when I was training to be an Americanist—I had already been struck by the opposition between historicist and ethicist criticism. It seemed to me then that James's soap-operatic plots and dramatic recognitions were at least adjacent, if not indebted, to the good-versus-evil showdowns and maudlin scenes of sentimentality of which many critics (including James himself) disapproved. I admired James more, but why exactly had he been nominated the apogee of novelistic development and the sentimental its nadir? Among ethicist scholars, James is tantamount to a patron saint; why didn't Stowe merit the position of at least a fairy godmother? And not only were ethicist critics not interested in sentimental texts; they were also not interested in anything happening in the world in which the book appeared. Learning the field as a student, I saw that many scholars of American literature were interested in both. In contrast to ethicists, Americanists read all sorts of texts, regardless of their literary prestige, and they seemed admirably self-aware about the contingency of their own interpretive values. I examine these scholarly camps in detail in chapter 5, but a preliminary account is appropriate here.

Americanists' own limitations emerged as I read their carefully historicized accounts of sentimentalism, beginning with Ann Douglas (who attacks it) and Jane Tompkins (who defends it).[40] In many ways both Douglas and Tompkins are models of the passionate historicism that I want to endorse for literary ethics. They read broadly; they read texts that lack modernist virtues; they read those texts as embedded in a specific time and place and treat them as collaborators in creating a picture of the world. They also read with great relish for the power of those texts' language, even when the language displeases them. These scholars of the sentimental give the lie to the ethicist critic's complaint that historicism ignores emotional life. However, such studies do not foreground the basic query of the ethicist program that attracted me: the question of what reading literature teaches us about intersubjectivity. Instead, the terms of the Douglas-Tompkins debate tie the value of the sentimental novel either to its subversion or its containment of a reigning ideology.

The decades of scholarship on sentimentalism that followed the Douglas-Tompkins debate showed the limits of that approach. Sensitive as such critics are to the complexities of historical archives, keen as they are to spot the bad ethics enforced by patriarchy, white supremacy, and market ideology, their inquiries focus on the broad cultural effects produced by these texts. Such critics do not treat sentimental novels the way ethicist critics treat the novels of Henry James: as eliciting from the reader a complex and valuable relationship. If canonical men were frequently brought down a notch by reading their novels as participating in ideological evils, sentimental women (and noncanonical writers of any gender or color) are seldom brought up a notch by the aesthetic and ethical readings that had long been accorded to James and Melville. There is little sense that reading such works might offer ongoing creative pleasure. Too much scholarship on sentimentality, in other words, does bear the faults that Felski assigns to critique and that Sedgwick assigns to paranoid reading. It can be reductive and high-handed. It tends to disavow the critic's emotional engagement with, and the agency of, a text. It treats as naive the view that reading is an encounter with otherness.

I have said that revelation and communion are equivalent in their claims to access transcendent difference. And if I aim to dethrone revelation, I do not wish to disavow it as a model of interpretive love. But the communion I see taking shape in nineteenth-century sources does have its advantages. As a model for interpretation, the love story of communion reduces the pressure on the text-as-other to reveal itself as eternal alterity. The self-transcending intimacy of communion emerges not by seeing (or almost seeing) the other's core, nor by grasping (or nearly grasping) the other's truth. Communion does not claim to know the other fully or deeply. Instead communion enables self-transcendence by enabling the self to see the other as a fellow mediator who crucially changes the self's relation to the world they both inhabit.

Communion thus avoids the potential aggression of revelatory reading. Ethicist readings often rightly warn against such aggression by enjoining the reader to accept the bafflement of his desire. But, in so doing, ethicist readings too readily deny the value of a reader's projections and exclude the possibility of the text and its context as collaborators with, rather than objects of, the reader's desire. The love story of communion shows how a reader's projections, refracted through the text and its context, may provide both an experience of transcendent communion and the payoff of a good interpretation.

Lest I make this model of love sound boundlessly positive, it is worth pointing out the limits of the model of communion and the limits of the works that make up this study. I chose these novels because they are key battleground texts for historicist versus ethicist approaches. To begin with Stowe and end with James is to demonstrate the split in American literary studies that I want to reconcile: an opposition that divides the culturally significant books worth knowing from the ethically compelling ones worth loving. But the Catholic-Protestant binary cannot explain all of American literary history. And while the novels in this study challenge the dominance of an ideal of revelatory intimacy, they do not extend that challenge beyond picturing different ways for white people to love one another.

This study's postsecular framework can, however, extend our analysis of the exclusions from the canon of African American and women writers.

The interiority and invisibility claimed by deep revelatory love serve to bolster white men's crucial privilege of seeing without being seen—of being a perfectly free, disembodied spirit over against a body marked black or female or both. I develop that point in chapter 3, in a discussion of the anxiety around portraits of masculine authorship. But, in brief, the Protestant representational economy of withheld revelation attached a raced and feminized otherness to Catholic practice. To the Protestant observer, Catholics made God the object of the gaze of the public eye—a position of disempowerment assigned more broadly to women and to dark-skinned persons. The love story of communion challenges this logic of invisible power. And to ask how a specifically religious hermeneutic shapes the emotional ideals we use for reading people and reading books is to raise a portable question, one that can be put to any set of texts produced in a given historical context. We could and should use this analytic lens to reconsider varieties of desire that circulate outside the world of elite white Protestants. By asking whether revelation is the one true way to encounter a text's otherness, we can begin to rethink what it means to love literature written anywhere or anytime.

The book is organized as a literary history framed by a methodological history. Chapter 1, "Love and Depth Canonized: Anti-Catholicism and the Shaping of American Literary Standards," begins that methodological survey. It examines how nineteenth-century anti-Catholic Protestantism informs early twentieth-century antisentimental aesthetics. The claim for revelation, for an ideal of unmediated private understanding, was crucial to nineteenth-century Protestant self-definition against a rising Catholic population. A conservative antihistoricist Protestantism carried forward the revelatory ideal through the turn of the century, and the work of early twentieth-century neo-orthodox theologians helped bolster the standards of New Criticism. The literary canon formed in those decades has long since expanded, its standards of artistic transcendence dismissed as naive. But revelation, whether framed as a positive goal or a forbidden fruit, continues to define our objects and methods of study.

Chapters 2, 3, and 4 constitute the literary-historical heart of the book. These historically contextualized readings establish the love story of communion that models the interpretive intimacy I call on literary ethicists to adopt. Chapter 2, "Sentimental Communion: Protestant Reading Meets

Catholic Worship in *Uncle Tom's Cabin* and *The Gates Ajar*," establishes the Catholic-inflected ideal of communion in two evangelical bestsellers. Harriet Beecher Stowe and Elizabeth Stuart Phelps offer explicit appreciations of Catholic practice. Seen in the light of Protestant guidebooks advocating deep reading of the Bible to get close to God, the vision of love in these two novels clearly resists the Protestant depth drive. The intimate bond between Eva and Tom, like that between Phelps's Mary and Winifred, emerges through their reading of theology, an ongoing work of interpretation that does not seek hidden answers but uses texts as a field for shared imagining.

The paradigm of communion shifts from character-to-character to reader-to-author in chapter 3, "Romantic Spectatorship: Self-Portrait as a Stranger's Head in *The Blithedale Romance* and *Pierre*." In those novels Nathaniel Hawthorne and Herman Melville portray depth-obsessed protagonists who are displaced self-portraits of the authors themselves. Reading these novels with contemporaneous debates about painted portraits of masculine power—images of George Washington and of Jesus—this chapter shows how communion's embrace of mediation can challenge a Protestant cult of invisibility. Both novels push their readers toward a model of intimacy as the shared spectatorship of a represented self.

The final step in this three-part literary-historical revision comes with a pair of authors who, despite the decades between them, both practice a protomodern psychological realism. Chapter 4, "Realistic Intercourse: Arranging Oneself for Another in *The Morgesons* and *The Golden Bowl*," shows Elizabeth Stoddard and Henry James imagining characters who deliberately make spectacles of themselves. In Stoddard and James the high visibility afforded by clothes and collectibles does not provide a map to the soul beneath, but neither do such trappings hinder real intimacy. Characters like Cassy and Veronica and Fanny and Bob love each other through shared representational projects: ongoing redecoration of costume and setting for the sisters, endless editing of their friends' stories for the wife and husband.

Chapter 5, "Love and Depth Revisited: History and the Ethics of Reading American Literature Now," returns to the methodological survey of chapter 1 and brings it up to the present. It offers a history of the ethical turn since the 1990s, showing how the Protestant depth drive lives on in the split between the historicism of American literary scholarship and the critique of that historicism by literary ethicists including Wayne Booth, Martha Nussbaum, Derek Attridge, and Heather Love. The most recent such critiques draw on new formalism, surface reading, and affect theory to charge historicism with mean-spiritedness. Although some historicist scholarship is reductive, it is a mistake to believe that emotional openness requires an ahistorical approach. Many historicists do read with emotional sensitivity. The book concludes with a call to literary ethicists (among whom I count myself) to adopt material and historical methods, as exemplified by chapters 2 through 4, and to expand their range of intimacies by expanding the range of texts they get intimate with.

The resistant love story of communion presented in *Love and Depth* is not a happier, heteronormative version of the canonical love story of frustrated desire between Queequeg and Ishmael or Jim and Huck. The novels I read here give us couples who are mentor and mentee, imaginary reader and imaginary author, sister and sister, and middle-aged wife and husband. These novels posit human relationship as the collaborative interpretation of a shared world. As we saw in the essays that Phelps and James wrote for *In After Days,* such an affectionally errant and curious variety of love is posited as capable of transcending the self, of becoming otherworldly, because the connection it forges between self and other can keep going on and on. The love stories I consider present these bonds as a worthy alternative—as truly intimate, as genuinely transcendent—to the withheld revelation that American literary studies has valorized for so long. Communion aspires to transcendence not because it sees an eternal truth beneath the surface, but because its shared interpretive work lets desire proliferate endlessly.

One

Love and Depth Canonized

Anti-Catholicism and the Shaping
of American Literary Standards

IN 1870, A REVIEWER FOR THE *Christian Union* objected to Elizabeth
Stuart Phelps's *The Gates Ajar,* a bestseller published two years earlier. The
novel's heroine worries that Protestants have drifted too far from Catholic
practice; the novel's reviewer accuses Phelps of drifting too far from Protestant propriety. Phelps's sentimental style has, for this reviewer, violated
what is identified as God's own aesthetic of withheld revelation: "This lady
is inexcusable in not knowing that God has restrained himself in his revelations, restrained his words, restrained his hand in his pictures, to outlines
only, in shadowy glimpses—awful, beautiful, tender. But Miss P. fills out the
utterances—completes the pictures, and makes them earthly and sensual,
to be laughed at by the world and grieved over by all who fear to trifle with
the Scriptures."[1] The reviewer, arguing for the superiority of awful shadowy
restraint over earthly sensual pictorialism, finds Phelps's prose objectionable for the same reason Catholic worship was objectionable to Protestant
commentators. Both sentimentalism and Catholicism made God's revelations publicly available to the world's senses. If revelation was not restrained, if it became a show anyone could see, it would lose the quality
that made it count as real intimacy: the quality of love that comes from the
sense that you alone have earned the right to see those shadowy glimpses.
The review demonstrates how a theological objection to excess entails an
aesthetic objection to excess. Both are linked by an ideal of intimacy where
restraint on one side provokes awed tenderness on the other.

    This chapter presents a bird's-eye view of the translation of the emo-
tional and interpretive ideals articulated by the *Christian Union* review
into the American literary canon. My aim is to show how a doctrine of
revelation that would become the ideal of American literary study in its

formative years found its motivating context in a conservative Protestant-ism that began as anti-Catholic and became antihistoricist. The logic of that conservative Protestant discourse, its claim for more intensely inti-mate interpretation, would repeat in New Critical claims for the greatness of Melville and James and Hawthorne. In brief, the ideal of withheld reve-lation emerges from conservative anti-Catholicism in the middle nine-teenth century, gathers fuel from theological antihistoricism in the late nineteenth century, and coalesces in the antisentimentalism of the New Critics' early twentieth-century American literary canon. At some mo-ments along this path, we can see the direct adoption by literary critics of Protestant principles. At other moments the influence appears indirect. Throughout, I mean to clarify the interdependence of the religious and literary ideals that define what it means to know and love a text.

I focus on a localized American episode in what could be construed as a very long story about the migration of revelation from Greek and biblical sources to German philosophy and Anglo-American poetics. We can source the language of revelation back to Plato's myth of the cave or to the through-the-glass-darkly rhetoric of Paul's letters.[2] We could track its development into an aesthetics of the sublime from Immanuel Kant to Samuel Taylor Coleridge to the American Transcendentalists.[3] In 1902, the conservative Protestant James Hall Brookes presented his own version of such a trajectory. Brookes blamed the liberal German theologian Fried-rich Schleiermacher for denying the Bible as revelation and recasting it as a sublime human achievement, a view Brookes saw as having spread virally to Coleridge and then to Matthew Arnold and his ilk, who "carried it to its unavoidable extreme" in a claim for the inspiration found in wind, trees, and cattle.[4] Such romanticism would also be rejected by the more broadly influential force of neo-orthodox Protestantism in the decades to come, when thinkers like Karl Barth would reassert the gulf between the merely sublime and the truly divine. The antiromantic rhetoric of neo-orthodox thinkers, finally, would bolster the antisentimentalism of emergent American literary studies. I end this chapter with the late twentieth-century debate over sentimentality—not the usual Douglas ver-sus Tompkins fight, but Douglas versus Sedgwick—and resume tracking the revelatory ideal in American literary studies in chapter 5, where it drives the tension between historicism and literary ethics today.

I begin by examining the logic whereby nineteenth-century Protestants proposed to get closer to God than Catholics did. A conservative, anti-Catholic brand of interpretation asserted its freedom from mediations both aesthetic (excessively visual or tactile aids to worship) and historical (church tradition or the contexts of the Bible's writing). The sign of properly unmediated reading was the experience of spontaneous, illuminating love—a felt contact with the divine—that rewarded diligent effort. On the contrary, for the Catholic-inflected model of communion, such transcendent intimacy was facilitated by mediations that appeal to the bodily senses and to a continuity with the past. Thus, in the love story of communion, as in *The Gates Ajar,* intimacy is experienced as enduring affection routed through a mediator (theological texts, in this case) rather than as a singular one-on-one transformation. The love story of communion resists anti-Catholic definitions of good reading and real intimacy and offers instead a distinctly unorthodox Protestant alternative.

In arguing for the Catholicized love story of communion as an overlooked tradition in histories of the American novel, I draw on the many excellent studies of how anti-Catholicism energized Protestant efforts to define nineteenth-century American culture. This chapter builds on such work by Jenny Franchot, Tracy Fessenden, Elizabeth Fenton, and Susan Griffin. Anti-Catholicism takes many manifestations. Mine is a necessarily limited treatment. I focus on the convergence of the emotional, aesthetic, and interpretive ideals disseminated by anti-Catholicism in American culture. Those ideals circulated broadly, seeking to define real love and good reading in multiple interpretive situations. In what follows, I take the sacrament of mass as representative of Catholic ways of getting close to God, and the reading of the Bible as representative of Protestant ways of getting close to God. I do not mean to reduce doctrinal differences between Protestants and Catholics to a contest between people who believe in words and abstractions and people who believe in wafers and crucifixes. But examining the polemical logic that built that contrast will help us understand the persistence of the false choice between literary historicism and literary ethics, between contextualizing and close reading, that still constrains our practice today.

Most broadly, Catholic tradition dictated that God's grace came through the sacrament of communion: tangible, publicly consumed, and, in the hands of a priest, capable of transubstantiation. Frederick William Faber, one of the most influential midcentury Catholic devotional writers, used language expressing the same fervent desire for union with God seen in Protestant texts: "We in Him, and He in us; He and we one together."[5] But, in contrast to the Protestant for whom such a merge with the divine would be sought through the pages of the Bible, Faber understood such union to occur through the mediation of church ritual.

By contrast, the Protestant argument for reading as a superior route to God was simultaneously an argument for the superiority of aesthetic restraint. Because words, unlike images, do not look like what they mean but must be deciphered inside a reader's head, they can claim a special propriety in rendering that which, like God, is held to be essentially invisible. In this account, the simplicity of the Bible's language could guarantee the exclusivity of the reader's access to the spirit that moved through the text. In that private space inside their heads, the intimacy that Protestants enjoyed through reading became a unique possession. Free from the mediation of priestly rituals and vivid images, free from the intervention of church tradition or biblical history, the love a believer felt for and with God was her very own. Reading thus enabled an unbeatable claim to religious authority, allowing Protestants to say, in effect, we are closer to God than you are because the love we feel with him is realer.

Certainly Protestants did not always act out their faith according to the anti-Catholic bias articulated by their theological leadership. (I present examples of official Protestant guidance for Bible study in chapter 2.) They did not always read their bibles seeking deep revelation. Reading out loud, and in groups, was the norm for consuming both sacred and secular texts.[6] And to some observers it seemed the Bible was scarcely read at all. Henry David Thoreau wrote that, despite "the bigotry with which [the New Testament] is defended," "I know of no book that has so few readers."[7] Martin Marty cites that line in arguing for understanding the Bible as an icon, "an object in the national shrine, whether read or not, whether observed or not: it is seen as being basic to national and religious communities' existence."[8] A family bible could be a "piece of furniture, a decorative addition" to the parlor, as Paul C. Gutjahr notes.[9] Nineteenth-century publishers competed to distinguish their offerings with "increasingly complex commentaries, luxurious illustrations, and ornate bindings"; such bibles would be displayed in the home to signal the family's gentility as much as its piety (41, 44). The traveling salesmen who distributed bibles for the American Tract Society reported instances of what looks like outright fetishization of sacred texts. One report told of a woman in rural New Jersey who had wrapped a tract in linen, apparently without ever reading it, and who wanted another copy.[10]

Such examples show that the Catholic-friendly Protestantism I find animating the love stories of major novels was not uncommon in ordinary practice. Ann Taves proposes that Protestant veneration of the Bible was a "functional equivalent" to Catholic devotions to the Blessed Sacrament.[11] Mary Kelley analyzes an early nineteenth-century example of what she calls "pen and ink communion": a Maine pastor and his family who metaphorically "[partook] of the host in the form of reading and writing" together.[12] These Protestant equivalents to communion try to graft materiality on to the virtuality of reading. But if they practiced mediated forms of worship, Protestants largely preached a doctrine of immediacy. That doctrine undergirds arguments by both theological conservatives and liberals. Phelps's conservative reviewer faults her for an unorthodox materializing of the Bible; liberal Protestants could fault a dogmatic piety for treating the Bible as a thing. Theodore Parker, a liberal who insisted on God's continuing revelation to his creatures, laments that more orthodox Protestants "regarded [the Bible] as the heathen their idol, or the savage his fetish."[13] It was this doctrine of dematerialized immediacy and its accompanying feeling of revelatory love that would later prove most adaptable to literary interpretation.

By sharpening the contrast between Catholic and Protestant ways of knowing the divine, I mean to illuminate an instance of what Tracy Fessenden calls the "consolidation of a Protestant ideology that has grown more entrenched and controlling even as its manifestations have often become less visibly religious."[14] One way Protestant ideology has become less visibly religious is in its evolution from anti-Catholic claims about how to read the Bible into antisentimental claims about how to read American literature. In particular, I argue, the characteristic marks of Protestantism—its iconoclasm, its distrust of rituals performed by authority figures—are the correlates of a specific definition of love. In effect, conservative Protestants constructed a love story between a reader and the God he found in his Bible. That story rejected crucifixes as distractions and the priest as a pander.

It also meant rejecting a prose style that threatened to manipulate the independence of a reader's feelings. We rightly think of sentimentality as a Protestant style, but it was a liberal Protestant style, and it was vulnerable to some of the same attacks that conservative Protestants leveled at Catholic worship. To more conservative Protestants, the sentimentalizing liberals in their own ranks could trivialize contact with God just as Catholics did by overtly mediating that contact. Later in the century, conservative Protestants would also blame historicizing liberals for materializing the transcendent.

The claim of potential revelation had to be protected by two kinds of immediacy. First, as already noted, aesthetic immediacy stripped away what were deemed excessive sensory appeals that might lay too heavy a hand on the reader's heart. The words on the page were sufficient. This aesthetic minimalism was guided by the perception of the scripture's unadorned concision, which kept its invitation to love discreet. Second, and equally important, was the claim for temporal immediacy. The potential for scripture as a source of private revelation meant reading it less as a historical document and more as a message received in the moment of the reader's encounter with the pages. An aesthetic minimalism and a suspension of history were requisite if this anti-Catholic love story between God and the reader was to end happily.

IN THE BEGINNING: PROTESTANT BIBLE
READING AS REVELATION

Susan Griffin reminds us that "Protestantism had, from its inception, emphasized the individual's unmediated relationship with God."[15] For the Puritan settlers, as David Holland writes, the Bible had recorded God's last official word and the sacred canon was closed. But within those bounds, direct messaging was still possible for believers: "passages of scripture" might "[bolt] into the mind of their own accord, as if the scripture were restated personally for them."[16] The emphasis on such immediacy was potentially disruptive. As Nathan Hatch writes, Protestants found the doctrine of *sola scriptura* "an effective banner to unfurl when attacking Catholics on the right, but always a bit troublesome when common people began to take the teaching seriously."[17] Anne Hutchinson and Joseph Smith, let alone Nat Turner, went too far in declaring new revelations. A still small voice, or a feeling of overwhelming love, was a more appropriate payoff. Horace Bushnell was accounted a radical at midcentury, but as decades passed his claim that any hungry reader of the Bible could find a revelatory love there—could "find his nature flooded with senses, vastnesses, and powers of truth, such as it is even greatness to feel"—would become widely acceptable.[18]

This Protestant emphasis on an unmediated relationship gathered polemical force, grounding claims for broad cultural superiority, as the Catholic outstripped the Protestant population in America. Sydney Ahlstrom writes that "by 1850 Roman Catholics . . . had become the country's largest religious communion," with 1.75 million members, and it would double that figure by 1860.[19] Many of these Catholics were newly arrived Americans, and, as Ahlstrom puts it, "every immigrant ship at the wharf made the older political elites more apprehensive about the country's future" (557). Reading the Bible came to seem a native-born right threatened by a foreign faith. The riots that would destroy "whole blocks of Irish homes, "two Catholic churches," "a convent," and a "seminary" in Philadelphia in 1844 were triggered by a false report that local authorities had allowed Catholics to "[ban] the Bible from the schools."[20] Alexander Campbell would argue in 1837 that the "Roman Catholic religion . . . is essentially anti-American" on grounds that it "oppos[es] the general reading of the scriptures . . . so essential to liberty and the permanence of good government."[21] Henry Ward Beecher would repeat that theme in 1861, preaching that "where you have had a Bible that the priests interpreted, you have had a king."[22] Roman Catholicism was enchaining; American Protestantism was liberating. What made the difference was reading the Bible.

If Protestants felt that Bible reading was a public good that needed sometimes violent defense, equally crucial was the right to read privately. As Claudia Stokes notes, "Private Bible reading" was a Protestant doctrine that "acquired particular currency" because it was felt to defend against "a perceived Catholic threat."[23] Elizabeth Fenton likewise observes that anti-Catholicism in nineteenth-century America broadly establishes "a logic of private and public that equates privacy with freedom and thereby treats 'Protestantism' . . . as the means of safeguarding liberty."[24] Privacy meant not only physical but intellectual solitude, a sense of oneself as the first reader. Alexander Campbell's preferred method was to read the scriptures "as though no one had read them before me." His father, Thomas Campbell, had likewise urged in 1809 that faith required believers "to see with our own eyes, and to take all our measures directly and immediately from the Divine standard."[25] The Campbells' "Restorationist hermeneutics," Mark Noll writes, "represented the extreme statement of a common position" (381). The widespread equation of reading with personal freedom grounded the sectarian claim for revelation as a Protestant prerogative.

Such immediacy assured that what the reader felt in reading was her own emotion, not facilitated by some go-between. Perhaps paradoxically, the spontaneous feeling that resulted from aesthetic minimalism required work. It was a hard-earned emotional payoff that was both the cost and the benefit of eschewing sensory appeals. Nativist preacher William Nevins makes the case for the invidious distinction between an overaccessible materiality in Catholic worship and a harder-to-come-by interiority in Protestant worship. As Nevins wrote, whereas Protestants "have to bring before the *mind* of the sinner the great saving truth of Christ *crucified*," Catholics "can *regenerate* and *pardon*" a worshiper just by "put[ting] the little *crucifix* in his *hand*."[26] The Catholic claim that the bread and wine a priest dispensed could transform the worshiper's soul made the soul dependent on the priest as go-between. By contrast, the mental labor that Nevins endorses projects a believer who is hardworking and independent. That difficulty was the sign that you had earned the experience of knowing and loving God. Those qualities made Bible reading an ideal activity through which to assert the Protestant claim to revelatory intimacy. That emphasis on effort, though, could push Protestants to defect. Jenny Franchot observes that converts to Catholicism often sought "a way of knowing and of being in society" that could resist "Protestant cultural validations of the willing self" who transforms himself just by wanting it enough (239).

Even among conservative evangelicals, the sacrament was downplayed: according to Ahlstrom, it was performed only "quarterly" and its efficacy was understood as a "subjective" matter; the real presence of Christ in the bread and wine "was not asserted" (625). Protestants whose liberalism veered into transcendentalist heresy, like Ralph Waldo Emerson, were equally adamant in rejecting aesthetic mediations as vitiating their intimacy with God. Emerson had been mentored by William Ellery Channing, who described a union with God that tapped "a depth in human love which may be strictly called unfathomable," a love that answered "the tendency of the soul to the infinite."[27] When Emerson resigned his position as a Unitarian minister, he named as one cause of that resignation his failure to feel deep enough emotion in administering the Lord's Supper.

Emerson's farewell sermon asserts that the point of reenacting the Lord's Supper is so that "men might be filled with [Jesus's] spirit," but he finds "the *use of the elements*" of bread and wine "is foreign and unsuited to affect us."[28] Emerson suggests that if Jesus personally told him that the sacrament of communion was the right way to worship him, and "yet on trial it was disagreeable to my own feelings, I should not adopt it"; he allows that Jesus might play the role of "an Instructor," which for him was the "only sense in which possibly any being can mediate between God and man" (75). But "in the moment when you make the least petition to God, though it be but a silent wish that he may approve you," then "the soul stands alone with God" (75). Even Jesus would disappear.

Such liberal Protestantism could turn, just as the conservative William Nevins did, to anti-Catholicism as a tool for filtering good from bad ways of reading for God's presence. Horace Bushnell, a liberal Congregationalist and an occasional nativist agitator, would develop a widely influential romantic theology of revelatory reading. Bushnell admired Samuel Taylor Coleridge's view of the Bible as poetic symbolism, particularly Coleridge's claim that the Bible, read rightly, "finds" its reader.[29] Bushnell explained scripture's power to find its reader by theorizing words as portals to an immaterial transcendence. Words understood as "analogies, signs, shadows" opened onto invisible abstraction, "the formless mysteries above us and within us" (*God* 77). But words abused by mechanical repetition became "earthen vessels" or "wooden statues" (48, 72). For Bushnell the Catholic Church had been an instrument of deadening, by formalizing, that mystery. The Roman faith had turned the living mystery of God's love into a "vast human fabric of forms, offices, institutions, and honors; a storehouse of subtleties and scholastic opinions, a den of base intrigues and mercenary crimes" (288–89). An 1894 remembrance of Bushnell gives a sense of his legacy: he is praised chiefly for the poetic images of Jesus that he inspired in his listeners, but also for fighting to deny public funding for Catholic schools.[30]

The counterargument from Catholic believers focused on the illogic of positing reading as a means to unmediated contact with God. Catholic doctrine allowed that reading the Bible might be salutary. But it was not the privileged source of revealed truth that it was for Protestants. John Carroll, an eighteenth-century Jesuit who was the first Catholic bishop in America, challenged Protestants "to prove either, that no more was revealed, than is written; or that revealed doctrines derive their claim to our belief" by virtue of "their being reduced to writing."[31] The idea that the mere text of the Bible could make a reader intimate with God was an absurd reduction to Catholic commentators. "Christ nowhere enjoins reading the Bible," the *Catholic World* reminded its readers in 1883, and "one may know the whole Bible by heart without being thereby closer to Christ."[32] A text could not be identified with its author: "No account of Christ is Christ. . . . nobody nowadays needs to be told that the contents of a book, whatever these may be, are powerless to place its readers in direct contact and vital relations with its author. . . . All effort is vain to . . . stop the cravings of a soul for the living Saviour with a printed book!" (4). Here the Protestant argument for intimate reading is refuted on its own terms: the notion that some deep reality lies in wait beneath the surface of the printed page is a fantasy. Rather than charge the reader with transforming paper and ink into contact with the divine, Catholic faith relied on church tradition to interpret the Bible and to mediate access to God.

Catholic doctrine also countered the logic of Emerson's claim that the Lord's Supper was emotionally deadening. The prominent German Catholic apologist Johann Adam Möhler argued that the purpose of the eucharistic ritual was not to provoke "human feelings, considerations, and resolves," although such provocation was "necessary" (279–81). Man was more than his feelings; "belonging to the world of sense," the creature requires a "sensible medium" to convey God's grace to his soul, and by receiving the sacrament "divine matter impregnates the soul of man" (279, 281). Rejecting the Protestant identification of privacy and invisibility with power, Möhler spoke of invisibility as a stumbling block to belief that God had mercifully removed. The presence of God did not depend on a reader's solitary emotional susceptibility but existed mysteriously in things that could be eaten and drunk: "Catholics firmly hold" that God "changes the inward substance of the consecrated bread and wine into the body and blood of Christ" (310–11). For

Möhler, as for his Protestant counterparts, the aim was union with God. But that aim would be achieved through the act of consuming the host. Matter, not words, was productive of transcendent intimacy.

Catholic apologetics thus articulated a faith that sensible media do not detract from but open up to genuine otherness, and that books alone do not offer special access to transcendence. Communion in the church depended on belonging to an institution and participating in long-established rituals. The Protestant logic of revelatory intimacy rejected such historical mediations as hindering the intimacy with God that was available through the immediacy of private reading. That faith in the revelatory power of reading, over against the idea that transcendent otherness could be mediated by matter and by history, is the starting point for the connection I am drawing between anti-Catholic interpretive claims and the formation of the American literary canon.

THE CRISIS OF HIGHER CRITICISM: HISTORY AS A THREAT TO LOVE

If Protestants rejected sensible mediation because it threatened to make God too available, historical context was a mediator that might make God unavailable. Indeed, where Catholicism threatened the cultural dominance of Protestantism, historicism seemed a threat to Christian faith itself. The nineteenth-century Catholic Church in America, for its part, "emphasized the immutability of the church's truth" and denied the legitimacy of biblical historicism.[33] What was known as "higher criticism"—a term denoting the study of the Bible in its historical context—had become the leading edge of scholarship in German universities since the later eighteenth century.[34] Mark Noll identifies higher criticism as stirring a "flurry" of interest among New England theologians in the 1830s and 1840s, when such historical research was seen as congenial to orthodox faith.[35] Conservative Protestant theologians like Moses Stuart welcomed historicism as an aid to Bible-reading faith. Printers included maps in bibles as evidence that scripture had been empirically verified.[36] Postwar, in the 1870s, the surge of interest in biblical historicism returned, this time more clearly as a threat.

By then the combined forces of science and history—personified, as Paul C. Gutjahr writes, in the figures of Charles Darwin and Auguste

Comte—were positing an increasingly comprehensive ground-level account of human life that required no divine intervention (167–68). The allure of Catholicism's excessively vivid, unprivate access to God might be dealt with by policing sentimental sensibilities within Protestantism. The potential authority of biblical historicism to dispute personal interpretation could not be handled so easily. The Protestant claim that Bible reading could produce immediate intimacy with God came under increasing pressure as liberal theologians and skeptical historians produced a picture of the Bible as a highly mediated text. The publication of a revised translation of the Bible in 1881 was a hit, selling, as Gutjahr reports, "over three million copies in the opening months of the version's release" (110). Its initial popularity did not last, but the publicity that attended its scholarly construction over the prior decade effectively destabilized the authority of the King James Version that had been the only voice of God for many of the faithful.

The possibility that historicism would take the Bible out of a reader's hands and heart aggravated the divide between conservative and liberal Protestants. For conservatives, reading the Bible in its historical context was a project that came to be viewed with more and more suspicion during the nineteenth century. For such Protestants the historicist theologian, like historical context itself, was a meddler in the private relationship between a believer and her Bible. From this perspective, historicist criticism and Roman Catholicism were both European imports gaining an alarming popularity as potential sources of authority. Both were declared illegitimate. An editorial in the *Christian Observer* proposes that the "School of Radical Critics" are setting themselves up as "the basis of infallibility" for Protestant faith, just as "Romanism" puts "the Church . . . above the Scriptures."[37] The clergyman Willis Beecher compares higher criticism to the Roman Catholic Church's "assumption that the Bible is not for Christian people except as officially taught them through the Church," which is of all its doctrines the one most "objectionable to Protestants."[38]

More broadly, the idea of historicizing the Bible struck many conservative Protestants the same way that historicizing literature strikes some literary ethicists today: as a self-serving denial of the agency of the text. Conservatives responded by reemphasizing the revelatory power of God's word and denouncing the arrogance of those who declared the Bible man-made. The theologians that Robert Moore-Jumonville calls "anti-critics" identified pride as the sin committed by biblical historicists.[39] James Hall Brookes, cited above, was a key organizer of "the annual Niagara Bible Conferences for prophetic study" that met during the last quarter of the nineteenth century.[40] He defended the Bible as fully verbally inspired. Brookes found "brazen impudence and self-conceit" behind an 1883 *Unitarian Review* essay urging readers to judge the Bible's contents in light of historical discoveries (27). Brookes named Germany as the birthplace of the view, "so fatal not only to inspiration, but to revelation itself," that the Bible's value lies merely in the "sublime thoughts" of the fallible men who wrote it (16). B. B. Warfield objected to such histories on grounds that "Christians ought to consider Jesus 'not as a child of his time, limited by the mental outlook of his day,' but as the Lord of all times and seasons."[41] For A. T. Pierson, historicist critics were victims of hubris who congratulated themselves on knowing more history than Jesus did. Such readers failed by relying on "intelligence" when love was the proper interpretive tool: "Only love will interpret many mysteries, and only Love can ever fully interpret God's Book."[42]

More liberal theologians embraced historicism. For some, historicism helpfully sifted the eternal seed of truth from the merely local husk of myth and tribalism that especially clogged the Old Testament. Such theologians compensated for now-outdated scripture with a Schleiermacher-style religion of experience.[43] William Newton Clarke, for instance, admitted that discoveries in geology toppled his view of the Bible as inerrant—"I had allowed the Bible to be altered for me to suit the facts"—but "it was thus becoming more intimately my own because it was more alive, and was more available for my use in the ministry of Jesus Christ."[44] Others tried to accept historicism without surrendering the Bible's status as a document of revelation. One such mediator was Charles Briggs, subject of "probably the best known heresy trial in American religious history."[45] That trial was prompted by an 1891 speech in which Briggs denounced Protestant bibliolatry and recognized the institutional church as a source of authority for the Bible. Briggs would spend his career arguing for the reconciliation of Catholic and Protestant churches.[46] Milton Terry was another mediating theologian who saw it as the task of the exegete "to disengage himself from the living present, and thus transport himself into a past age" ("not an easy task," Terry admitted).[47] For Terry, the historical reality uncovered by critical biblical study added to, rather than subtracted from, faith: "Seeing Palestine is, indeed, a fifth gospel" (234). But the reader today needed to maintain a critical distance to rightly see the Bible as a timebound document. In reading the texts left by men who had heard God's word, "the biblical interpreter should not allow his vision to be so dazzled by the glory of their divine mission as to make him blind to facts of their history" (232). This mediating position did not finally provide a stable middle ground, and the split between conservative and liberal approaches grew wider.

The antielitist, a-man-and-his-book strain that characterized conservative reactions to biblical historicism would be institutionalized early in the twentieth century in James Gray's "synthetic reading" program. President of the Moody Bible Institute from 1904 to 1934, Gray advocated a rigorous program of close reading. Just as the New Critics would prescribe, in 1904's handbook for synthetic reading *How to Master the English Bible* Gray promotes reading the Bible—"at first at least"—independently of outside aids.[48] It is too easy, he warns, for readers to fall down critical rabbit holes and lose what should be a sustaining view of the whole biblical landscape. An independent reading also enables the reader to feel for himself the text's "most precious and thrilling experiences of spiritual illumination" (49–50). Gray assures his readers that the Bible is "wondrously self-interpreting," such that questions raised in the epistle to the Hebrews can be answered by returning to Genesis, if they would "simply read" it and "submissively follow the channel laid out by its divine Author" (42). Gray advises the faithful to read each book of the Bible in one sitting, ignoring the chapter breaks, and to read it over and over (45–47). The organizing structures of chapter and verse, Gray reminds his readers, are man-made, implicitly contrasting the language itself (though Gray acknowledges the fact of translation) as God-given.

The title of Gray's 1904 handbook promises mastery, not intimacy. But Gray prefaces his rules for reading by telling us that this method is not the product of scholarly expertise but a technique he learned from a layman. The layman's story, as Gray recounts it, describes reading the Epistle to the Ephesians "twelve or fifteen times," alone, "lying down under a tree," until he felt himself "lifted up to sit together in heavenly places in Christ Jesus" (18). In the end, the layman tells Gray, Ephesians possessed him, not vice versa. For all of this original reading scene's pastoral romanticism, though,

Gray's aim is to create a portable pedagogy. Gray succeeds in answering what he describes as an institutional need to find a replicable, universally applicable, method of teaching reading (25). Timothy Weber cites Gray's guide as an influential text for the fundamentalist movement against historical criticism.⁴⁹

It is worth noting here how antihistoricist close reading responds to parallel institutional pressures: Gray's biblical close reading succeeded as a teachable and scalable interpretive method, much as literary close reading did in the mid-twentieth-century university. In that case, as Gerald Graff has observed, as student populations swelled, administrators favored teaching that did not rely on intensive historical or philological training. The result was that "the general education program and the New Critical program gradually merged, and a new kind of division became institutionalized between literature and history."⁵⁰

NEO-ORTHODOXY, NEW CRITICISM, AND THE FOUNDING OF THE AMERICAN CANON

In the wake of the historicist crisis, a more theologically conservative Protestant movement—an elite counterpart to the fundamentalism developing in institutions like the Moody Bible Institute—consolidated. The theologians who would be identified in the early decades of the twentieth century as neo-orthodox were socially progressive, not nativists. What neo-orthodoxy retrieved from a more conservative strain of nineteenth-century Protestantism was an emphasis on the unmediatable distance between man and God. As earlier anti-Catholic Protestants had done, neo-orthodox thinkers rejected what they saw as illegitimate facilitators between God and man. They rebuked the you-can-find-God confidence that they saw expressed by Transcendentalists as much as by biblical historicists. One such rebuke appears in Albert Schweitzer's *The Quest of the Historical Jesus*, which surveyed nineteenth-century efforts at discovering Jesus in his own time and concluded that the result of such historicism was "a figure designed by rationalism, endowed with life by liberalism," a false domestication of one who was truly a "stranger and an enigma."⁵¹ Biblical historicism, on this view, enabled a self-regarding complacency. Once again, pride was the besetting sin of liberal interpreters. The theological cure would be a reemphasis on man's fallenness and God's transcendence, a gulf that no historical research could bridge.

My aim, again, is to show the convergence of literary and theological reading styles around the time that literary critics were assembling the great books that would professionalize the study of American literature. Neo-orthodoxy revives the ideals of ahistorical immediacy that motivated nineteenth-century anti-Catholicism. And, as with nineteenth-century anti-Catholicism, twentieth-century neo-orthodoxy understands that immediacy in terms of revelatory intimacy—though with the difference that this intimacy is less positively asserted, more often withheld. Neo-orthodoxy updates the reader-text love story that anti-Catholic Protestants had constructed. The Bible might not grant full spiritual illumination to even the most loving reader, but it is still a revelatory document, and the act of reading it might afford a soul-shivering sense of contact with the divine.

It is not that neo-orthodoxy and anti-Catholic Protestant conservatism hold the same view of language and revelation. Conservative nineteenth-century Protestantism rejected historicism on the common-sense grounds that words are straightforwardly referential and that the Bible is thus an accurate record of God's revelation.[52] Twentieth-century neo-orthodoxy rejects historicism on the modernist grounds that the medium of language itself can have disclosive power. As Lynn Poland puts it, neo-orthodox theologians hold that scriptural texts are "not straightforward renderings of events but disclosures of the significance of events. Unlike the historical Jesus, the Christ of Faith is, so to speak, an interpretation."[53] Reading becomes an event productive of revelation, not the decoding of a prior revelation.

The neo-orthodox view of the radical gulf between history and the divine found traction in the early decades of the twentieth century among some literary critics who were equally ready to discard liberal confidence for a more austere program of interpretation that emphasized the text as radically other and autonomous. Poland explains the crossover from neo-orthodoxy to New Criticism by way of T. E. Hulme's influence on T. S. Eliot. The fundamental crime with which Hulme charged the romantics was their failure to appreciate the gulf between man and God. Eliot funneled Hulme's charge into a theory of textual autonomy that New Criticism would codify. New Critics, too, shared Hulme's urge to take the religion that romanticism had spilled and return it to an appropriately high shelf.[54] Much as "literary modernists assert the autonomy of poetry," Poland writes, "these theologians declare God's Word to be autonomous, neither derived from nor interpreted on the basis of historical facts or principles, but by revelation and responding faith alone" (464). That move, despite the neo-orthodox distaste for romanticism, effectively revives Coleridge's sublime. The difference is that the sublime has been scrubbed of its uplifting qualities and designated a bracing chastisement. Still, the revelation withheld of a Barth or Hulme, like the revelation achieved of a liberal like Emerson or Bushnell, were equally "antipositivist"—equally insistent on seeing religious and poetic vision as an expression of freedom that broke through the determinism of history (Poland, 461–62).

Neo-orthodoxy had its detractors, who characterized the movement by its "flight from reason, from history, and from time, to authority and eternity—from personality to a totally other," in the words of a reviewer in the *Journal of Bible and Religion* in 1946.[55] But its own key figures spoke of a faith renewed by substituting the historicist confidence that liberal Protestants like Clarke, Briggs, and Terry had espoused for the fear and trembling idealized by Søren Kierkegaard, whose work was first introduced in America in 1923 (Ahlstrom, 937).

In rejecting the liberal embrace of biblical historicism, neo-orthodoxy instead envisioned the temporal distance between God and man as a radical gulf that no church tradition or historical research could possibly mediate. Such mediation was merely cover for a wishful self-projection onto the text. To Swiss Reformed theologian Karl Barth, the godfather of neo-orthodoxy, historicist criticism allowed readers to dismiss as mere local color the hard Christian truths of Paul's doctrine. Barth defended his own study of scripture from the charge of "imposing a meaning upon the text" because he read the Bible in light of Kierkegaard's sense of "the 'infinite qualitative distinction' between time and eternity."[56] As did Kierkegaard, the neo-orthodox turned the historicist demolition of the Bible's authority into a virtuous uncertainty that forced the believer to cling to the impossible paradox of God's infinitude made flesh and blood in history. To be wholly cognizant of, to wholly feel, this revelation was still the only ideal worth yearning for. But for neo-orthodoxy, man was too fallen to come close. Revelation was not attainable by cultivating one's likeness to

God, and God was not immanent, as Transcendentalists and liberals had affirmed. One could only hope to love God by embracing Christianity's fundamental offense to human understanding and by willing the downfall of one's own self-love.[57]

But the impossibility of consummating a revelatory intimacy provoked its own powerful emotional response. Self-dissolution or anguished desire, the marks of revelatory love, signaled that one was really approaching God's truth. Paul Tillich describes the affect of true faith in such terms. In *Dynamics of Faith*, Tillich writes that the "ultimacy" of Christian faith is signaled by the "ecstatic attraction and fascination" it elicited. Tillich, like Barth, posits history not as a bridge between God and man but as a gulf across which God was impossibly distant; the incompatibility of God's infinity and man's temporality is the proper measure of "man's relation to the holy," and only by recognizing that impossible distance can the believer paradoxically experience "the feeling of being consumed in the presence of the divine."[58]

This love story would prove appealing to American literary studies. Ann Douglas frames the neo-orthodox movement as the necessary intellectual backdrop to the formation of a worthy American canon. She calls neo-orthodoxy an "[attempt] to rectify the vitiation of serious intellectual and religious endeavor" and aligns its revived Calvinist theology with the aesthetics that enshrined the great American romantics; she writes that "it is especially fitting that *Billy Budd* was exhumed and published in 1924, as Karl Barth, Paul Tillich, and the Niebuhr brothers were beginning their careers," and she explicitly connects "the long-overdue rediscovery of Melville [that] took place in the 1920s" with the resurgence of this purified Protestantism.[59] Her account lay down enduring battle lines for the study of sentimentality in American literature. Douglas also importantly prompts us to see the shared investment, made by both nineteenth-century anti-Catholicism and early twentieth-century literary canonizing, in emotional and interpretive immediacy.

One sign of the congruence Douglas points out between American literary study and neo-orthodoxy is their shared enthusiasm for Calvinist theology. That shared enthusiasm is notable in accounts of Jonathan Edwards, an object of admiration whose achievement for both theologians and literary critics is specified in terms of the same emotional state of a half-painful, half-wonderful unknowing. H. Richard Niebuhr saw in Edwards a Kierkegaardian vision of the agonizing uncertainty caused by man's sinful distance from God's love. Edwards, wrote Niebuhr, "recognized what Kierkegaard meant when he described life as treading water with ten thousand fathoms beneath us."[60] Niebuhr's description mirrors the Edwards of Perry Miller's 1949 biography; Miller admires Edwards's will to push ever toward the unthinkable and unsayable, praising Edwards's writing as "an immense cryptogram."[61] In Miller's hands, Edwards the theologian comes to resemble the distant, mysterious god that Edwards theologizes about. "The way [Edwards] delivered his sermons," Miller says, with "no display, no inflection, no consideration of the audience . . . is enough to confirm the suspicion that there was an occult secret in them" (50). Such admiration helped to establish the emotional standard of American literature in its formative period by identifying the feeling of withheld revelation as the signal of literary merit.

Beyond such explicit appreciations of American Protestant orthodoxy, we also find a broader give-and-take of shared principles linking neo-orthodoxy to contemporaneous literary criticism. As Niebuhr and Miller admire Kierkegaard and Edwards for their view of puny man suspended over the fathomless depths, so do other critics admire Melville and other canonical writers. According to critic H. M. Tomlinson, the author of a preface to a 1929 reprint of *Pierre*, that novel keeps the reader "poised over an abyss of darkness most of the time."[62] In 1950, M. O. Percival would interpret Melville's Ahab as an instance of Kierkegaard's analysis of the problem of despair.[63] Roland F. Lee would use Kierkegaard to explicate what he calls Emerson's "theory of communication" in 1957.[64]

Major literary journals of the time offer more evidence of the congeniality of Christian orthodoxy to the rising orthodoxy of literary formalism. As Anthony Domestico shows, under T. S. Eliot's editorship, the *Criterion* (1922–39) presented modernist literature (*The Waste Land*, Proust, Yeats) alongside modernist theology, both neo-Thomist Catholics and neo-orthodox Protestants.[65] These Catholic and Protestant movements shared an aim to roll back Protestant romanticism by reemphasizing man's fallenness and God's distance. Despite the *Criterion*'s reputation among its contemporary readers as stuffy and pious, it employed major writers like William Empson, Ezra Pound, and Marianne Moore. It was "thanks to Eliot's editorial practices" that the "*Criterion*'s readers were aware of the confluences between Barth and Eliot, Auden and Niebuhr" (35). And over the years the *Criterion*'s book review section effectively adapted Karl Barth's neo-orthodoxy for cultural criticism (25). An essay by V. A. Demant, for instance, finds in Barth an opponent of the historicist determinism of Marxism. For Barth, Demant claims, "truth speaks in timeless acts breaking in upon man and by his response he is lifted out of history. This utter break between the eternal and the temporal order is the dialectical opposite of the humanism it supersedes."[66] Domestico argues that Demant has exaggerated Barth's theology here, but the essay suggests that neo-orthodoxy had an intellectual prestige that could be put to work validating broad arguments for how to understand the world ahistorically.

Picking up in the year the *Criterion* left off, the *Kenyon Review* "so successfully enshrined a literary agenda that its successes and failures still shape our concerns," in Gordon Hutner's estimation.[67] Edited by John Crowe Ransom from 1939 to 1959, the *Kenyon Review* set the standards of literary merit and shaped "the way we think of American literature— writing it and studying it—as a way of arguing about society" (Hutner, 102). Ransom gave us the name for New Criticism in his volume of 1941; Ransom's 1937 essay "Criticism, Inc." was, as Catherine Gallagher argues, a successful marketing plan for New Criticism's hold on professionalizing literary study.[68] And his argument there—for a criticism that would treat literary texts as ahistorical "metaphysical maneuvers" created in an "agony of composition"—makes the work of the poet sound like the work of the neo-orthodox god.[69] A dozen years before the affective fallacy would be codified as such, Ransom also lays some groundwork for antisentimentalism by declaring the illegitimacy of feeling in criticism. "It is hardly criticism to assert" that a text "causes in us some remarkable physiological effect," Ransom writes—for instance, "the flowing of tears, visceral or laryngeal sensations, and such like." Even "spiritual ecstasy" or "catharsis of our emotions" are out of bounds to proper criticism (597). Such reader responses propose that the text aims to make the reader feel something. Those feelings thus deny the "autonomy of the artist" and "the autonomy of the work itself as existing for its own sake" (598). Like the Calvinist God, this artwork is sublimely indifferent to its audience.

Indeed, Ransom had already registered his own argument for a return to a more austere faith in 1930, in *God without Thunder: An Unorthodox*

Defense of Orthodoxy. That book laments the "soft modern version of the Christ" and argues that "the only real God there is"—"the only God we can ever really love"—is a god "whom we can never familiarly nor intelligibly possess."[70] Ransom is ecumenical enough to consider Eastern Orthodoxy, Judaism, and Roman Catholicism as possible outposts of a truer faith. He rejects them based on a frank admission of tribalism. Ransom admits to occasionally "feel[ing] envious of [the] spiritual advantages" enjoyed by converts to Catholicism, but he reminds his readers that "we have for a good many generations cultivated a powerful antagonism" against the Catholic Church, and even if he could "overcome these prejudices," Ransom suspects his "friends and kind" would not follow suit (326). Better, he concludes, to lobby for demodernizing one's own congregation.

Eliot, it is true, found a certain old-school Catholicism congenial to his vision of the literary tradition once he stood on British ground. But, as Ransom's advice to return to Protestant orthodoxy suggests, strains of anti-Catholicism still drove American efforts to shape the canon. Paul Lauter's account of Melville's canonization describes the social context of nativism that helps account for the convergence of American literary canonizing with anti-Catholic theology. As it had done in the mid-nineteenth century, so in the 1920s, Lauter writes, immigration "encouraged" a "variety of efforts to reassert the hegemony of Anglo-Saxon society."[71] One way to counter the potential for demographic shifts to disrupt white cultural supremacy was to update Melville's identity from that of an adventurous globetrotter to that of a "lone and powerful beacon against the dangers presented by the masses" who were "dark, foreign, and numerous" (6). Lauter adduces as one such effort Raymond Weaver's 1921 biography, which paints Melville as a heretical prophet.

Henry James's reputation was also boosted by critics who linked him to this new version of Melville as prophet. The Melville revivers speculated that the youthful James must have drunk up Melville's late works. Carl Van Vechten wrote that Melville shares with James a "metaphysical" and "self-revealing" quality.[72] By elevating the authors they study to metaphysical giants, such critics render themselves "new disciples" and chosen "interpreters of a modernist secular writ" (11). Lauter notes that one of the rare dissenters from Weaver's portrait of Melville is a reviewer in the *Catholic World* who "excoriates both [Weaver's] failure to account for Melville as 'a

religious man' and for his view of humanity as 'the herd'" (13). Lauter identifies this Catholic view as "a traditional religious position" (13). I would
identify it instead as a specifically Catholic allegiance to communion that
counters a specifically Protestant claim to revelation. And I would further
identify the modernist secular writ preached by the Melville revivers as
another iteration of the conservative Protestant ideal of revelation.

ANTISENTIMENTALISM AND THE CASE
OF *BILLY BUDD*

My concern at the end of this chapter is to prepare the ground for the
early twenty-first-century debate over historicism and ethics—a debate I
examine in chapter 5—by showing the early twentieth-century interplay
between neo-orthodoxy and those literary scholars whose views would
make American literary study an antihistoricist, antisentimental, and revelatory affair.

   We are in a position now to appreciate the significance of the continuity
between the *Christian Union*'s disapproval of *The Gates Ajar* and the New
Critical disapproval of such novels. Orthodox Protestants (whether in the
1870s or 1920s) and literary critics alike privileged revelation withheld in
the name of a hard-eyed view of man's fallenness. Readers of the Bible, like
readers of Melville or James, would struggle to understand the text and
would probably fail. As with earlier anti-Catholicism, that view of the gulf
between reader and text paradoxically bolstered a conviction of the reader's autonomy. To confront, in reading, such a gulf of understanding was to
feel the freedom of standing alone before a vast mystery. The conservative
Protestant ideal of revelation withheld provoked emotion through obscurity. In light of that ideal of the sublime, sentimental conventions are bad
mediators, verbal props that make for easy understanding and easy feeling.

   We can see that emotional protocol become an academic program in
a textbook like *An Approach to Literature,* which had a decades-long life
span as a literary anthology (first copyrighted in 1936, its fourth edition
published in 1964). Coedited by Cleanth Brooks, John Thibault Purser,
and Robert Penn Warren, the text codifies the Protestant aesthetic of deep
love as unmediated textual encounter. Its introductory essay is gendered
in all the predictable ways that riled feminist literary critics back in the

1980s. Yet the editors prescribe an emotional repertoire that literary ethics still largely endorses. Setting up a case study in the contrast between the artist and sentimentalist, the introduction pits Robert Browning against an imagined hack journalist dubbed the "sob sister."[73] The sob sister, write Brooks et al., "wants to make us feel the pathos" of a murder story, but all she can think to do "is to overwhelm us with pitiable pictures and adjectives": she "shouts [at the reader] what to look at and what to feel about it" (6). When a poet like Browning writes about murder (in "Porphyria's Lover"), he "merely directs the imagination of the reader so that he feels that he has discovered the meaning of the experience for himself, and consequently feels it to be much richer" (6). Browning's poem organizes the sensation of revelation to the reader. The consequence of that experience of independent discovery is that the text feels more like art.

This diagnosis of the emotional unfreedom brought on by the bad mediation of sentimentality echoes the *Christian Union*'s 1870 claim that Elizabeth Stuart Phelps turns what should be an invisible mystery into a glaring picture. The objection that excess visibility hinders real feeling echoes in the antisentimental polemic Ann Douglas would launch more than a hundred years after that negative review. Douglas is no New Critic. But the emotional and aesthetic ideal of withheld revelation that operates in *The Feminization of American Culture* (1977) mirrors that of the New Critics. Phelps appears in *Feminization* as an author whose sensuous detail threatens a transcendence that must remain hidden. Phelps misunderstands transcendence, says Douglas, because she misunderstands history not as large-scale progress but as stasis. Douglas admires the view of history "common to Hegelians and to Calvinists" that "combin[ed] . . . a sense of tragedy with millennial hope" (171). By contrast, Douglas observes that Augustine "had believed . . . that the Christian should direct his thoughts toward the eternal 'City of God' and ignore the flux of his earthly home" (171). In *The Gates Ajar* Phelps is guilty, Douglas says, of "dilat[ing] heavenly time" into a moment of "prolonged close-up" (226). My reading of Phelps, as I note in the introduction and develop in the next chapter, sees her picturing change within eternity. But Douglas does not consider that sentimentality's effort to "dislodge a linear" view of history for a "cyclical pattern" (195) might be an attempt to recover something like an Augustinian, Catholic view of history. Instead, Douglas concludes that "for Phelps . . . heaven, like history itself, is a civilian affair, a matter of individuals and their tastes and needs" (188). This is, for Douglas, an illegitimate way to view either heaven or history. What makes it illegitimate is its smallness, which prevents the large-scale view of change that conveys man's only true sense of freedom.

Douglas's chief complaint against sentimental smallness is its privileging of private experience (158). But her preferred aesthetic experience of being overwhelmed by immensity also reinforces the value of privacy. Douglas's analysis of *Billy Budd* praises Melville's refusal of "interior views" (325) and his shaping the narrative climax to a standard of "'inviolable privacy and 'holy oblivion'" (326). Douglas's reading makes clear her identification of great American literature with what she identifies as a Calvinist model of withheld revelation. Douglas barely glimpses a mighty and incomprehensible God through Melville's pages. Critics who dislike the unfriendly God that Melville presents here are, Douglas says, "in part guilty of just the liberal heresy which Melville opposed" (324)—language that suggests the strength of Douglas's literary investment in the principles of her theological heroes.

Melville's channeling of this Calvinist God is what generates the tremendous force of *Billy Budd*. Here, says Douglas, "there is absolutely none of the sensuous detail which over-runs and destroys the narrative" of Melville's earlier novel *Pierre*. What makes *Billy Budd* "extraordinarily helpful" to its readers is its "bigness." In *Billy Budd* we cannot grasp or see the truth, but "we attain . . . a sense of its dimensions, the space it occupies" (326)—which is very large and very far away. This is not a God whose revelation in the Bible was conditioned by historical circumstance (as higher criticism argues), nor one whose historical reality as the incarnate Son allows us to relate to him as a particular man in a particular setting (per the historical Jesus approach). This is certainly not a God whose presence should be mediated by the ritual theatricality of Catholic practice. The reader's encounter with this God of withheld revelation proves the private emotional freedom that defined both antisentimentalism and anti-Catholicism.

Some thirteen years after *Feminization*, well into the era of the American canon's deconstruction, Eve Sedgwick refuted Douglas's reading of *Billy Budd* and challenged the ideal of withheld revelation. For Sedgwick, *Billy Budd* is a sentimental text, and Melville's Captain Vere actually shows us how "the privacy effect" relies on the public performance of suffering to maintain its special allure.[74] What Melville is telling us, says Sedgwick, is that hiddenness is always an advertisement of itself. *Billy Budd,* rightly read, proves that the privileged interiority Douglas admires Melville for respecting is itself really a theatrical performance. Whereas Douglas charges sentimentalism with, as Sedgwick says, "degrad[ing] . . . American culture" so that "public and private have become fatally confused" (115), Sedgwick wants to show that public and private can never be disentangled. The charge that some artwork or feeling is sentimental is only a way of saying that that artwork or feeling has inconveniently reminded us that privacy depends on public performance.

Sedgwick proposes that, in *Billy Budd,* as in Christianity more broadly, this unwelcome deconstruction of privacy is most offensive when it is provoked by the figure of a male body in pain, whether Billy's or Christ's (125, 140–41, 148). In both cases the transgression is demonstrated by the bad desire it provokes: vicarious feeling, "a structure of relation, typically one involving the author- or audience-relations of spectacle" (143). Vicariousness is characteristic of sentimentality, and Sedgwick notes its ongoing status as degraded feeling. She cites by way of example a then-recent *New York Review of Books* essay on kitsch that dismisses the popular Protestant song "And He Walks With Me" as "nastily flavored religious jello."[75] Sedgwick argues that the song offends the reviewer because it posits a too-easy intimacy between Jesus and believer. In Sedgwick's analysis, there is a shared motive behind the distaste for both Catholicism, called fetishism by critics who espouse conservative Protestantism, and the distaste for Protestant sentimentalism, called kitsch by critics who espouse a modernist aesthetic. Both are forms of representation that take what should be transcendent and make it a spectacle, mediate it into consumable form, and thus eliminate the sublime feeling that we need to assure us both of the transcendence of the object and of our own autonomy. Both Catholic fetishism and Protestant kitsch are guilty of denying our autonomy and provoking vicariousness, a feeling that substitutes for one's own private emotion the "*reflexes of the impulses of others*" (150).

For Sedgwick, antisentimentalism, in its rejection of the spectator relationship, partakes of a broader homophobic logic that rejects vicariousness. Homophobia sees vicariousness as a bad form of desire because it threatens the claim to the autonomy of self and other. Vicariousness, as Sedgwick describes it, aligns with what I have been describing as communion. This congruence appears in the accusations of fetishism and narcissism deployed both by antisentimental and anti-Catholic logic. In both cases the fear is that of making the other too visible and thus too readily assimilated to oneself. Such fear, like homophobia, prohibits desiring the same kind of object you yourself identify with. For the ethicist literary critic, this is a moral fear, the fear of failing to recognize difference, and an interpretive fear, the fear of not having learned anything from a text, of simply seeing yourself in it all over again. The depth of feeling that we attribute to a text's depth is the assurance that we have not failed. It signals that we have not fully assimilated the text and that a hidden surplus is still out there.

Critics like Sedgwick and Jane Tompkins prevailed over Douglas, insofar as the project of expanding the canon beyond its initial great white Protestant men succeeded. But in that contest, the Protestant ideal of revelation withheld as the sign of literary value was not challenged so much as it was either reversed into a project of revelatory exposure or simply abandoned. The initial canon developed by the New Critics, which promised to secularize American literature by omitting the overt pieties of sentimentality, instead standardized a defensive strain of Protestantism. The later deconstruction of that canon by the New Americanists—though it exposed the covert religiosity of claims for Hawthorne's or James's sublimity—kept in place a methodological reverence for the hidden truth of ideology. The depths revealed by ideology critique and symptomatic reading would in turn provoke the protective instincts of literary ethicists, who from varying angles would call again for revelation to be withheld, asking readers to be humble in the face of the unknowable. That is where I pick up this story in chapter 5, after examining the love story of communion across six novels in three broad literary-historical categories.

Two

Sentimental Communion
Protestant Reading Meets Catholic Worship
in *Uncle Tom's Cabin* and *The Gates Ajar*

HOW DO EVA AND TOM LOVE EACH OTHER? Harriet Beecher Stowe's narrator does not claim to know exactly. "It would be hard to say what place [Eva] held in the soft, impressible heart of her faithful attendant," the narrator tells us, but Tom both "loved her" and "almost worshipped her."[1] Catholic adoration provides an analogy for Tom's feeling: "He gazed on her as the Italian sailor gazes on his image of the child Jesus—with a mixture of reverence and tenderness" (266). As for Eva, her feelings are even less definable. She reciprocates Tom's devotion by reading the Bible "to please" him (267). The Bible itself becomes both an object and a mediator for her passion. Eva's "earnest nature threw out its tendrils, and wound itself around the majestic book; and Eva loved it, because it woke in her strange yearnings, and strong, dim emotions, such as impassioned, imaginative children love to feel" (267). This transfer of love for Tom to love for the Bible is not unexpected, since Tom himself is a "black morocco"–bound compendium of virtue, as Eva's father describes him (155). But Eva and Tom "felt just alike about" the Bible (267). Both favor "the Revelations and the Prophecies," sensing in these texts "a wondrous something yet to come" (267). The Bible is the engine of their intimacy, a third party in what seems a very Protestant love triangle.

But *Uncle Tom's Cabin* offers a distinct resistance to Protestant norms even as it maintains faith that reading can save one's soul. When it was translated and published in Italy in 1852, it was read widely and enthusiastically. However, the Catholic press took exception to its theology. One newspaper, *La Civiltà Cattolica*, objected to Stowe's portrayal of "sentiments so noble and virtues so marvelous [being acquired] by the *sole* reading of the *sole* Bible, which seems to be the predominant fixation of the author."[2] This judgment is no mistake. The scene of Eva and Tom reading the Bible next to Lake Pontchartrain, for instance, represents an ideal of Protestant devotion, and it consecrates in advance the characters' upcoming deaths. The newspaper reminds its audience that the Catholic faith does not promote salvation through reading. But it also faults Stowe for taking inspiration from "the immense treasures of Catholic hagiography" to feed the "fervid imagination" embodied in a "sentimental novel."[3] That critique echoes, from the opposite side, the Protestant protest that *The Gates Ajar* (1868) had wrongly embellished God's restrained pictures. From the Catholic view, though, Protestant sentimentalism looked more like cultural appropriation.

That appropriation is necessary to Stowe and to Phelps in their vocation as both novelists and practical theologians. Wanting to win their readers to the abolitionist cause or to console them for the losses of the Civil War, they take it that reading can save the soul, a foundational Protestant view that inspires their projects as authors. But the reading they imagine goes against the grain of orthodox Protestant injunctions to sit alone and pore over the pages. Communion, as opposed to revelation, configures devotional reading as a communal and emotional, a visual or even tactile, experience. As noted in chapter 1, many Protestants, in practice, did read together; many did treat the Bible as an icon or fetish, not only as a conduit to God's divine truth. Ronald Zboray and Mary Zboray's study of antebellum New England readers shows that before the Civil War, especially, the default for everyday reading was sociable: "Sequestered readers . . . were by far rarer than readers surrounded by social activity" (169). And readers cared about books and bibles as material objects. One seminary student, writing to his wife-to-be, justified his "extravagance" in seeking out the finest editions by asserting that "to you as well as to myself there must be an increased satisfaction in reading an elegantly printed book" (226). The materiality of the word did not disappear for such readers.

But the reading of the Bible, or of sermons or tracts, could also motivate a distinctly private reading practice. The Zborays find many readers who designated devotional reading as its own category, one that "required" "mental focus and engagement." They write, "Inattentive devotional reading could verge on impiety, and it would certainly disrupt the clear transmission of the word from text to devotee, so the practice was avoided"

(170). Focused attention is promoted again and again in the Protestant guidebooks I discuss below, which ask readers to approach the Bible in solitude, focused on the word alone. Such guides adhere to the ideal of revelatory reading, aiming to produce an invisible, private intimacy between God and the believer. Against that ideal, *Uncle Tom's Cabin* and *The Gates Ajar* imagine reading as communion, a shared ritual dependent on visual and material texts. The Protestant doctrine of *sola scriptura* shifts in these novels to resemble Catholic worship. This holds both for the kind of reading Stowe and Phelps portray in their fiction, and for the kind of reading their fiction aims to generate in its own readers.

Certainly both Stowe and Phelps are possessed of impeccable Protestant credentials. Stowe was daughter and sister, respectively, to prominent clergymen Lyman and Henry Ward Beecher; Phelps was raised in a family of two generations of Andover seminarians. Stowe's Protestant influences have been persuasively and extensively tracked, as have Phelps's.[4] But there are explicit signals in the pages of both novels of the appropriation that the Catholic press objected to. Stowe draws her key characters as religious hybrids. Little Eva's grandmother was a pious Huguenot and the "direct embodiment . . . of the New Testament," but St. Clare recalls her playing Catholic hymns (232). Eva wants to save her slaves' souls by teaching them all to read the Bible, but she settles on preemptively handing out relics, locks of her own hair, from her deathbed. At St. Clare's home in New Orleans, Tom is half-seriously described by the narrator as resembling a "Bishop of Carthage, as men of his color were, in other ages" (186). By the time Tom is at Legree's plantation, the convent-educated Cassy calls him "Father Tom," treating him unironically as confessor and spiritual director (404).[5]

Phelps, for her part, was proud to own her upbringing in a faculty family at the conservative Andover Seminary. Her memoirs recall a visit from Emerson, whom she suspects thought them all "barbarians" of a primitive faith.[6] She denies having strayed from Protestant orthodoxy to become a Spiritualist (8). But in *The Gates Ajar,* her characters openly voice appreciation for Catholicism. The hero of *The Gates Ajar,* Winifred Forceythe, worries that "in our recoil from the materialism of the Romish Church, we have, it seems to me, nearly stranded ourselves on the opposite shore."[7] Winifred's daughter Faith kisses a portrait of her dead father nightly, as if it were an icon, an act of devotion that startles the narrator, Mary Cabot, when she first sees it. A reviewer in the *Catholic World* for one of Phelps's later *Gates* novels concludes that novel describes the decidedly extra-Protestant realm of purgatory.[8] We can think of both Stowe and Phelps as helping enact a counterreformation from within Protestantism, anticipating the "movement toward Catholic forms" that Jackson Lears describes as marking "the late-nineteenth-century crisis of [Protestant] cultural authority."[9] One of the speakers that Lears identifies with this movement, the Congregationalist minister Lyman Abbott, remarked in 1909 that "perhaps we Puritans have reacted too far from the sacerdotalism of medievalism and need to retrace our steps," echoing the sentiment Winifred had expressed in Phelps's fiction four decades earlier.[10]

This chapter shows how the theological hybrid that adapts the "immense treasures" of Catholicism for Protestant reading plays out in fiction, in a love story of communion that resists the ideal of revelation. *The Gates Ajar* and *Uncle Tom's Cabin* both put outsize pressure on the question of how to read and how to access the sacred. Both show how Christian doctrinal differences influenced the imagination of reading and of intimacy in the sentimental novel. By recuperating elements of Catholic practice and relaxing the Protestant depth drive, Stowe and Phelps portray true love as a couple's ongoing work of piecing together texts to build an account of the meaning of life and death. When Tom and Eva read the Bible together, they are reading their way to salvation, like good Protestants. But the interpretive work that constitutes their love is not figured as a hermeneutic dive into God's word. They connect biblical imagery to hymns and to the landscape around them and thereby recreate the text as a shared spectacle. Mary and Winifred's discussions of heaven in *The Gates Ajar* are similarly imagistic and culturally specific. Their intimacy is not based on a transformative one-on-one realization that shuts out the world, but on a day-by-day collaboration that requires the inputs of both a theological library and the lives of their neighbors.

Neither of these novels tells a conventional love story. Stowe imagines a little white girl and a grown black man as her model of true love. In asking her readers to accept these characters as models of love, she is adapting familiar Christian admonitions to be like a child and like a slave. Phelps's model couple carries less symbolic weight. Her more realistic pair comprises an aunt and a niece: one bereaved woman who teaches another how love endures. Neither of these mentor-mentee relationships is characterized as erotic, nor is the love between Eva and Tom and between Mary and Winifred portrayed as a privileged soul-to-soul revelation. They love each other by reading and talking together. They are in love not with what is inside each other, nor even with what is inside the books they read, but with the interpretations they generate from the books they read. The intimacy thus developed between the two couples is, however, presented as both tender and intense. In its dependence on mediation, their communion might be said to partake of the triangular structure of René Girard's mimetic desire; it also recalls Eve Sedgwick's description of vicariousness.[11] Communion does not frame the love object in an isolating halo of singularity; it posits real love as facilitated by cultural signifiers that shape and feed desire.

That description suggests the outlines of what I am calling the love story of communion in American fiction. But since I begin my account here, with *Uncle Tom's Cabin* and *The Gates Ajar*, it will be helpful to clarify the boundaries of the term. Communion may be one version of the "intersubjective transcendence" that Marianne Noble sees the sentimental novel aiming to produce.[12] However, communion is not the self-shattering jouissance that Noble proposes readers might experience in imagining Tom's death. Communion is what Tom and Eva achieve in their reading together, an intimate understanding that is neither violent nor sexualized. And while communion emerges in American fiction with these two novels' overt efforts to Catholicize a Protestant vision of transcendent love, it is not continuous with sentimentality. Not every text we might categorize as sentimental portrays communion. To take another landmark bestseller as an example, the love story between John Humphreys and Ellen Montgomery that Susan Warner tells in *The Wide, Wide World* aligns more closely with revelatory reading. Ellen's formative Bible reading is private, unlike Eva's with Tom; her conversations with John tend toward abstraction. The heaven that John describes to Ellen is orthodox, not packed with carnations and gingersnaps, as Phelps's novel has it.[13] Second, and more important, one of the key claims of this book is that communion is a model of intimacy that jumps over literary-historical boundaries. Though it begins with the overt Christian theologizing of these sentimental novels, communion as a structure of loving and knowing appears in romanticism and realism too.

What makes communion an identifiable alternative to the canonical model of love as revelation withheld? As a Catholicized form of encountering radical otherness, communion relies on mediation. Such mediations translate to the narrative form of the love story in three broad ways. First, unlike the intimacy of revelation, the intimacy of communion puts faith in the visible mediation of appearances. In telling the love story of communion, novelists' characterizations rely on what Karen Halttunen calls "sentimental typology," the prevailing nineteenth-century belief that "all aspects of manner and appearance were visible outward signs of inner moral qualities."[14] The popular acceptance of phrenology and physiognomy provided a reliable visual vocabulary—ways to describe eyes and noses and foreheads—that could convey abstract personality traits.[15] In *The Gates Ajar* and *Uncle Tom's Cabin*, though, such descriptions are not presented as appearances that need decoding. In cataloging the details of faces, clothes, and the things that surround a person, these novels render characters as manifest selves whose interiors are externalized. One could call such characters flat. But the point is that they do not have to unpeel each other's self-presentations to get to know each other. Whatever makes a character worth loving is there to be seen.

Any fiction requires imagery to function. In the love story of communion, though, imagery is presented with an earnestness and an excess that distinguish it from more standard realistic or romantic treatments. As we will see in later chapters, obsessively detailed materiality is crucial to the world-building in both Stoddard's and James's fiction, and while the protagonists of *Pierre* and *The Blithedale Romance* try to penetrate appearances, Melville and Hawthorne make those efforts look vain, confirming the importance of what can be seen and touched. We have already seen that *The Gates Ajar* was criticized for its unconstrained vividness. And *Uncle Tom's Cabin* aspired from its inception to be a book of pictures. In a letter to the editor of the *National Era,* which first published the novel in serial form, Stowe wrote, "My vocation is simply that of a *painter,* and my object will be to hold up in the most lifelike and graphic manner possible slavery. . . . There is no arguing with *pictures,* and everybody is impressed by them, whether they mean to be or not."[16] Though Phelps focuses on her protagonist's interior life, the conversations that build Mary's intimacy with Winifred develop an intensely detailed picture of heaven. Both novels, in their reliance on visual mediation, present intimacy not as the pleasure of diving deep but as the pleasure of sharing images.

Second, the love story of communion puts faith in the interpersonal mediation of performance. In other words, it posits self-other understanding as a process of ongoing spectatorship. This is a consequence of communion's trust in appearance: exterior signs, more than inner states of being, are charged with emotional weight and allure. Versions of this spectatorship mark all the novels I consider. In each case, in communion, falling in love is not the quest of a solitary self in search of the other. Rather, the self in love appreciates how the beloved plays to, and with, the culture around her. Emotion is performative, rather than expressive. Understanding comes from gauging audience reaction more than from introspection. Characters who are in love will trade the roles of performer and appreciative audience member. Their performing responds to and interprets the world they inhabit together. This interpretive work is collaborative; it may be repetitive. Whatever elements of their context the couple works to understand—the Bible, theories of the afterlife, family histories, friends' affairs—their understanding does not arrive at the payoff of a definitive insight that unites them in private mutual knowledge. The transcendence of communion relies instead on the promise that a couple's shared interpretation could go on forever.

Finally, the love story of communion trains its own readers to accept such mediations. Reader-text intimacy here is no longer a personal encounter with the sublime but an ongoing project of interpretation that spreads into public culture. The love story of communion encourages readers to conceive their emotional responses as part of a network of shared emotions, rather than to cherish their fascination with textual mystery. *Uncle Tom's Cabin* and *The Gates Ajar* offer a contact with otherness that does not require us to strike through the mask of fiction to the real author, as we might be tempted to do with the Melville of *Pierre* or the Hawthorne of *The Blithedale Romance*. Those novels, I will argue, actually encourage spectatorship by showing how badly wrong the unmasking impulse can go. In Stoddard and James, the reader's spectatorship is fostered by the authors' foregrounding of their novels as staged arrangements. In each case, the text itself, rather than the real or implied author, becomes the other that performs for the reader.

That may seem an odd claim, given that Stowe "drew her own dockside crowds, had her travel plans publicly announced, packed her own halls, appeared before audience after audience as her celebrated self."[17] Stowe's in-person availability to her readers was clearly crucial to the book's success. But however much Stowe could travel, her text, translated into Uncle Tom shows, traveled further and lasted longer. The theatrical afterlives of *Uncle Tom's Cabin,* like the merchandising and sequels of *The Gates Ajar,* allowed Stowe's and Phelps's readers to go on cultivating intimacy with the text-as-other. A revelatory text holds out to readers the possibility of a road-to-Damascus epiphany or the feeling of suspension over a forbidding depth. Communion does not organize the reader-text relationship around mystery or insight; communion does invite readers to keep reinterpreting and reimagining the text. As it emerges in the sentimental mode, communion enables that ongoing interpretive work through material artifacts and ritual performances.

Such spin-offs help clarify the Protestant-Catholic tension that drives the love story of communion. Seen as an effort to correct the Protestant "recoil from the materialism of the Romish Church," as Phelps's Winifred puts it, the theatrical and material spin-offs that each novel generated take on a theological appropriateness. On this view, Uncle Tom shows are like passion plays, ritual reenactments of sacrifice. Such theatricalization is the proper extension of a fictional technique that downgrades the privilege of private reading in favor of public worship. The merchandising of *The Gates Ajar,* the funeral wreaths and cigars that Phelps will recall with both disdain and "tenderness" years later, might be the tangible means whereby readers attained a kind of grace from the novel.[18] Such spin-offs frankly subverted the Protestant insistence on literacy as prerequisite to receive a soul-saving message and indirectly contradicted the anti-Catholic caricature of unreasoning, illiterate Papists. Just as a Catholic need not understand a Latin mass to be saved by the Eucharist, one did not have to know how to read to be moved by a performance of *Uncle Tom's Cabin.* And one need not read *The Gates Ajar* to recognize the title as a signifier of enduring love.

Though I see Stowe and Phelps as imagining a form of love that reappears in gothic romanticism and in psychological realism, my reading of their novels generally aligns with the literary defense of sentimentality.

I broadly support the effort to "[define] sentimentalism in terms of an anti-individualist ethos that emphasizes connective over autonomous relations," as Elizabeth Dillon puts it.[19] I build on the work of critics like Glenn Hendler and Mary Louise Kete, as well as that of the sentimental novel's early champion, Jane Tompkins, who emphasize the group subjectivities that the sentimental produces.[20] Those group subjectivities are encouraged by the structure of communion, which asserts that intimacy can be public, mediated by material props, and still offer real contact with otherness. That assertion runs contrary not only to Protestant orthodoxy but also to scholarship that sees the marketing of such props as proof of sentimentalism's false emotion. As Lucy Frank observes, Phelps's novel "shows that the spiritual and commercial realms were complexly intertwined, not separate and incompatible."[21] Frank draws on Karen Sánchez-Eppler's argument that "the public and the emotional need not be viewed solely in oppositional terms."[22]

Frank and Sanchez-Eppler are arguing against a purported divide between real private feelings on one hand and false public emotions on the other, a divide that I see as conditioned by nineteenth-century Protestant anti-Catholicism. But to describe these novels in the religious terms of communion and revelation is not simply to rehash the contest between the social values of communitarianism versus individualism, nor is it to ask, from a different angle, whether Stowe and Phelps served or resisted patriarchy and capitalism.

The sentimental novel's gestures toward social change and solidarity may be judged as in bad faith if, like Ann Douglas reading *The Gates Ajar,* your measure of good faith is whether a text resists market consumerism, or if, like Gillian Brown reading *Uncle Tom's Cabin,* your measure of good faith is whether a text that resists market consumerism can also accept African Americans as full citizens. Those are legitimate ways to measure novelistic power and they are important questions to ask about American fiction. (I return to Brown and like-minded critics of the sentimental in chapter 5.) Stowe's and Phelps's novels did participate in an emotional economy that served the needs of white readers above all.

But *Uncle Tom's Cabin* and *The Gates Ajar* did more than that. Stowe and Phelps wrote these two novels in part as queries about how people can access God through a text. I treat them as projecting a competing Catholic-inflected ontology, a different view of the relationship between the world and the transcendent. My interest is in how that projected relationship plays out in the intimacy between self and other. I am not trying here to measure the degree of good or bad faith that these two authors invested in their appropriation of Catholic worship habits. My chief question is whether, given that appropriation, these novels offer a viable alternative to Protestant ideals of knowing and loving. On that score, they succeed.

Moreover, that successfully imagined alternative does offer distinct values in contrast to revelation's model of interpretive intimacy. The love story of communion challenges a Protestant logic of invisible power by suggesting the potency of what is visible; it challenges an ideal of spontaneous personal will by proposing that ritual and repetition are what move people. And communion insists that contact with otherness can be achieved without stripping away cultural context, without demanding that an essence shine forth. It recognizes a degree of social constructedness as enabling, not hindering, intimacy. It also recognizes that two persons in love are themselves social actors who can reinterpret, if not actually refashion, the world around them.

The analysis of Stowe and Phelps that follows aims to generate a triangulation of critic, text, and historical context: a reading model that could serve as a template for a hybrid of literary historicism and literary ethics. The archives I use to illuminate the novels comprise both Protestant Bible reading guides and defenses of Catholic worship. But my adducing this historical context is not motivated by the will to expose that literary ethics laments. I am not trying to lock down these novels' meanings as much as build a bigger story about an obscured form of desire in American literature. In accord with ethicist aims, I am reading for potentially portable models of human relationship. My reading does not displace one like Frank's, which takes *The Gates Ajar* as a "revealing example of" the ways fiction "can register the impact of—indeed, be generated by—traumatic national events and rapid social change" (165). But I do not read these novels chiefly as windows on, or as products of, historical movements. Religious history is a context within which to understand how Stowe and Phelps created fiction that might, without buying into the Protestant ideal of revelation, make good on reading's implicit promise to move us beyond ourselves.

GOING DEEP: PROTESTANT BIBLE READING

Chapter 1 covered the general principles whereby Protestants claimed a superior intimacy with God based on their reading of the Bible. In what follows, I consider the application of those principles as laid out by Bible study guides circulating during the time when *Uncle Tom's Cabin* and *The Gates Ajar* were published. (James Gray's 1904 *How To Master the English Bible*, cited in chapter 1, marks a later example of the genre.) To claim reading as the route to a revelatory love of God, these guides relied on the binaries of inside and outside, surface and depth, public and private. Reading done properly could allow the reader far enough into the text to feel the contact with God's otherness that might yield salvation. An 1869 edition of *The Bible Hand-book*, by English Baptist clergyman Joseph Angus, exhorts readers, "First, we are not to contemplate this glorious fabric of Divine truth as spectators only. It is not our business to stand before Scripture and admire it; but to stand within, that we may believe and obey it. In the way of inward communion and obedience only shall we see the beauty of its treasures. It yields them to none but the loving and the humble. We must enter and unite ourselves with that which we would know, before we can know it more than in name."[23] Real intimacy here is communion, but it is qualified as "inward communion." It is achieved not through the mere spectatorship that Catholics (according to Protestants) contented themselves with in adoring the Eucharist. For Angus, deep reading allowed the reader to unite "more than in name" only with the spirit that authored the book. Truth is compared here to a fabric we could admire, and reading to the discovery of beautiful treasures, but Angus admonishes us to stop merely admiring such beauty. The focus is on the abstract virtues that are both the prerequisite to, and payoff of, good reading: love, humility, obedience. Such reading helped the Christian to grow stronger in understanding and in loving the God that she met in the pages of the Bible. The Bible's richly complex language here becomes a lure that threatens to derail belief and obedience. To admire meant remaining outside, knowing God only in name, forfeiting union with his divine truth.

For Angus, the Bible yields its treasures only to the especially loving reader. This is hardly a call for aggressive reading. Other Protestant guides put more stress on reading as labor. In 1844, for instance, the Massachusetts Sabbath School Society published a guide urging believers to read beneath the surface. Ordinary reading, as of a "common book" or newspaper, would fail to attain the proper depth; at best the reader would "gather up, perhaps, a few fragments that lie upon the surface."[24] The ideal reading, by contrast, would feel more like diving into dark water and finding a gem: "As by steadily and intently gazing into waters which at first appear dark and fathomless, you by degrees penetrate their depths, and see the lost jewel that lies at the bottom, so by dwelling with earnest meditation upon the deep things of God, light comes to the mental eye" (55). The reward for such reading-as-diving was an illuminating merge with the true meaning and spirit of the text. This is intimacy as mutual penetration. The good reader penetrates the depths of the text, and by trying "to find the treasure which is there hidden from the world," that reader in turn might "be penetrated and filled with the spirit and life of the Divine word" (56). Reading could spiritually incorporate the word and afford contact with that word's author. The promise that such revelatory reading might fill a reader with divine life effectively elevated it to the level of a sacrament.

To foster such a relationship with the divine in the first place, the reader is directed to isolate herself for a one-on-one encounter with the text. The Sabbath School Society guide recommends that readers "lay aside all the cares and business by which our attention is liable to be diverted . . . and seek a place of stillness and seclusion, where we may listen undisturbed to the voice that speaks from heaven" (45). In the Protestant ideal of revelation, it is up to the reader to be properly susceptible to God's presence in the pages of the Bible. There are no material props, such as Catholics availed themselves of, to aid the believer in feeling that presence. "We need, therefore," says Angus, "to supply by our thoughtfulness and solemnity, the feelings which were produced of old by sensible images of the Creator's presence and authority" (65). This truer, more progressive belief no longer requires images to feel that God is near; it generates that feeling from words alone. The feeling of intimacy becomes a private possession under these circumstances. But if the reader can claim for himself the love he feels with God, so he can be faulted if his reading fails to produce the right emotion. Charlotte Bickersteth Wheeler admonishes the young women who are her audience that "if a chapter does not seem to speak to you, to have any message for you, it is generally because you have not been searching it. You have not read it in a prayerful spirit, but with your mind's eyes partly shut, or even looking another way; or your heart has been full of something else."[25] Looking around the text rather than searching it deeply cuts off the believer from God's voice. Deep reading, on the other hand, has the power to make the text speak and deliver its messages.

The titles of the works of two English Nonconformists—Rev. Thomas Watson's "The Bible and the Closet" and Rev. Samuel Lee's "Secret Prayer Successfully Managed," reissued together in 1842—clearly signal the alignment of privacy with devotion. Like Wheeler, Watson warns against shallow reading. "Some can better remember a piece of news," he writes, "than a line of Scripture; their memories are like those ponds where the frogs live"—muddy and shallow—"but the fish die" for lack of deep water (24). The more deeply the mind absorbs the word, the more vitally nourishing the word can be for the reader. Indeed that word must move from the head, where it first enters, deeper into the body, to the heart, where it can take full effect. As the bee sucks honey from a flower, Watson says, so "by reading we suck the flower of the word," an image that relegates the form of the text to an empty husk devoid of meaning.[26] Watson argues that, properly internalized, God's word should "not only *inform* you, but *inflame* you" (39). The analogy of reading to falling in love finds its full extension in Watson's interpretive guide. He calls the Bible a love letter from God: "The Spirit is God's love token; the word his love letter; how doth one rejoice to read over his friend's letter" (31).

For Catholics, by contrast, the Church is primary, both in the sense that it pre-dates the Bible and that it is the route to genuine contact with God's otherness. As the German Catholic apologist Johann Adam Möhler observes, to ask (as Protestants did) that the Church justify itself by appeal to the Bible was absurd. For the Church to undertake such a justification "she would fall into the most absurd inconsistency. . . . she would be like the man, that would examine the papers written by himself in order to discover whether he really existed!"[27] To feel connected by love to God was not achievable by reading but through communion, a ritual instituted and consecrated by the Church.

And communion was emphatically a work of group participation. It de-emphasizes the individual's inward feeling. As Möhler explains it, "It is not however the interior acts of thanksgiving, adoration, and gratitude, which [the church community] offers up to God"; these feelings "are deemed unworthy to be presented to God." Rather "it is Christ himself present in the sacrament" that enables the sanctifying work of grace (314). The worshiper here becomes a go-between who returns the Son to the Father, participating in the circuit of love that mysteriously binds the Trinity. Such sacramental participation is performed by a social self: "The community, in the person of the priest, performeth this" (314). Such a model of community performance is absent from Protestant Bible-reading guides, where individual feeling authenticates the sacrament of deep reading. Angus's *Bible Hand-book* stresses that truth comes to those who are emotionally moved by what they read. Feeling serves as an interpretive tool: we cannot "*know* those truths which are revealed only to those who feel them" (148).

Given that insistence on intense feeling as requisite for real knowing, and given the logic that intense feeling would only come with an immediacy achieved by private depth-diving, apologists for the Catholic faith were obliged to make the case that mediation could enable true love and real faith. In an 1883 polemic titled "Protestantism versus the Church," the *Catholic World* charges that "man is not a bodiless spirit, and a sacrament without a sensible sign or medium is not fitted for the twofold nature of man."[28] Without "sufficient external appliances and supports," religious devotion risks falling prey to perversions like the Salvation Army and revivalism. Such reactions of misguided enthusiasm naturally would follow the stripping of the tangible and visible from worship practices. The Protestant will to keep the spiritual separate from the material "betrayed heretical tendencies" and threatened to "end in spiritual death" (11). The idea that surfaces (whether images, the materiality of earthly "supports," or the Bible's glorious rhetorical fabric) had to be abjured or broken through to achieve contact with God was a harmful reduction to the Catholic mind.

The sentimental novel is built on the premise that feeling produces knowledge; its epistemology yokes, rather than splits, emotion and cognition.[29] Stowe and Phelps assume further that feeling comes from what is visible, tangible, and shared in public. Their fictional reliance on sensible imagery aligns with Catholic warnings against the consequences of

Protestant inwardness. The revelatory reading that Protestant Bible guides prescribe to achieve intimacy with God is not like the reading that generates intimacy in the love story of communion that Stowe and Phelps tell. As novelists they have an investment in salvation through reading, and their novels aim to help readers access sacred truth. But they write less with the idea of either promising or withholding revelation than with the aim of prompting the ongoing process of interpretive collaboration that is communion.

EVA AND TOM IN LOVE

Shortly after *Uncle Tom's Cabin* was first published, the French novelist George Sand observed that "the only love-story, the only passion of the drama," was that between Little Eva and Uncle Tom.[30] Hortense Spillers, reading the novel nearly 140 years later, sees that passion revealed in Eva's request to buy Uncle Tom: "I want him," she tells her father. This, Spillers writes, is a stunning assertion of desire that subverts Stowe's carefully desexualized affection between Eva and Tom. (When her father asks what she wants him for, Eva answers, "to make him happy" [156].) In that line, says Spillers, Eva voices a "daring and impermissible desire" that is the "[symptom] of a disturbed female sexuality that American women of Stowe's era could neither articulate nor cancel."[31] It was white America's favorite love story, still capable of producing news in 1933 when the original Eva (Mrs. Cordelia MacDonald, who had played Eva in 1853) met, in real life, the current Uncle Tom (the white actor Otis Skinner, who performed in blackface).[32] Eva and Tom's love maintained its cultural traction no doubt because it allowed a covert celebration of a disturbed white sexuality. But theirs is also, importantly, a love story about reading. It was pictured as such again and again.

To identify Eva and Tom's relationship as the novel's central love story is to find a nonviolent model of intimacy in *Uncle Tom's Cabin*. That is not to deny the plausibility of Marianne Noble's 1997 argument for the sadomasochistic fantasies that the novel sponsors; her application of psychoanalytic paradigms to the novel makes a compelling case for a revelatory "sentimental wound" that allows a reader to merge with a fictional other in pain. Noble uses the work of Jacques Lacan and Julia Kristeva in order

Opposite page: Images of Eva and Tom from 1852 (*top*) and 1853 (*bottom*); *this page:* images from 1855 (*top*) and 1933 (*bottom*, depicting Otis Skinner as Tom for the Alvin Theater's revival). (Harry Ransom Center, University of Texas at Austin)

to "excavate" a possibly feminist account "from beneath" the language of "disembodied transcendence" she sees as Stowe's Calvinist baggage (302). In her response to Noble's essay, Elizabeth Barnes registers doubt about the applicability of such frameworks to mid-nineteenth-century readers.[33] I share that doubt. I am not convinced that the scene of Tom's death offers, as Noble proposes, a "fantasy of perfect access to the other's 'real presence'" (304). If his injuries are meant to make readers identify with Tom as a person, then Barnes is right to say that "Stowe had to have [Tom] beaten to death in order to prove that he existed" (324).

But the violence wreaked on Tom's body is not, I think, meant to make us identify with Tom. By the time Tom is martyred, he is scarcely human at all; he has become a black Christ. Read through the lens of contemporaneous Protestant-Catholic tensions, Tom's pained body demonstrates less an invitation to merge with Tom than an effort to replace a bare Protestant cross with a Catholic crucifix. Indeed, Protestant objections to the vividness of Catholic portrayals of Christ testify to a wish to protect, by keeping invisible, white male authority (a point I discuss in the next chapter). If Stowe radically rewrites the savior in the figure of a black slave, it is also true that by making Tom an object of veneration she keeps white power unexposed. And if Tom is a Catholicized, vivified Christ figure, he is just as available as Noble's argument suggests for readers' sadomasochistic fantasies. My point, though, is that this final vision of Tom is an apotheosis, not meant to make us love him as a particular man but to monumentalize his suffering for our sins. Tom's humanity is established earlier, in the scenes that Stowe draws of his life, above all in his intimacy with Eva.

To the degree that my argument resists Noble's reading, it also resists Barnes's proposal that sentimentality fosters a scapegoating intimacy whereby white spectators feel redeemed by witnessing the pain of others.[34] The key template for such sacrificial vicariousness, as Barnes says, is the Christian narrative of God giving up his son to crucifixion. But, for all its lurid violence, Stowe's work (let alone the Bible) aims to do more than make readers feel redeemed by somebody else's suffering. As Michael Gilmore argues, Stowe's rhetoric seeks to reclaim an eighteenth-century model of literary authority that fuses word and action. For Gilmore, Stowe's "sacramental aesthetic" wants to transform readers, much as Ophelia is changed by Eva and Cassy is changed by Tom, into actors themselves.[35]

Noble's and Barnes's work is revelatory scholarship, both in the sense that it produces insights into the structures of feeling that Stowe's work enables and that it belongs to the mode of symptomatic reading that ethicist scholars want to counter. Hortense Spillers's critique is also revelatory, exposing *Uncle Tom's Cabin* as a landmark work in the history of white Americans' ceaseless efforts to deny their destructive yearning for black bodies. But the novel is no less a landmark work in the history of Protestant efforts to imagine how to love God and how humans should love each other. Read in light of the competition between Protestant and Catholic ideals, between positing sacraments as interior acts versus as a community performance, the Eva-Tom bond is most remarkable not for how much but for how little it hides.

To restate my general point about sentimentalism with respect to the particular case of *Uncle Tom's Cabin:* it is worthwhile to read Eva and Tom's love story as a sincere Christian fantasy, because to analyze that fantasy on its own terms helps us discover alternatives to the dominant Protestant ideal of revelation. Such an analysis can also add to our understanding of how religion shapes categories of race. Stowe is typical of socially liberal nineteenth-century Protestants in describing Catholics in the same romantically racist terms as black Americans. *Uncle Tom's Cabin's* narrator speaks of the "vivid and pictorial" imagination of the "negro mind" (35). In *Agnes of Sorrento* Italians are born with "the instinct of painting" and the saintly heroine is notable for her "impressible imagination."[36] But Stowe does not only patronize such a mind; she attempts to emulate that mind as a writer, and to proffer it as a model for her readers' interpretive and emotional practice.

One sign of that emulation is Stowe's stated aim, in writing to her editor, to be a painter as she composes *Uncle Tom's Cabin.* The language of that letter suggests the irrationality Protestants associated with the visual mediations of Catholic worship: Stowe says she wants to write in pictures because pictures cannot be reasoned with. Some of the contemporaneous resistance to *Uncle Tom's Cabin* can be traced to Stowe's willingness to write like a Catholic—which was also to write like a woman. Both sentimentalism and Catholicism were viewed as feminized deviations from true Christianity because of their appeals to emotion through the senses, rather than through a disembodied intellect coded as masculine.[37]

Here I take exception to Michael Gilmore's account of Stowe's sacramental aesthetic. For Gilmore, Stowe remains staunchly Protestant in that the "real presence" called forth by her novel depends on the reader's will to receive that presence, just as "in Reformed sects, as opposed to the Catholic Church . . . communicants must take the Savior into their souls" on their own accord instead of relying on a priest (71). I am also not sure that Stowe is "contemptuous of the notion that things lack reality unless they can be physically seen and heard" (70). Stowe's rhetoric appeals to the senses in an effort to bypass the personal choice that was enshrined by Protestant faith. Rather than contempt for readers' desire for physical evidence, her language expresses an understanding that we do desire material proof. She knows that, like Thomas in the Gospels, we want to touch the wound. As Stowe says in the letter cited above, her imagistic language means to leave readers "impressed, whether they mean to be or not." Her use of vivid detail aims to overcome the reader's willed intentions—to corral them into belief in her characters' pain—by impressing their senses.

That reading aligns with the response of contemporaneous reviewers who both admire and disapprove of the way the novel's prose seemed calculated to assault readers' imaginations. The most critical accuses Stowe of peddling pornography, "paint[ing] from her own libidinous imagination scenes which no modest women could conceive of" and offering "thinly veiled pictures of corruption" that would make "a lady of stainless mind" "blush."[38] More appreciative reviews are still ambivalent in their praise. *Littell's Living Age*, for instance, observes that Stowe, "the clever authoress," skillfully deploys "the instinct of her sex": she "takes the shortest road to her purpose, and strikes at the conviction of her readers by assailing their hearts. She cannot hold the scales of justice with a steady hand, but she has learnt to perfection the craft of the advocate."[39] A review in the theologically conservative *Mercersburg Review* says the novel "carries you along whether your judgment assents or not," a privileging of feeling "so natural in a woman."[40] By ascribing the novel's emotional appeal to Stowe's gender, the review confirms the unfitness of women to handle serious debate and echoes Protestant judgments of what was substandard about Catholicism.

We have seen that Protestant Bible reading guides urge solitude to achieve the feeling of God's love. Stowe's novel resists those prescriptions by making understanding an event that functions through and with an audience. In ways that anticipate James's emphasis on the "scenic" quality of fiction, Stowe builds into her novel a dramatic quality that would help propel it to the stage. Bible reading becomes a performance: the young George Shelby reads from the book of Revelations to the slaves on the Shelby plantation (35); after Eva's death, St. Clare loves for Tom to read to him and to pray for him (311). The narrator tells us that Senator Bird's conversion—his decision to help Eliza escape in defiance of the Fugitive Slave Act—is the triumph of "private feelings" (85) over against Congress and the Union. But his private feelings were generated amid an audience who all witness the same tableau of a beautiful mother and son, two refugees immobilized by exhaustion. Eliza's testimony there produces "the magic of real presence," and Stowe's narrative eye pans around the members of the Bird household, cataloging the range of response to that presence. Eva's deathbed scene, another occasion when a crowd of spectators is transfixed by a female's suffering body, is also laid out with careful attention to setting. We readers are told that Eva's room is furnished "in a style that had a peculiar keeping with the character of her for whom it was intended" (291). We get details of the window hangings, the design of the rug, the bamboo furniture, the color scheme of rose and white, and the knickknacks themed on angels and lilies. Stowe seems to take it that, to register Eva's death fully, readers need to visualize the surfaces that surround and in effect compose her. The model of communion posits that scenery cannot be divorced from character.

The match between Eva and her decor, and the dispersal of her hair, are elements that the love story of communion borrows from the Catholic faith's presumption of the continuity between spiritual and material. These are examples of what we could call the transitive property of subjectivity: a faith that the body and the things that surround it extend a person's subjectivity out into the world. (We will find that assumption in full effect in Stoddard and James.) In the love story of communion, prolonged physical proximity enables the spread of selfhood from the animate to the inanimate. If subjectivity is not dependent on the hidden depths that we understand, say, furniture to lack, then it follows that things can speak as well as persons.

Thus Rachel Halliday's rocking chair has a life of its own, which it shares with Rachel. Stowe can shift seamlessly from a description of Rachel's loving brown eyes to personifying the chair Rachel sits in, which "had a turn for quacking and squeaking,—that chair had." The need to add the specifying tag admits to the possible confusion between chair and woman, a confusion the narrator extends comically by proposing the chair suffered "from some asthmatic affection, or perhaps from nervous derangement" (140). The description is humorous. But Stowe presents both the chair and Rachel as worthy of love: the chair's "subdued 'creechy crawchy'" is beloved by the family because "for twenty years or more, nothing but loving words and gentle moralities, and motherly loving kindness, had come from that chair;—head-aches and heart-aches innumerable had been cured there,—difficulties spiritual and temporal solved there,—all by one good, loving woman, God bless her!" (140). The agency hovers around the chair at the beginning of the sentence and only settles distinctly on the "good, loving woman" sitting in it at the end. What makes Rachel lovable is hard to separate from her chair. Such a description breaks down the ideals of depth and inwardness promoted in Protestant Bible guides.

Certainly for Stowe the things we own and wear are worth loving, in spite of—or perhaps because of—their lack of depth. Philip Fisher observes that Stowe's original subtitle for the novel identified Tom as "a man that was a thing" and argues that the work of the novel is to render Tom human by extending sentimental feeling to include him within its humanizing circle.[41] But this transitive subjectivity can also, as Gillian Brown shows, serve as an apology for enslavement. By Stowe's logic, "humanity [can be] vested in a subject by virtue of . . . an intimacy and identification developed in the history of a proprietorship."[42] Stowe's vision of a domestic world blissfully sealed off from the marketplace cannot finally accommodate black Americans because, for Stowe, blackness is an indelible marker of commodity status. African Americans have a place in Stowe's domestic economy only as well-cared-for possessions (56).

Brown's analysis explains why Topsy, whom Stowe describes as "one of the blackest of her race" (245), must be shipped off to Africa in the end. Topsy's case shows the limits of the liberating potential in the counterindividualist structure of communion. Stowe's narrator presents Topsy as a "thing" with a "veil" over her features and as an "image" (246, 249). She performs on command. (Given her superior stage presence in St. Clare's household, it is no surprise that many posters advertising Uncle Tom shows gave pride of place to Topsy's name.) Yet, even as Stowe's descriptions of Topsy dehumanize her character—Topsy gets none of the Shakespearean gravitas that, for example, Melville gives to Pip—Stowe shows that Topsy has accurately reckoned her own dehumanization by the legal and economic system of slavery. In response to Ophelia's battery of questions, Topsy tells Ophelia that she is a product "raised by a speculator," not a person born of mother and father (249). Ophelia, though, does not appreciate the acuity of Topsy's judgment; Ophelia needs to be enlightened by love for Topsy. Eva's touch is the instrument of Topsy's redemption, and in turn Topsy's touch becomes the instrument of Ophelia's redemption. That grants her character a crucial, if only temporary, power in the circuit of embodied salvation Stowe imagines.

Given the logic of communion, it is fitting that Tom and Eva read each other with a vision that takes in appearance, manner, and surrounding props. They grow closer and closer, but not by virtue of seeing more and more deeply into each other. Neither one possesses any depth to see into. Neither they nor we readers are privy to their interior states of mind. If Tom gazes at Eva like an Italian gazes at an icon, that image does not prompt Tom to search for her soul. That she resembles, to his eyes, a familiar sacred image is the sign that he loves her for who she really is. If the love story of communion renders Eva depthless (as depthless in her way as Topsy), she is nonetheless easy to love, and to appreciate as a spectacle. Indeed, spectacular appreciation seems equivalent to love. One need not dive into the depths of Eva's soul to find the gem hidden there. Stowe's characterization follows that premise throughout the novel.

Likewise, the interpretive work accomplished by Tom and Eva's communion is not penetrative but appreciative. When Eva begins to learn, through Tom's influence, to read the Gospel, the effect is magical. This is the passage cited at this chapter's opening: "At first, she read [aloud] to please her humble friend; but soon her own earnest nature threw out its tendrils, and wound itself around the majestic book; and Eva loved it, because it woke in her strange yearnings, and strong, dim emotions, such as impassioned, imaginative children love to feel" (267). Eva's yearnings and emotions are here invisible and internalized, appropriate to Protestant depth-reading. But the winding tendrils Stowe invokes to describe Eva's reading hint at a different model. Eva's interest in the Bible takes the form of a plant-like embrace that wants to hold and grasp the book, rather than penetrate its interior.

In the case of Tom's reading, Stowe tells us he marks up his bible—"bold, strong marks and dashes" in "a variety of styles and designations"—to indicate "the passages which more particularly gratified his ear or affected his heart" (151). The feeling of gratification that Protestant depth-reading aims to produce here expresses itself in a decorative embellishment that layers image on top of word. Tom's stylized marginalia may serve as a reminder that he is new to literacy and still reads with a neophyte's pictorial imagination, but they seem also to suggest a desire to illuminate the scripture, to translate the text from words into something closer to pictures. This is not an exegesis but a visualization of text. Tom and Eva both find satisfaction not by merging with the depths of the text, but by playing it (to borrow Roland Barthes's term), reproducing it as a new, more vivid and concrete, text. Something similar happens when they write together: it does not exactly signify, but "it really begins to look beautiful," according to Eva (244).

The narrative follows its description of Eva's and Tom's reading methods with an account of what might be called the Protestant sublime. Stowe's narrator here reflects on an ideal experience of reading the book of Revelations. Setting aside the story's thread, Stowe's narrator asks us to imagine a generalized "soul. . . . a trembling stranger" caught "between two dim eternities" of past and future, trying to understand "the voices and shadowy movings which come to her from out the cloudy pillar of inspiration" (267). This language evokes the Protestant ideal of revelation withheld: here on earth, the cloudy pillar stays cloudy, its "mystic imagery" remains illegible, "so many talismans and gems inscribed with unknown hieroglyphics" (267). The believing soul has faith that these things will be made plain "when she passes beyond the veil" (267).

The scene that follows that image of the Protestant sublime is Tom and Eva's climactic love scene. Their reading of the book of Revelations is wholly unlike the trembling encounter with a hidden mystery that has just been described. It is not alluringly dim but satisfyingly vivid. Eva and Tom do not actually pierce the veil, see the mystery, and thereby fulfill their love. Instead, their reading recreates the scripture by drawing on other texts they both know, a shared cultural vocabulary of devotion. They associatively build on the text without deciphering it.

Their reading becomes, in fact, a spectacle itself. The scene of Tom and Eva reading by the lake, first engraved by Hammatt Billings for the novel's 1852 American edition, became the single most popular image generated by *Uncle Tom's Cabin*. Jo Ann Morgan writes that, out of "scores of scenes in the story, generated for more than 150 years, illustrations of Tom and Eva together in gardens or courtyards, huddled over the Bible, have been the most reproduced."[43] We have already seen a few such images of their devotional reading, which would be used to advertise Uncle Tom shows for years to come.

The language Stowe uses to describe this scene reinforces the reading method Eva and Tom enact—that is, the description of the scene emphasizes horizontal movement across surfaces, rather than the vertical surface-to-depth penetration imagined by Protestant Bible guides. There is no diving to the bottom here: "It is now one of those intensely golden sunsets which kindles the whole horizon into one blaze of glory, and makes the water another sky. The lake lay in rosy or golden streaks, save where white-winged vessels glided hither and thither, like so many spirits, and little golden stars twinkled through the glow, and looked down at themselves as they trembled in the water" (268). This horizontal spread—horizon stretching out, vessels gliding across the surface—resists hermeneutical prying. The reflective quality of the lake's surface makes the vertical distance between sky and lake blur into indistinctness: the "water" is simply "another sky." The water and sky both become a shared representational space wherein Eva and Tom reimagine and visualize the Bible text. They are not hoping to merge with the soul of the text or to unite here and now with its author. Instead the two are trying to make the Bible concrete and visible and thus shareable.

When Eva reads, "'And I saw a sea of glass, mingled with fire,'" she interrupts herself: "'Tom,' said Eva, suddenly stopping, and pointing to the lake, 'there 'tis.'" She shows him how the lake is that sea of glass, and Tom sees it. In response he sings a verse from a hymn about how "bright angels should convey me home, / To the new Jerusalem." When Eva asks him where that Jerusalem might be, Tom says, "O, up in the clouds, Miss Eva." Eva responds to the suggestion by seeing what he says the text means: "'Then I think I see it,' said Eva. 'Look in those clouds!—they look like great gates of pearl.'" She asks Tom to sing another hymn, and again to his verse describing angels "robed in spotless white," she declares "Uncle Tom, I've seen them," and claims further that she is going there (268–69). Tom asks where, and in response Eva stands and points to the sky.

This moment of shared rapture appears where a love story of revelation would instead portray the satisfaction of an erotic merge or make us feel the anguish of a consummation just missed. In this love story of communion, Tom and Eva understand each other, and they understand the Bible. They are not, however, looking into each other's souls; they are using the mediation of the text to build a picture of the transcendence manifest in the world. They have not dredged up meaning from the depths of the text, but they have refashioned the Bible's words into a shared spectacle. If their expectation of attaining grace through reading the gospel is Protestant, the character of Eva and Tom's reading—their shared materialization of the biblical text—is tinged by Catholic practice. This hybrid reading, an understanding that is full without being deep, demonstrates the structure of love as communion.

REMATERIALIZING IN HEAVEN

The narrator of *Beyond the Gates* (1883)—the second in the series that began with *The Gates Ajar*—visits heaven and finds fictional characters among its inhabitants. Among them is Tom (though Eva is missing from the celebrity roll call that includes Hester Prynne and Jean Valjean).[44] If *Uncle Tom's Cabin* had a performative afterlife that could put its titular hero in another author's vision of heaven, *The Gates Ajar* also produced a cultural momentum that demonstrates the enduring reader-text intimacy characteristic of communion. To create that intimacy, the *Gates* series relies on the mediation of merchandising and the continuity of its sequels, *Beyond the Gates* and *The Gates Between* (1887). The three novels each feature different characters, but they carry on the reader's relationship with the ideas that Phelps puts forward in *The Gates Ajar*.

All three of Phelps's *Gates* novels might be subject to the disapproval registered in a review of *The Gates Ajar* in the *Ladies' Repository*. That review observes that "the heaven [Winifred] pictures would be . . . delightful to an unconverted worldly man, who . . . had a taste for books, paintings, statues, and natural scenery" and concludes with the repeated admonition that we cannot know, till God's kingdom comes, the "immense realities of heaven."[45] Like the reviewer for the *Christian Union,* this writer objects to Phelps's aestheticizing faith. Phelps, even more than Stowe, seems to such reviewers to approach what Jenny Franchot calls the "dangerous plenitude of a fleshly sublime" (199) that Protestants associated with Catholicism.

The reading program that Phelps portrays in *The Gates Ajar* is more sophisticated than Eva's and Tom's. But as a form of communion, it maintains a rejection of the ideal of revelation. Interpretation here remains collaborative, vivid, and concrete; it does not aim for the private and shadowy. Like Eva and Tom, the novel's interpreter-in-chief Winifred Forceythe takes an interest in the book of Revelations. She contends that it has been too literally interpreted by her fellow Protestants. Her niece Mary Cabot, whose brother Royal ("Roy") has just died in the Civil War, wants to believe in Winifred's vision of a heaven where Roy may have met President Lincoln and from where Roy watches over Mary now, but Mary must be persuaded to believe such a vision is theologically sound. Early on, sensing Winifred's departure from the orthodox view of the afterlife, Mary cites the biblical support for that view: "The harps and choirs, the throne, the white robes, are all in Revelation" (45).

Winifred responds with evident impatience: "Can't people tell picture from substance, a metaphor from its meaning? That book of Revelation is precisely what it professes to be—a vision; a symbol" (45). Such images are not, she goes on, "*empty* symbols." To read the true fullness of a symbol, Winifred shows, we cannot dematerialize the vehicle to tenor, decode harps and thrones as meaning "love," and stop there. A symbol's fullness of meaning entails its potential to change. The same meaning signified by robes and harps can be retranslated back into different but equally significant, equally legitimate, vehicles. Winifred rematerializes the tenor into another vehicle, one more legible to the human heart: the bodies and creature comforts that are necessary for love to function.

Winifred's critique of Protestant literalism effectively anticipates and inverts the critique of *The Gates Ajar* as erring by aestheticizing God's word. Gail Smith suggests that the conservative Deacon Quirk, an officious church elder who thinks he is protecting a properly spiritual understanding of heaven from Winifred's literalism, can be seen as a proxy for Phelps's own conservative critics.[46] His insistence on sticking to the letter of Revelation's imagery founders on Winifred's rebuttal that her claim for pianos in heaven is no less spiritual, and no more material, than the Bible's claim for harps in heaven. Winifred's practice suggests that such critics are committed to an impoverished and incomplete reading.

Winifred's frustration with overliteral Bible readers might extend to contemporary literary critics, as Smith points out. Surveying more recent accounts of the novel by scholars from Ann Douglas to Lisa Long, Smith argues that "*The Gates Ajar* is not fairly judged as literal-minded. If anything, the novel is much closer to a celebration of figuration . . . it encourages its readers to engage in their own picture-making, as Mary and [Winifred] do, expressly for the support of faith by analogy" (116). Generating a shared pictorial response to a text is, as we saw for Eva and Tom by the lake, key to the communion that this novel both portrays and provokes. To create such a response requires an interpretive method that aims not for abstraction but for concretion. If, as Smith puts it, for Winifred "Revelation's figures are based on material things," "that doesn't make them any less figurative. When spiritual figures are read correctly . . . their concreteness is seen correctly as simile and metaphor intended to draw the soul to God" (108). The effectiveness of this program for drawing believers toward contact with transcendence is demonstrated by Mary's experience. After months of talking with Winifred, Mary finds that God has shifted from being an "abstract Grandeur" to a "living Presence, dear and real" (110). The mediations of visual imagery have produced a more, not less, profound intimacy with the transcendent.

Phelps's novel develops not only the role of visual mediation in communion but also portrays the quality of ongoingness that marks communion. Cindy Weinstein analyzes the challenge that Phelps faces in trying to narrate a paradigm shift that "means making the past present, keeping the dead here, collapsing then and now."[47] That shift induces "an incoherence about time" in the sentences of Mary's diary as Mary struggles to evoke the unimaginable enduring present that God promises (65). But as Winifred trains Mary to speak of the dead in the present tense, Mary learns to think of death as a beginning, as Christian doctrine promises.

The proposal that an end is a beginning also serves to recast intimacy not as an upward learning curve but as a repetitive cycle. Communion is not teleological, driving from a better to the best understanding of a loved one. Like the serial story of friendship Phelps commends in her essay for *In After Days,* this is a vision of a seemingly endless routine that nonetheless fluctuates, made dynamic by its sensory particulars. As Weinstein observes, Phelps's narrative subverts the usual novelistic drive toward discovery and closure. *The Gates Ajar* counters Peter Brooks's classic account of novelistic structure because it offers "a competing masterplot"—namely, "God's plot, which is *the* crucial historical context that Phelps brings to her understanding of narrative" (68). It helps further to read this novel in the more specific historical context of Protestant-Catholic tension; in that context, we can see Phelps resisting conservative Protestantism by borrowing Catholic ideals that recast ritual and the material not as hindrances to be triumphantly overcome, but as fit vehicles of transcendence.

In *Uncle Tom's Cabin,* as we saw, Stowe hypothesizes a revelatory reading for the afterlife: the Bible's mysteries will be readable when the believer enters heaven. With Winifred's materialist reading method as a model, Phelps takes on the task of realizing that hypothesis. Her novel discovers that whatever depth might be imagined for selves in the afterlife is irreducibly mediated by flesh and blood, furniture and flowers. To arrive at that embrace of materiality, though, requires a struggle for Phelps's heroine Mary.

That struggle is the story the novel tells. Mary at first prizes her deep, private feelings, but she tries to empty herself of egoism. She hates idolatry, but she only knows and loves others through what she can see and touch. Phelps's version of communion is complicated by her choice to frame the novel as Mary's diary, a form that promises us privileged access to the narrator's secrets. Phelps finally repudiates that promise, but the diary form means that *The Gates Ajar* is a less theatrical novel than *Uncle Tom's Cabin.* Mary never gives a catalog of interior decoration in the course of her diary entries; the action and dialogue take place in vaguely pleasant rooms and gardens. And because Mary never describes herself to her diary, we are forced to think of her as a disembodied voice, a vague interiority. Disembodiment is the problem for Mary: deprived of the materiality of her brother's physical self, she feels cast into a void of abstract doctrine that cannot sustain her love for him. Her healing will take shape through conversation with Winifred—shared reading and dialogue that, day after day, generate a picture of the afterlife that is material. Only in such a material afterlife is love actually possible.

The story of Mary's coming to accept communion as real intimacy—to believe, like Catholic convert Orestes Brownson, in "the more authentic reality of mediated existence"—begins in grief.[48] Her diary begins by recording Mary's anguish after she hears of her brother's death in the Civil War. In the immediate aftermath of the news, she pictures herself as in solitary confinement: "Those two words—'Shot dead'—shut me up and walled me in, as I think people must feel shut up and walled in, in Hell" (5). She rejects the efforts of the community to ease her pain and resists the social conventions that would govern her emotion. We take these pages as Mary's private thoughts, truer than what she can say to the condolence callers she resents. But Mary will not remain so private and deep. After less than two weeks she condemns her own introspection and quits the diary. (The hiatus will last only three days.)

She quits it, curiously, for reasons that are in conflict with each other. On the one hand Mary stops writing because she realizes that the journal is cultivating a self-involvement that for her amounts to selfishness, an indulgence of the "luxury of grief" (15). Her brother, she reflects, would not approve. On the other hand Mary distrusts her journal writing as a record of the mere surface of her emotion: "On looking over the leaves [of the journal], I see that the little green book has become an outlet for the shallower part of pain" (15). The trouble with Mary's journal is that it threatens to make her both too deep and not deep enough. She fears that writing will overprivilege her most profound self; she fears that her writing will shortchange her most profound self. This conflict, which will eventually push Mary toward the mediated intimacy of communion, is built into the Protestant depth drive. That depth drive privileges immediacy, simultaneously denying the value of appearances and wishing for some visible truth. The depth drive defines revelation as an ever-vanishing point. The truest truth is always invisible; any apparent form becomes a shell of some deeper reality.

Mary's initial faith in this ideal of revelation withheld comes through most sharply in her reaction to Dr. Bland's sermon at the Homer First Congregational Church. Bland's heaven is built on universal, not particular, love; he speculates that in the joy of contemplating infinite truth, a man might forget to think of his wife for thousands of years. There will be no individual depths, but a perfect transparency of each soul to every other. Bland proposes that in heaven "the soul will have no interests to conceal, *no thoughts to disguise. A* window will be opened in every breast, and show to every eye the rich and beautiful furniture within!" Mary records this idea with scorn: "I wonder if he really thought *that* would make 'a world of bliss'" (41–42). The transparent selves and universal love that Bland anticipates, by revealing interiority, would effectively destroy individuality for Mary and Winifred. Such individualism was not a key issue for Stowe, but in Phelps's novel love and understanding depend on recognizing the particularity of the self. Aunt Winifred's love of her is more valuable, Mary says, because "she seems to love me a little, not in a proper kind of way, because I happen to be her niece, but for my own sake" (34). Real love must be love of the unique individual according to its private quirks and merits, not according to conventional forms.

When she and Winifred parse Dr. Bland's sermon later, Mary brings up this transparency of heart and its accompanying universalization of love as a cause of anxiety: "I would rather be annihilated than to spend eternity with heart laid bare,—the inner temple thrown open to be trampled on by every passing stranger!" (46). The interior is sacrosanct here—the self is no mere container but a temple. Winifred agrees. She calls Dr. Bland's notion "nonsense" because it would destroy the self by rendering its depths as surfaces for all to see; Winifred argues that transparent hearts and indiscriminate loves "would destroy individuality," leaving us "like a man walking down a room lined with mirrors . . . till he seems no longer to belong to himself, but to be cut up into ellipses and octagons and prisms" (46). This passage reaffirms the Protestant privilege of depth and the unreliability of surface. Faced with fragmentary reflections of ourselves, we would lose our crucial sense of private self-ownership and go mad. Winifred concedes that in heaven we will have extra moral legibility to one another, but such legibility could not violate the privacy of one's own hidden self.

But if Phelps begins her novel favoring invisible depths of self, those depths will yield to her interest in models of faith and of selfhood that match Winifred's appreciation of Catholicism. Winifred's little girl kisses a photograph of her father at night as if he were an icon; after reading a hymn to Mary, Winifred urges that "we may learn something from that grand old Catholic singer," who is "far nearer to the Bible" than later "innovators" (98). The social self invoked in the Catholic mass will play a role in reintegrating Mary into the community as it moves her attention from the inside to the outside, from depth to surface.

To begin with, Mary must lessen her investment in privacy and adopt a more publicly available selfhood. If it is too absurd to imagine a man who no longer belongs to himself in heaven, as Winifred says in repudiating Dr. Bland's sermon, much of the guidance she provides to Mary nudges her precisely not to belong to herself, at least while she lives on earth. Instead she urges Mary to belong to others. When Mary revives her journal it is in the interest of cultivating selflessness. She returns to her diary only when Aunt Winifred arrives, and only then, she says, for the "excellent reason" that "I have something else than myself to write about" (16). We know that Mary is healing when we see her reach out to others; it is a sign she is regaining her true self, which, as Phelps's novel progresses, comes to mean her communally constituted self. It is a sin to sit upstairs meditating on one's interior life rather than to respond to dull Mrs. Bland's social call. By the end of the novel Mary has achieved selflessness. Her diary no longer records her inner pain, only her anticipation of a heavenly union with Jesus and her brother.

Winifred, like Stowe's characters, takes the Protestant view that salvation comes through reading the Bible. But Winifred, in a manner more in line with the Catholic reliance on tradition than with the Protestant doctrine of *sola scriptura*, understands the Bible through spiritual authorities, never reading alone but with a community of earlier interpreters. Widow of a Congregationalist minister, she has read a library's worth of theologians. She calls up names and cites passages by heart: Thomas Chalmers on "spiritual materialism," Isaac Taylor, even Swedenborg (whom she likes but does not accept). Under Winifred's influence, Mary trades her private reading of German romantics for conversations about Christian texts. Being able to externalize rather than internalize the text becomes the point for Mary. In this way Phelps resists the Protestant Bible guides' emphasis on reading alone.

Moreover, Phelps, though she gives over much of her novel to theological speculation rather than concrete imagery, values the physical as much as Stowe does. Although Mary never becomes the sort of icon that Eva does, appearance remains a reliable index of character. Winifred, for instance, simply looks more spiritual than the "earthy" Deacon Quirk (88).

The inner temple that Mary abhors to imagine laid bare is inconceivable without the hair, eyes, and arms that embody it. What Mary misses in her brother, what makes him lovable, is his eyes, arms, smile, hair, the weight and cadence of his walk. If Stowe managed, as Spillers points out, to hide the white woman's desire for the black man in plain sight, Phelps can be said to keep carefully implicit an incestuous desire. In the early stages of her "physical repulsion" from the fact of his death, Mary invokes Roy's presence by naming the parts of his body she misses: "Roy, with the flash in his eyes, with his smile that lighted the house all up; with his pretty, soft hair that I used to curl and kiss about my finger, his bounding step, his strong arms that folded me in and cared for me" (7). It grieves her above all to imagine that body "laid out there in the wet and snow,—in the hideous wet and snow,—never to kiss him, never to see him any more!" (7).

The novel wants to preserve the idea of sacred depths, but the love that makes those depths sacred demands faces, hands, and hair to love; it demands strawberries and gingersnaps, as well as houses and pianos, to love with (103, 82). Winifred assures Mary that "the spiritual body is real, is tangible, is visible, is human," though changed somehow (69). She recommends that Mary read Thomas Chalmers's "On the New Heavens and the New Earth," a sermon arguing that we will have new and sin-free bodies in heaven. In Chalmers's words, to expunge our bodies of original sin "the old fabric must be taken down, and reared anew," but "not of other materials, but of its own materials, only delivered from all impurity, as if by a refining process in the sepulcher."[49] Our bodies in heaven must be solid material, but of some better and brighter kind. After his death, Winifred reasons, Jesus returned in a recognizable body, ate fish, and talked with his friends; thus we can be sure we will be capable of the same. The Bible makes clear we will have bodies in heaven, and what, Winifred asks, "would be the use of having a body that you can't see and touch?" (66).

Mary's diary tracks her growing intimacy with Winifred. That intimacy grows through an appreciation of Winifred's style. Here too there is tension: Winifred both arouses surface desire (and frequently sanctions it by telling Mary that of course she and Roy will have bodies in heaven) and denies it. Before she meets her aunt, Mary is drawn to Winifred's letter for its specifically material and formal qualities as much as for the ideas it communicates. Mary loves Winifred's handwriting, her careful choice of words, and then her voice and her face. And in the voice and handwriting, she loves the form of Winifred's words, the vessel in which those words find delivery. Their love also relies on reticence. Winifred wins Mary's heart at crucial moments by not speaking—by holding her or stroking her hair instead. Such reticence might seem to privilege depth over surface by suggesting that what is deepest suffers diminishment by surfacing into expression. That was the fear that partly motivated Mary to quit her diary early on. But in Phelps's novel reticence instead yields space for the physical to promote real self-other understanding; at crucial moments, the body and hands communicate more effectively than the abstractions of mind and words. During Dr. Bland's sermon about heavenly transparency, Mary recounts, "Aunt Winifred slipped her hand into mine under her cloak. Ah, Dr. Bland, if you had known how that little soft touch was preaching against you!" (41). Phelps makes this touch effect a mutual understanding across the body's surfaces, as the model of communion posits.

Yet Phelps never stops plying the tension between the surface of the body and the depth imagined within that body. Near the novel's end, after Winifred has schooled Mary in her notion of heaven and brought her safely back to the fold of the community, Winifred wonders aloud about the keepsakes from the dead—the "lock of hair to curl about our fingers; a picture that has caught the trick of his eyes or smile; a book, a flower, a letter"—that the living hold dear. "Yet who loves the senseless gift more than the giver,—the curl more than the young forehead on which it fell,— the letter more than the hand which traced it?" (111). By casting the choice here in terms of material relic versus real person, Winifred distances herself from idolatry. Winifred acknowledges that "Roman Catholic nature is human nature, when it comes upon its knees before a saint" (54), but adds that such adoration risks idolatry. In this moment she sounds like Deacon Quirk, who earlier warned Mary that "poor human nature sets a great deal by earthly props" (11). Despite her sympathy with Catholicism, Winifred here invokes the usual Protestant distinction between Catholics' worship of mere mediating props and Protestants' worship of the true God.

Although Winifred's analysis of the keepsake seems to downgrade the physical relic, the terms of her comparison suggest that real love is a matter of favoring one physical surface over another, the body over the traces it leaves: the forehead more than the hair, the hand more than the hand-writing on the sheet of paper, the eyes or smile more than the photograph of them. Reading the same passage, Lucy Frank observes that the novel portrays "the physical traces of" Roy as "part of an associative network, acting as interconnected reminders of his ongoing, materialized spiritual being and of God's presence" (174).

For the paradox of materialized spirituality to work—for it to help solve Mary's problem of choosing between love of God and love of Roy—requires the sanctification of the physical. That sanctification was con-ferred by Christ's incarnation, which, Winifred says, "dignified forever" our bodies (68). That sanctification enables the believer to avoid idolatry, because it remakes Jesus from the glorious and inscrutable deity into a man at whose sandaled feet you can sit and listen. Winifred ultimately trades revelation for a "communion with God" she defines as *"friendship of the man Christ Jesus"* (112). Such friendship, because it is mediated through the physical, is expansive enough to include one's brother along-side the man Jesus.

The Gates Ajar shows that love can only function through material mediation. This version of communion amounts to a somewhat uneasy Protestant doctrine of transubstantiation. Ultimately Mary and Winifred solve the problem of surface and depth by making selfhood a matter of materiality, though it is a materiality that is only fully sanctified in heaven, where Christ's body redeems it. Beginning from a model of self that favors depth, Winifred and Mary arrive at a self that is constituted bodily and socially. Even in heaven depth is unimaginable without surface. To put it another way, love for Phelps is finally strong enough to make the distinc-tion between surface and depth—a distinction that Protestant faith and its hermeneutics would otherwise oblige her to insist on—irrelevant. Phelps, like Stowe, thus makes a novelistic virtue of the insight that real love, love that endures, requires visual and emotional mediation. Both authors en-able fiction to make a claim to speak God's truth precisely through fiction's ability to present a world of vivid surfaces, whether on heaven or earth.

Three

Romantic Spectatorship

Self-Portrait as a Stranger's Head
in *The Blithedale Romance* and *Pierre*

FOR HIS 1850 REVIEW OF Nathaniel Hawthorne's *Mosses from the Old Manse*, Herman Melville takes on the identity of a nameless Virginia tourist. In that anonymous disguise, he makes the case for authorial disappearance. If only "all books were foundlings," then "we could glorify them, without including their ostensible authors."[1] Yet, if he initially wants to glorify books minus the persons who write them, Melville's reviewer goes on to claim that "if you rightly look for it, you will almost always find that the author has somewhere furnished you with his own picture" (2316). This hidden self-portrait turns out to be the real prize for the reader who knows how to look. The Virginia tourist finds that prize in Hawthorne's *Mosses*. The stories offer enough "clews" to allow the reviewer to "enter a little way into the intricate, profound heart where they originated" (2310), and from there an erotic connection develops. The reviewer feels Hawthorne "[drop] germinous seeds into my soul" and "[shoot] his strong New-England roots into the hot soil of my Southern soul" (2317). This sense of insemination revises the reviewer's initial impression of Hawthorne. This is no longer the "pleasant" and "harmless" Hawthorne that most readers see (2311). This more dangerous author is visible only to a gifted reader: "There is no glimpse to be caught of it, except by intuition," but he is full of "the blackness of darkness" (2312). The intuition of Hawthorne's darkness transforms the reviewer, whose tone takes on a soaring confidence. This invisible revelation consummates an intimacy that empowers both the reader and the author.

Melville's "Hawthorne and His Mosses" tells a love story between an author and his reader that pays off in the revelation of a potent hidden depth. That love story of revelation is appropriate to dramatize the merging of two writers who would become twin stars of American romanticism. It stands as a model of how the romantic mode imagines revelatory intimacy, and it contrasts with the sentimental novel's love story of communion. As we saw in the last chapter, in *Uncle Tom's Cabin* and *The Gates Ajar* characters do not track down clues to burrow into each other's hearts. They bond by talking about the Bible and theology, and we are assured that their interpretive work will continue in the afterlife. Their communion is ongoing and triangulated through a shared text. But in "Hawthorne and His Mosses," the mediating text of the stories drops out as the reader approaches the dark heart of the author. The romantic love story of revelation claims to transcend the self and bind with the other not through an endlessly shared creativity but through a transformative moment of contact.

That romantic vision of love will be mocked by Melville in *Pierre* and by Hawthorne in *The Blithedale Romance*. Both published in 1852, these novels critique the romantic mode and at least half-endorse a sentimental authorship. *Blithedale* and *Pierre* make vivid how disastrously wrong the depth drive can go as a motive for human interaction. That critique of revelation comes through in the love plot in each novel, wherein a depth-obsessed hero destroys his chances at real intimacy. These fictional love stories serve as cautionary tales to the reader to beware insisting on revelation.

The novels themselves also provoke, and frustrate, their readers' drive to find the depths of Hawthorne and Melville. On the face of it, *Blithedale* and *Pierre* seem designed to furnish pictures of their authors. Both are semiautobiographical accounts of the writing life. Like other critics before me, I read the novels' protagonists—poet Miles Coverdale and experimental novelist Pierre Glendinning—as alter egos for Hawthorne and Melville. Writing in 1926, Amy Louise Reed argues that "Miles Coverdale is really an autobiographical character."[2] In 1983, Michael Paul Rogin reads Pierre as a barely fictionalized analogue for Melville.[3] But for any reader hoping to meet the author frankly in these pages, to learn what Hawthorne really thought of his experience at Brook Farm or how Melville struggled to find his voice as a writer, these novels do not deliver. Miles and Pierre, instead of unveiling their authors' real selves, become vehicles for a critique of the pretensions of romantic authorship.

It might sound, then, as if these novels are case studies in revelation withheld—wielding their fictional status like the dark veil Reverend Hooper wears to the grave in Hawthorne's story "The Minister's Black Veil." But the more accurate parallel is the translucent silvery veil that Zenobia throws over Priscilla to seal the effect of her own narrative. The novels deliberately play with the power of revelatory promises; they do not present the austere unknowability that we saw neo-orthodox theologians praise and that we will see Levinas-inspired literary ethicists admire. The tone of these novels is self-aware, verging on campy: think of Miles's gasped final confession about Priscilla, or the filigreed Romeo-and-Juliet scene of Pierre wooing Lucy at her window. If Miles and Pierre are at times tragic, they are also occasionally ridiculous. They are not only bad lovers but misguided artists. Hawthorne and Melville make them look that way by contrast with the women they are most attracted to. In *Blithedale* and *Pierre,* the artistry of Zenobia and Isabel, both creative women who know how to use mediation and artifice, offers a counterexample to the masculine depth drive and its aesthetic program.

Each novel partway endorses that feminine counterexample and even inhabits it to a degree. In doing so, each novel makes possible a happier love story, a nonrevelatory intimacy between author and reader. *Blithedale* and *Pierre* structure the possibility of the reader and author looking together at the spectacle of the novel itself. This shared enjoyment of the performance of the narrative is Hawthorne and Melville's adaptation of sentimental communion. I am not saying they make this relationship with the reader easy or altogether pleasant. But the novels make that structure of mutual spectatorship available. How *Blithedale* and *Pierre* generate this variant of the love story of communion between themselves and their own readership is the subject of this chapter.

That is a quite different reader-text love story from the one Melville writes in response to "Hawthorne and His Mosses." At the end of this chapter, I consider some of the complexities in the language of love to be found in Melville's letters to Hawthorne. My aim here is to let the review stand as an example of consummated reader-author revelation, in contrast to the love story on offer in Stowe and Phelps. I mean for that contrast to illustrate how an emotional hierarchy supports a gendered aesthetic. The shift from the previous chapter to this one reminds us of the familiar split between the Byronic male creator versus the sweetly sentimental author-ess. And it shows how the greater prestige accorded to romanticism over sentimentalism depends on the greater prestige accorded to the intimacy of revelation over the intimacy of communion. To follow the pictures of Eva and Tom reading by the lake with the dark germination of "Hawthorne and His Mosses" is to experience sentimentality's reputed aesthetic shortcoming as a deficit of feeling.

The sense that the love to be found in communion is less moving or less real than the love Melville's reviewer finds with Hawthorne marks another example of how the Protestant privileging of revelation can shape literary judgments. The idea that only revelatory intimacy really gets beyond the self to the other relies on the logic of nineteenth-century anti-Catholicism examined in chapter 1. Melville's review itself suggests a religious connection. The depth that makes Hawthorne so attractive is intensely Protestant, identified with "Puritanic gloom" and a "Calvinistic" appreciation of the power of sin (2311). Indeed, at the start of the review, we are reminded that Jesus's power was invisible: "Not even in the case of . . . our Saviour, did his visible frame betoken anything of the augustness of the nature within" (2308). The lack of visible divinity secures Jesus's true nature deep inside, where its invisibility fuels the impossible desire to see it. What is true for God the Author is also true for mortal authors.

In particular, then, the iconophobia of anti-Catholic logic helps explain the emotional and aesthetic shift we feel in moving from Stowe and Phelps to Hawthorne and Melville. Such logic dictates that keeping God invisible—though capable of potential revelation—is the only way to protect his claim to transcendence and to protect the emotional freedom of his worshipers. This logic sets boundaries both for proper representation and for proper interpretation. It holds that if God is hyperrepresented (e.g., as an anguished body on a cross), then the believer is forced to underinterpret and underfeel. Catholicism's mediated worship threatens a crucial Protestant feedback loop whereby the believer's private emotional response proves his capacity for spontaneous deep feeling at the same time that it proves God's capacity to evoke such feeling. On this view, the ritual and imagery endorsed by Catholic practice disempowers both God and his creatures by cheapening the emotional transaction between them. By making God too sensually available, Catholic practice disempowers the divine and threatens the autonomy of believers.

In this way Protestants could cast the superiority of their interpretive approach as a manful striving to see through obscurity by contrasting it with the feminine passivity it assigned to Catholic worship practices. As Jenny Franchot writes, Catholic "image[s] of the male body in extremity" were for Protestants "a taboo representation of erotic arousal and moral degradation."[4] Much more than reading did, such images threatened to collapse the believer's will. "Catholicism's dominating theatrical displays," with their "power to enthrall and control . . . could finally issue in the 'feminization' of the self by breaking down its emotional reserves" (239). Protestantism's alluring gloom protects masculine authority; Catholicism's vivid intensities turn believers into swooning women. We saw one application of that logic at the start of chapter 1, in the review of *The Gates Ajar* that claimed Phelps's pictorialism had trivialized God's majesty.

It is worth noting that, among mortals, such invisible power is the prerogative not just of men but of white men. In these novels about authorship, Hawthorne and Melville implicitly identify invisibility as a white male privilege, whether it is seized sheepishly (as in Miles's anxious defense of his right to peep) or defiantly (as in Pierre's determination to sequester himself as an urban hermit). The novels indirectly acknowledge the disempowering visibility of race by heightening the contrast between the dark women, Zenobia and Isabel, and the pale good girls, Priscilla and Lucy. Zenobia's and Isabel's not-blonde female bodies are powerful enough in their sensory appeal to threaten the will of Miles and Pierre. The protagonists protect themselves by holding out for invisible and empowering depth. Hawthorne and Melville let us see that resistance to Zenobia and Isabel not as an admirable refusal but as a defensive maneuver.

Moreover, both Zenobia and Isabel model an alternative mode of creative power to which their male lovers are oblivious. We know from "The Tartarus of Maids" that Melville could lament the exploitation of a female creativity that was obliged to serve male authorship. We also know that Hawthorne, for his part, resented the overproduction of female creativity he saw in the "damned mob of scribbling women" he complained about to his publisher; if he feared offering his own soul for his readers' consumption, Hawthorne deplored a woman putting herself before the public eye in print, an act he likened to "stark naked" prostitution.[5] But I read Zenobia and Isabel as performers whose methods Hawthorne and Melville try on for size in these novels. Both women put on a show, self-consciously parrying or fulfilling their audiences' expectations. Through the figures of Miles and Pierre, Hawthorne and Melville experiment with appearing before the public in the self-aware way that Zenobia and Isabel do.

I develop this thesis by examining a case study in masculine portraiture that shows how Protestant iconophobia works and how it could be overcome. That case study concerns two portraits of masculine authority at its most exalted: Jesus and George Washington. The former of these painted portraits was deliberately left undone; the other was successfully achieved. Mid-nineteenth-century debates about these paintings demonstrate how the dominant Protestant culture imagined that a viewer's feelings could confer power on, or withdraw power from, the object it viewed. That context helps us register the force of the dissent against the Protestant depth drive that is lodged by the performative self-portraits of *Blithedale* and *Pierre*.

Comparing the verbal portraiture of *Blithedale* and *Pierre* with the literal visibility of painted pictures helps specify what authorial visibility means—what it threatens or offers—in the broader culture of the mid-nineteenth century. Protestant anti-Catholicism did not just direct Bible reading or church worship. The assumptions that anti-Catholicism makes about representation and interpretation spread beyond that specifically religious discourse into the judgment of visual and verbal media. Tracking that spread helps reinforce my broad argument that Catholic-Protestant conflict is not just a context but a source for the interpretive and emotional hierarchies that would organize American literature from the start.

My reading of these novels argues that Hawthorne and Melville generate an author-reader intimacy that resists the Protestant logic of invisible power. What that intimacy might look like crystallizes in a moment from the end of *Pierre*. I will return to this scene later, but I include it here as an image of the version of communion that both novels produce: the mutual spectatorship of reader and author gazing together at a representation that is strange to both of them. Near the end of *Pierre*, Pierre and Isabel are looking together at an unknown portrait—a picture of a stranger's head. Both are deeply moved, but their reactions are entirely separate: "Though both were intensely excited by one object, yet their two minds and memories were thereby directed to entirely different contemplations." Melville's narrator does not present this scene as a tragedy of failed mutuality. He suggests it is "unreasonabl[e]" for one person looking at a picture to believe another person looking at the same picture is "occupied by one and the same contemplation."[6] That acceptance of disjunction is in line with communion, which requires two distinct perspectives on a shared text in order to keep the work of interpretation going. This moment of spectatorship—sharing the same object but not the same feeling—does not satisfy Pierre's wish for revelation. Melville, however, lets it stand as a wry comment on the paradoxical wish that our emotions should be both intensely private and magically shareable.

PICTURING MAXIMUM AUTHORITY

In midcentury America, the question of how to paint Jesus, God the Author incarnate, was answered by some Protestants with a simple prohibition: don't do it. There were broader reasons in the economy of American art to discourage such an undertaking. Portraiture as a genre of painting still carried the whiff of work for hire,[7] and the increasing accessibility of daguerreotypes seemed poised to make painted likenesses obsolete.[8] For an ambitious artist aiming to paint a transcendent subject, Barbara Novak writes, landscape offered a way to limn God by representing the grandeur of his creation.[9] But the ultimate argument against painting Jesus was emotional. It would mean a loss of feeling to portray a subject whose transcendent power and allure required invisibility.

We have seen the argument against excessively pictorial language applied to Phelps's novels. Using the same logic in a disapproving review of a book that considered the Bible as poetry, a writer for the *North American Review* argues for the superior capacity of plain language over the artificiality of poetry, saying that even John Milton falls "far short of what the simple prose of the Gospels" (e.g., the brevity of lines like "Jesus wept") "develops."[10] The problem with the intrusive mediation of poetic language is its failure to invite the reader in: "We turn away from the *poems* named above, with our minds dissatisfied and all but displeased." The reviewer argues that fancy language makes bad intimacy by asking us to consider the even less satisfying visual medium, asking: "How can painters copy the face of him, from which beamed an intelligence, a kindness, a dignity, an energy, and a glory which no mortal man ever did or could possess?" (249) Abstract nouns do all that can be done to represent Jesus's virtues. Even a "proposed. . . . portrait" is a "detraction" from the "Son of God," says the reviewer, because "our *ideal* so far exceeds the efforts or darings of the pencil" (249). Given the reviewer's claims that a portrait is a direct copy and the original is transcendent, these strictures make sense. But this case for the ontological impossibility of a portrait of God relies on emotional response. The proof that the ideal exceeds what art can dare is there in one's disappointed feelings in response to the art.

It is not surprising, then, that the painter Washington Allston, who had made some sketches toward a picture of Christ healing the sick, opted not to complete the work. Allston's explanation cites "the universal failure of all painters, ancient and modern, in their attempts to give even a tolerable idea of the Saviour" before adding, "Besides, I think His character too holy and sacred to be attempted by the pencil."[11] The painter Robert Weir showed even more discretion. Uncomfortable with the "unbridled imagination" confronting him in "Catholic life as he saw it in Italy," Weir said that "I painted the *Two Marys at the Tomb,* but left the figure of Christ to be imagined. I have often so left it. One feels a delicacy in even attempting the delineation."[12] Such delicacy helped maintain the maximum emotional power vested in the undelineated figure of Jesus.

Those artists who did attempt painting Jesus might find themselves blamed for their emotional deficits. The *Literary World*'s "Fine Arts" column finds Horatio Greenough's *Head of Christ* "wholly deficient in that expression of sublimity which we inseparably connect with our idea of the Saviour."[13] Greenough, the reviewer feels, has the skill but not the spirit for the task. A review in *Godey's,* otherwise enthusiastic about religious paintings, finds that the Jesus in Benjamin West's *Christ Healing the Sick* proves the painter's "comparative incompetency."[14] To capture Jesus's true nature, the painter himself must feel properly awed, and West had not risen to the occasion. The writer speculates, "The cherubim were not invoked [by the artist] to impart their sacred fire, nor did the hesitancy of self-distrust cause the dilated heart to tremble." In these cases, the problem is the lack of fire in the artist's heart. Because it was not painted with sufficient passion, the picture fails in turn to make the viewer feel grandenough feelings.

Such responses show how the biblical claim that God's invisibility is the necessary correlate to fallen human perception (if you see his face, you will die) could become a Protestant emotional rationale that made unsatisfiable desire the proof of God's greatness. Writing an introduction to her brother Charles Beecher's novelization of the Bible, *The Incarnation; or, Pictures of the Virgin and Her Son* (1849), Harriet Beecher Stowe praises her brother's choice to describe all the Bible characters except Christ.[15] Christ's appearance is "a subject where all words, as well as all artistic representation, whether by pencil or chisel, must forever fall short of the expectations and desires of the soul that appreciates his glory" (vii–viii). Stowe's fiction, as we have seen, would later develop a pervasive sympathy for Catholic practice and a deliberate pictorialism. But this early document aligns with an anti-Catholic logic spelled out by a figure like the Scottish minister John Cumming, whose *Lectures on Romanism* was published in America in 1854.

Cumming articulates as one reason not to paint Jesus the common-sense assumption that a portrait requires the presence of its subject. And Jesus never posed for any artist.[16] The Bible, by contrast, is an unmediated representation. "If I wish, therefore, a portrait of Jesus, I will not take what man has painted," writes Cumming, "but that which God has sketched, as it is exhibited and portrayed in every page of His own inspired and blessed Word" (463). Catholics, Cumming argues, debase God to the merely sensuous with their pictures and props. The full truth of God's power is conceptual, not material. A painter might paint Jesus "bearing the cross," but could not paint him "bearing our sins away," the central fact to be understood about Jesus (462). This bias against pictorial mediation matches Cumming's refusal of any ecclesiastical mediation of God's word, which he views as "a letter from my Father to me, his child" (432).

Cumming's logic aims to protect the emotional autonomy promised by revelation in two ways. First, to insist on presence is to make the sitter's being there, not the mediating power of the artist's imagination or skill, the key to a portrait's success. Second, to prefer words to pictures is to prefer private ownership of one's response to God. Pictures are publicly available to all eyes alike, whereas the decoding of words takes place in the dark space of a reader's mind. A believer can thus take more possession of a verbal encounter with God than a visual one. A painter's representation could only intrude on the "filial joy" and "confidence" of the father-child intimacy that Cumming describes as real faith (452–53). This happy familial relationship does not sound like the intense longing of romantic revelation.

But Cumming's case against bad representation still relies on invisibility to preserve good love, free and deep love, between God and believer.

Another brother of Stowe's, celebrity minister Henry Ward Beecher, articulates this Protestant emotional rationale from a more moderate position. Beecher was a liberal Protestant and an appreciative viewer of pictures, as he reported in a series of letters written during his travels in Britain and Europe in the early 1850s and published in the New York *Independent*. Beecher says "the finest head of Christ" he found on his trip is one by Guido Reni, in the National Gallery in London, of a young Jesus with John the Baptist. Jesus is "calm yet vivacious, with a look of dignity THAT IS TO BE." A comparable picture by Leonardo da Vinci, Beecher says, is good, but "it is not Christ," whereas "one imagines that Guido's *is*, or might have been."[17] Beecher seems willing to be moved by art, but no picture is able to make him feel intimate enough with the savior.

Walking through a gallery at Christ Church College, though, he comes close. Beecher is most moved here by a "head of Christ" he does not identify by artist. It was "not," he clarifies, "that it met my ideal of that sacred front, but because it took me in a mood that clothed it with life and reality. For one blessed moment I was with the Lord. I knew Him. I loved Him. My eyes I could not close for tears. My poor tongue kept silence, but my heart spoke, and I loved and adored" (52). Beecher is careful to attribute this moment of revelatory intimacy to his own emotional agency. It is Beecher's mood that clothes the picture with life, not the mediation of the painter, which fails to meet Beecher's ideal. But gazing at this picture produces a bond both painful and joyful: "For one moment there arose a keen anguish, like a shooting pang," as Beecher considers his unworthiness, but that awareness of sin passes when "there seemed to spring out upon me, from my Master, a certainty of love so great" as to "leave me shining bright" (53).

Despite what sounds like an experience of transformative love, not unlike what Melville's reviewer felt in reading Hawthorne, Beecher stops short of fully endorsing this or any image. After his tour of the National Gallery he concludes that "love was the true nature of Christ," and "it is this very element that painters have failed to depict" (82). He reflects that "in almost all the heads of Christ which I have seen, there is much to admire but nothing to satisfy. They are more than human, but not divine. They carry you up a certain distance, but then leave you unsatisfied. If they are majestic, they are stern; if severe, they are flat and expressionless; if loving, they are effeminate. Many of them, by old masters, are absolutely *shaggy and repulsive*" (81). This is a way of describing, Goldilocks-style, the just-right kind of intimacy a Protestant wants with God. And though Beecher's will to adore and merge with an image marks the point where evangelical sentimentality approaches Catholic habits of worship, Beecher keeps on the Protestant side of the fence by insisting on the not-quite-rightness of portraits of Jesus. He finally disavows even words as poor vessels for the "thoughts and feelings that nothing but the heart itself had power to utter" (53). Beecher's affective self-analysis demonstrates the Protestant logic by which real power is marked by an invisibility that leaves the viewer free to feel an endless—because impossible to satisfy—desire. Even a great portrait can be shown to fail by positing the deeper emotional response that could be achieved by encountering the unmediated original.

This iconophobic logic would be refuted by Gilbert Stuart's Athenaeum portrait of George Washington. As a masculine authority figure, Washington was held to be only slightly less potent than Jesus. Though his official apotheosis would not be painted until 1865 in the Capitol Rotunda, Rembrandt Peale and Horatio Greenough had both already aligned Washington with the god Jupiter in their portrayals.[18] Moving the association from the pagan to the Christian deity, William Powell's 1864 painting *General Washington Receiving His Mother's Last Blessing* led one reviewer to compare Mrs. Washington to the Virgin Mary, suggesting that her son, too, had saved the world. According to the text that was printed along with the engravings of Powell's pictures, "No woman since the mother of Christ has left a better claim on the affectionate reverence of mankind."[19]

So it is not surprising that a popular biography of Gilbert Stuart frames the task of painting Washington using the same terms of unsatisfied longing operative in discussions of painting Jesus. The biographer writes that, when the former president first sat for Stuart in 1795, "Washington was, as his name ever will be, the idol of every lover of liberty, and the world were anxious to have a correct likeness of him.... They had seen what were called likenesses of this great man ... but still were not satisfied; nothing, as yet, had been produced that reached their idea of him."[20] To produce the president as an idol, Stuart would have to both attain a correct likeness and reach the idea of Washington. That the likeness and the idea were separable—that getting the face right was different from getting across the right idea—was something that audiences surely understood but could forget while they were looking at the picture. By enabling that forgetting, the Athenaeum portrait succeeded at its task. As early as the 1810s, a Russian diplomat noted that success, observing that "every American considers it his sacred duty to have a likeness of Washington in his home, just as we have images of God's saints."[21] For their first president, Protestants could trade their iconophobia for iconophilia.

Viewers moved by the portrait, though, could maintain allegiance to Protestant antipictorialism by asserting that Washington's presence, not Stuart's artistic mediations, was responsible for their powerful feelings. That is because Stuart painted Washington from life; he had the advantage of in-the-flesh presence. Popular appreciations of the Athenaeum portrait pointed not so much to Stuart's technical skill but to his emotional acumen. He was credited with "an alertness and precision like magic" that could "[transfer] the vital identity of his pre-occupied and fascinated subject, with almost breathing similitude."[22] But Washington was hard to bewitch. Newspaper accounts and volumes of popular biography circulated the story of Stuart's struggle to get his famous sitter to reveal himself in conversation. By one such account, Stuart ran through all the topics he had at command until "the painter struck on the master-key"—the subject of horses—"and opened a way to [Washington's] mind which he has so happily transferred to the canvass with the features of his face."[23]

The idea that great portraiture owes more to skill at psychic exposure than to talent with the brush repeats in *Pierre,* in Aunt Dorothea's tale of how a scandalous portrait of Pierre's father was painted. That portrait, which seems to expose his father's adulterous lust for a Frenchwoman, comes to serve for Pierre as a paternity test, proving that Isabel really is his illegitimate half-sister. Its power to offer these truths is explained by the story that it was made while his father was unaware that he was being painted. In the fictional as in the real-life account of a portrait's genesis, the picture's ability to reveal truth is attributed not to art, but to the special emotional access opened up between a sitter and a painter. In both cases, too, this explanation equates visibility with vulnerability, an exposure of what the subject would ordinarily keep private. Such explanations uphold the promise of revelation by asserting that a portrait's power is produced by the subject's exposed depth rather than by the artist's clever manipulation of paint.

The logic of presence as a guarantee of depth perception—the reasoning that legitimized a viewer's feelings of intimacy with a picture by downplaying artistic mediation—can be tracked in part through a debate that occurred two decades earlier, in Congress. In 1832, the superiority of Stuart's Athenaeum portrait was in doubt as members debated whether to use Stuart's picture or a portrait by Rembrandt Peale as the basis for the face in a new full-length picture of Washington that they were commissioning. One congressman argued that Stuart's picture was inaccurate. Peale's, though painted after Washington's death, "bore a much closer resemblance especially about the eyes."[24] Peale himself lobbied hard for the superior likeness of his portrait, publishing a pamphlet that compiled statements from Washington's contemporaries testifying to its accuracy.

Athenaeum portrait, Gilbert Stuart, 1796. (National Portrait Gallery, Smithsonian Institution; owned jointly with the Museum of Fine Arts, Boston)

Patriae Pater, Rembrandt
Peale, 1824. (US Senate
Collection)

These included Chief Justice John Marshall, who said that Peale's portrait "is more Washington himself than any portrait I have ever seen," and a Judge Peters, who cited his emotional response as a measure of accuracy when he affirmed that "I judge from its effect on my heart" (343). Peale, though, ultimately lost the contest. In the 1850s, when the Capitol Building was remodeled and Congress moved to a new venue, Peale's portrait was left behind in the old chambers. The picture bearing Stuart's version of Washington's face was "taken along" to the new building, as art historian Egon Verheyen remarks, "and remains a constant reminder of the way in which the nation wants to think of its first president" (137).

The question of likeness was hard to gauge not only because there was no photograph of the first president, but because Washington's face was, to some observers, most notable for being so generic. In 1784, Joseph Mandrillon wrote that there was no "one striking feature" to

Washington's face, leaving a visitor "the remembrance only of a fine man"; the Marquis de Chastellux said that "it [is] impossible to speak particularly of any of [Washington's] features, so that in quitting him, you have only the recollection of a fine face"; and Brissot de Warville likewise observed that Washington "has no characteristic traits in his figure, and this has rendered it always so difficult to describe it: there are few portraits which resemble him."[25] For all the assertion of the authenticity of the Athenaeum portrait, its likeness to Washington is not decisive; the measure of likeness is in its effects on the viewer's heart.

The analysis of later scholars helps us appreciate how Stuart got around the Protestant iconophobia of his viewers and made them feel intimate with Washington. In fact, Peale and his defenders may have been right about the greater accuracy of Peale's image. Dorinda Evans compares Stuart's portrait with the features recorded in a life mask of Washington to show that Stuart adjusted the president's face, shrinking "the size of the large eye sockets and the prominence of the cheekbones" to avoid making Washington look too "sensitive" or "haunted," qualities that might hinder viewers' feeling of beholding majesty.[26] Stuart did not just copy; he invented. Verheyen writes that, whereas Rembrandt Peale's portrait tried to "show Washington in a much more clearly defined way" (136), Stuart strategically recast Washington's image by using "Renaissance compositional devices": "Choosing a three-quarter view, yet fixing the eyes on the viewer, ignoring the hands and thus implying an above-average size man, places the spectator at the same time at a distance from, but also in direct contact with, the person represented" (133). Stuart's mediation is also made plain by his evident brushstrokes and by blank spaces left on the canvas where he stopped painting.[27] Nineteenth-century psychology also provided conventions Stuart could draw on. As Christopher Lukasik observes, the widely accepted theories of phrenology and "physiognomy created the very faces it claimed to interpret" by generating the categories that people used to read those faces.[28] Popular guidebooks like the Fowler brothers' *Illustrated Self-Instructor in Phrenology and Physiology* analyzed scores of printed portraits, thereby becoming visual lexicons that trained readers to see noses, chins, and foreheads as signifying particular traits.[29] Yet Washington's powerful spirit coexists here with established rules and evident artifice. The net effect is distant but direct contact. Stuart's choices maintain a soft-focus veil that balances intimacy and mystery, benevolent familiarity and distant majesty.

Stuart's successful use of invention and convention helped the Athenaeum portrait become what Adam Greenhalgh calls "a devotional cult image, an 'icon' in the strictest sense of the word" for "America's civil religion" (272). Contrary to the logic of a private encounter with otherness, this picture's revelatory intimacy coexisted with mass reproduction. The proliferating copies of the Athenaeum portrait through the nineteenth century and into the twentieth did nothing to stop its viewers from feeling they were in contact with the real Washington (290–91). To a reviewer reconsidering Stuart's picture in 1855, this image, now "distributed over the globe," is "majestic, benignant, and serene," a "master-piece" that captures "the absolute character and peculiar example of Washington."[30] As an icon, the power of Stuart's picture is not diminished by the mediation of copying technologies. As an icon, too, its power defies the anti-Catholic logic that makes invisibility the key to maintaining masculine authorial power. Contra the Protestant faith that the only God worth loving is an invisible one, Washington maintains his measureless power not despite but because of the mediations and replications that make his spirit widely visible. It would take Protestants almost a hundred years before they could embrace their own iconic image of God in Warner Sallman's *Head of Christ* (1940).

As with *Blithedale* and *Pierre*, Stuart's work is a portrait of authorship that does not hide its mediations but that nonetheless produces real intimacy. The intimacy feels more satisfying, to be sure, in the case of the Athenaeum portrait. Self-portraiture, whether for painters or novelists, invites irony, and certainly *Blithedale* and *Pierre* exploit such irony in their off-putting fictional self-portraits. What the novels do share with the representational strategy of the Athenaeum portrait is a disregard for the Protestant logic of invisible power that forbade painting Jesus. That is not to say that Hawthorne and Melville embraced visibility; far from it. We might see these fictional self-portraits as protests against the new technologies feeding a market demand for more authorial visibility. The daguerreotype posed a double threat: its mechanical process seemed to record the objective truth of its subject (thus Holgrave in *The House of the Seven Gables* can reveal Judge Pyncheon's hidden cruelty), and its cheapness and accessibility put those true selves into mass circulation (thus Melville's narrator in *Pierre* decries the cheapening effect of such pictures).[31] As participants in the publishing economy, Melville and Hawthorne did have their portraits made. Hawthorne submitted to both painter and camera with more apparent good grace than Melville, who in 1851 refused to have a daguerreotype made for *Holden's Dollar Magazine*.[32] But Hawthorne and his wife Sophia kept hidden an 1848 daguerreotype by John Adams Whipple that they felt made Nathaniel look unpleasant.[33] Such gestures bespeak the authors' tension—between an urge to be known and an urge to protect their power by staying invisible.

But the novels they write, *Blithedale* and *Pierre*, work to reject the choice—a choice enforced by the logic of anti-Catholic iconophobia—between protecting the true self by hiding it, or else revealing and weakening it. Hawthorne and Melville avoid that either/or choice by taking advantage of the way self-portraiture enables the artist to alienate himself. That self-alienation, surprisingly, founds the possibility for intimacy with their readers. Insofar as Miles and Pierre are avatars for their authors, they become objectified selves. But the alienated self projected by each novel enables an author-reader communion in the form of shared spectatorship. These displaced self-portraits let the authors play both subject and object, the gazer and the gazed-at. *Blithedale* and *Pierre* present an otherness both strange and true, as foreign to their authors as it is to us.

THE BLITHEDALE ROMANCE: THE APPEAL OF PAINT AND PASTEBOARD

Hawthorne had his likeness made several times throughout his career, from the image of the fresh-faced young man painted by Charles Osgood in 1841 to the more imposing elder statesman captured by Mathew Brady's camera in 1860. Apart from these visible offerings of his personality to his readership, Hawthorne conducted an enduring love affair with his readers in the prefaces he wrote to his works. Presented in his own name rather than in the voice of a narrator, these prefaces reveal the author at work. The introduction to *Mosses from an Old Manse* presents Hawthorne ruminating on creativity among squashes in the garden and mulling over literary longevity among old sermons in the attic. "The Custom House," introducing *The Scarlet Letter*, shares his struggle with writer's block and the archival find that got him over it. Hawthorne's final preface, to *The Marble Faun*, expresses his wish to reconnect with that "one congenial friend," the "all-sympathizing critic" that Hawthorne admits he has always fantasized.[34]

The Blithedale Romance is his only full-length drama of the writer's life. As such, it extends these prefatory questions about what kind of intimacy the author should offer his reader. It takes a current-day plot (Hawthorne's first novel to do so) borrowed from Hawthorne's life (as the preface reminds us) and adopts a first-person narrator (the only one among his novels) to tell it.[35] Miles Coverdale is purpose-built as an alter ego for his author. But—at least according to the rules for author-reader intimacy laid out in "The Custom House"—this portrait of himself must keep the "inmost Me" veiled. Hawthorne will not, like some other authors, "indulge [himself] in such confidential depths of revelation as could fittingly be addressed . . . to the one heart and mind of perfect sympathy."[36] We readers may get close, but we will still be left guessing. Both Hawthorne's wish for sympathy and his wish to stay unrevealed combine in his construction of Miles, a figure Irving Howe calls a "highly distorted and mocking self-portrait."[37]

I argue that, by structuring *Blithedale* as a displaced self-portrait, Hawthorne can imagine himself as both the object and subject of spectatorship. The spectatorship the novel produces is marked not by isolated distance but shared appreciation of the novel as an estranged image of himself. A contemporaneous review of *Blithedale* in the *Knickerbocker* recognizes such a relationship between Hawthorne and his reader. The reviewer describes a shared spectatorship that emerges from Hawthorne's role as a gentle satirist: "He never flees from you with a diabolical jeer at the demolition of a revered fiction. He mourns with you over the wreck he has made, and putting himself within your 'sphere' by his kind sympathy, gently points the way to a truer philosophy."[38] The reviewer specifies that the wreck he speaks of is the ruin of the political idealism that had led Hawthorne to join the Brook Farm experiment in his real life. But Miles too is a wreck, and *Blithedale* also asks the reader to mourn over and jeer at this disappointing writer who both is and is not Hawthorne himself.

Howe reads Miles as the self-exorcism of Hawthorne's "tendency to withdrawal" (170). Similarly, Amy Louise Reed sees Miles as a character whose habit of distanced observation, as in Hawthorne's own notebooks and letters, is both a source of relish and a cause for self-criticism.[39]

His 1831 sketch "Sights from a Steeple" proposes that "the most desirable mode of existence might be that of a spiritualized Paul Pry," a character who sounds like a sprightly emotional vampire. This creature passes his time "hovering invisible round man and woman, witnessing their deeds, searching into their hearts, borrowing brightness from their felicity and shade from their sorrow, and retaining no emotion peculiar to himself."[40] Paul Pry may be presented ironically. We know that in works like *The Scarlet Letter* Hawthorne abhors depth-diving. But he also enjoys being on the outside looking in.

Dramatizing the urge to get inside a stranger, however, is a good way to insist that there is an inside that needs protecting. Such an insistence belongs to the logic of Protestant iconophobia I described above. To the Protestant mind, Catholicism's sensual allure threatened to overwhelm the boundaries of a believer's interiority. Hawthorne manifests this logic in his response to his travels in Italy. Despite his professed ravishment by the landscape and art, Hawthorne adopts a detached position common to many visiting American tourists of the day, who relished Catholicism's splendor from a patronizing distance. As Jenny Franchot notes, when it came to "the possibility of actually subscribing to Catholic faith, of believing in the literal as well as aesthetic authenticity of St. Peter's, Hawthorne observed: 'It would be but compelling myself to take the actual for the ideal; an exchange which is always to our loss'" (200). As dramatized in *The Marble Faun*, Hawthorne's tale of Rome, what helps Protestants maintain their purity of heart against the false show of Catholicism is an assiduously distanced observation. The virginal Hilda in her lofty dovecote maintains that distance as much as Paul Pry in his steeple.[41] Spectatorship serves as a way to keep one's inner ideals intact and to prevent falling for the merely actual.

Miles Coverdale—who shares the name of a prominent sixteenth-century English clergyman and translator of the Bible—also speaks for the Protestant logic that opposes public appearances to hidden truths. Like Hawthorne, he wishes to protect a private will that is autonomous and at least potentially inviolate. His will to maintain emotional autonomy accounts for his visceral disgust for the perfectly groomed impresario, Professor Westervelt. Westervelt is both too plainly revealed and too fake: Miles shrinks from the "naked exposure of something" in his eyes (105), yet his teeth turn out to be dentures, and Miles wonders if his face

is not "removeable like a mask" (107). One of Westervelt's most dangerous powers, as Miles presents it, is his ability to spread emotional effects
like a "contagion" (107). When Westervelt laughs at his own portrayal of
Hollingsworth's gold-digging seduction of Zenobia, Miles cannot help
laughing too. He feels shame afterward for having "lost the right of re-
senting [Westervelt's] ridicule of a friend" (108).

Likewise, Miles laments the "mystic sensuality" of mesmerism because
it denies the right to feel and deploy one's emotions at will (182). Miles's
allegiance to hidden emotional truth registers in his "horror and disgust"
at the mesmerists who would reveal the secrets of the human heart (183).
Three examples of feminine love (the virgin, the widow, the mother) that
vanish under hypnosis fuel Miles's conviction that "if these things were to
be believed, the individual soul was virtually annihilated" (183). Not only
is "all that is sweet and pure, in our present life, debased" (183); religion's
promises of eternity, and of a transcendent source of the moral life, are
gutted if we cannot privately possess our feelings.

Given how much Miles stakes on a woman's love, it is not surprising
that his frustrated fascination with Zenobia forms the dramatic center of
Hawthorne's critique of the depth drive. Early on, Zenobia, who knows she
is being studied by him, "let[s]" Miles "look into her eyes, as if challenging
[him] to drop a plummet-line down into the depths of her consciousness."
But Miles is disappointed. He tells Zenobia he sees "nothing . . . unless
it be the face of a sprite laughing at me from the bottom of a deep well"
(72). Later, he longs to know whether Zenobia's costumed or unadorned
self is the realer one. Miles is correct to understand Zenobia as performing
herself, yet Miles incorrectly applies the binary of real versus false to her
method of representation, which confounds that opposition. What he does
not understand, but the novel makes clear, is that Zenobia's performance is
a legitimate kind of authorship.

For Miles, all of Zenobia's costuming and accessorizing must refer to
something deep inside her. The flower she wears daily in her hair cannot
remain merely a "brilliant," "rare," and "costly" touch that sets off Zenobia's beauty. The flower, by the revelatory logic whereby the outward sign
indexes inward truth, must be "a subtile expression of Zenobia's character"
(70). This could be the only explanation for its persistence in his imagination, Miles thinks: the flower could only matter to him so much if it

actually expressed some hidden aspect of the real woman. He also assures us that he is only interested in her because bachelors like him are always interested in virgins who got away. What he feels is not love, could not be love, to Miles's way of thinking, because it has no secure connection to depth. Hawthorne lets us see that Miles's faith that his is a higher standard of love really amounts to a failure of love on Miles's part.

Furthermore, Hawthorne consistently calls into question Miles's depth drive as an authorial method. When Miles is overtly stymied as an author, as when Zenobia pulls the curtain down on his peeping, his defense is to assert his superiority as a hermeneut: "God assigned" him these friends to watch so that Miles might "learn the secret which was hidden even from themselves" (155). The hope of prying out such secrets seems to be what makes his friends worth paying attention to. Miles's claim that, as a creative type gifted with "generous sympathies" and "delicate intuitions," he is exempt from "vulgar curiosity," is patently self-justifying (155). And Miles concludes his narrative with what seems intended as a climactic big reveal, the information that he has always loved Priscilla: "I—I myself—was in love—with—PRISCILLA!" (218) That final declaration seems most of all calculated to make us think he was all along holding something, anything, back. The last-ditch, breathless promotion of this revelation, one that his foregoing story has given us no particular reason to believe, makes the concept of keeping, or baring, such deep secrets seem risible. As Jordan Stein argues, Coverdale's persistent self-misunderstanding finally "does not reveal anything about the narrator other than that he *has* a personal style."[42] That could never be enough for Coverdale, who stakes his claim as an author on delivering revelations.

Indeed, Hawthorne lets us see that Miles is not only sexually attracted to but also professionally jealous of Zenobia's artistic talent. In recording her story about the Veiled Lady, Miles says that Zenobia is guilty of flamboyant excesses that his retelling will omit. But in the tale of Fauntleroy that follows (prompted, it seems, by some one-upmanship after Zenobia's performance), Miles tells a highly embellished story that condemns a man for being highly embellished. Miles cannot celebrate embellishment, though, because to praise such artifice would undercut the power of the final revelation of his heart; neither can Miles admit that Zenobia's attractive force might be the effect of a well-designed costume. More important, he cannot admit that being attracted to her self-presentation might amount to real love, might be just as profound an intimacy as the revelatory consummation he expects if he could discover "the mystery of Zenobia's life" (71). When he sees Zenobia alive for the last time, he registers how "the effect of her beauty was even heightened by the over-consciousness and self-recognition of it" (203). In other words, he recognizes that beauty can be beautiful not simply when it is passively and unconsciously there for the taking. Beauty's force can be heightened by the self-aware cultivation of it.

In that moment Miles gets a glimpse of a mutual spectatorship that could be far more satisfying than his voyeurism. He sees, in that last look, how Zenobia appreciates his recognition: "She understood the look of admiration in my face; and—Zenobia to the last—it gave her pleasure" (203). Zenobia recognizes Miles's fitness as an appreciative audience and wonders aloud why she had not thought of wooing him. She had earlier tested, and approved, Miles's appreciation of her costuming powers in the scene when she presents him with Priscilla decked out in flowers. Miles spots the false note, the one stray weed Zenobia mixed in, immediately. Although Miles can identify his role in a circuit of nonrevelatory intimacy, he can only describe it. He does not let himself participate in or enjoy it. That is the mistake, the failure to enjoy the communion of shared spectatorship, that *Blithedale* wants to point out. We will see that in Stoddard's and James's love stories, audience appreciation is the modus operandi for a lasting relationship. Here, because of Miles's depth drive, it fails as the basis for intimacy.

Zenobia's narrative, "The Silvery Veil," demonstrates a crucial link between her storytelling practice and Hawthorne's in *Blithedale*. Like Hawthorne convicting himself of coldhearted voyeurism via the figure of Miles, Zenobia uses her tale indirectly to confess her sins. Through fictional displacement, she convicts herself of returning Priscilla to bondage under Westervelt. But, alongside that confessional impulse, Zenobia knows how to manage a stage. The veil is a prop, no more than a "piece of gauze" that "managed . . . to increase the dramatic effect" of her narrative (122–23). Her use of the veil also suggests that Zenobia knows how to gratify the Protestant hunger for stories of cloistered nuns and the wizardly priests who spirit them away. By the end of *Blithedale*, though, Hawthorne flips that script by putting Priscilla in charge of the formerly dominating Hollingsworth and by leaving Westervelt, like Coverdale, in the position of a disappointed commentator. Thus, *Blithedale's* version of spectatorship departs from the smug Protestant detachment we see both in Hawthorne's Italian notebooks and in much of Miles's practice. *Blithedale* is not in favor of a voyeurism that denies its participation in a spectator culture as Miles does.

By making his protagonist an instrument of self-criticism, Hawthorne produces a complicated relationship with his readers. The novel is not just satirical; it is intimate too, because in looking at Miles and his faults we are still looking at Hawthorne. Miles is not so dogmatic in his insistence on keeping reality separate from fantasy that he fails to see the price he pays for that insistence. His self-importance as a chronicler of other people's lives competes with his self-deprecation as a chronicler of other people's lives. He understands that his will toward depth makes him mean-spirited. He takes pleasure in well-arranged surfaces, but he resists that pleasure strenuously. Westervelt's highly polished manner and dress provoke equal parts disgust and envy in Miles. He enjoys picturing himself as a spectacle for future utopia-dwellers, but he resents Zenobia's implication that his poetry is mere artifice. He admires the mystifying techniques of the Veiled Lady, but he wants to attain the true-to-life. He wrings his hands over the way his microscopic examinations of his friends must violate their privacy; he can think of no other way, though, to understand them. He watches them carefully, and while he will resort to the expedient of inventing whatever he cannot observe, he is always shamefaced about this, thinking of his "exaggeration" as "error" (89). Unlike Zenobia's, Miles's authorship does not revel in its capacity to invent and embellish.

The critique of Miles's depth drive should prompt us to reconsider how much *Blithedale's* preface, as Hawthorne's prefaces usually do, insists on the distinction between reality and romance. To reread the preface in light of the critique of the depth drive is to see Hawthorne as an author who values romance not because of its protective function of hiding depth, but because romance is productive of its own "improved effects" (38). *Blithedale's* preface makes the claim that Hawthorne's real-life experience at Brook Farm was "essentially a day-dream, and yet a fact" (38). That "and yet" is less emphatic than saying "it was both a day-dream and a fact," a formulation that would deny any meaningful difference between reality and fantasy. But neither is it a dogmatic either/or binary that would sort the dreams from the facts as cleanly as Miles wants to. It also refutes the claim of "Hawthorne and His Mosses" that the real Hawthorne is the dark one and that the light sentimentalist is just a public pose. The story Hawthorne has Miles tell in the novel goes out of its way to muddy the distinction between fiction and reality, which is especially the case in the scene when Priscilla, bearing a letter from Margaret Fuller, reminds Miles of Zenobia. This is a deliberate step out of Faery Land into history, an overt invitation to compare Zenobia, the creature of imagination, to the actual Fuller, who had only recently died.[43] In conversation with Westervelt, Miles confirms that Zenobia is only "her name in literature." Though Miles tells us that he "mention[s] Zenobia's real name" a moment later in that scene, he does not record it in the narrative (106). That omission testifies to Miles's will to keep truth hidden, his teasing maintenance of the allure of a depth he will not reveal.

Blithedale suggests that, for Hawthorne, romance is the appropriate form for self-portraiture, not because romance keeps the real truth veiled behind a false show, but because the veil's embellishment, like Stuart's painterly modifications of Washington's face, pushes us to accept representation as both fact and fancy. To its readers, *Blithedale* never reveals Hawthorne clearly, but it grants an indirect communion between reader and author. The novel does so by letting us watch the author invent, critique, and pity an alien version of himself. And it suggests that Hawthorne needs our admiration as Zenobia needs Miles's. Although that feedback loop does not afford the power of revelation, it does bind the creator and his audience together through the shared project of spectatorship, a project that requires both an audience that knows it is looking at a performance and a performer who can trust he is playing to an appreciative crowd. Hawthorne's self-portrait as Miles Coverdale leaves us gazing along with Hawthorne at the spectacle of a depleted author still trying to impress us with the secret of his true love.

PIERRE: LOOKING AT A STRANGER'S HEAD

In the winter of 1851–52, after Melville had finished *Moby-Dick,* while he was preparing to write the novel that would be *Pierre,* he wrote to Hawthorne that "Leviathan is not the biggest fish;—I have heard of Krackens."[44]

Melville chose a different image to describe the project to Hawthorne's wife, Sophia: a letter to her said his next fiction would offer not saltwater but a "rural bowl of milk."[45] The dissonance between these two images for Melville's novel-to-be forecasts the tension in the relationship that the novel would strike in its readers. It suggests the tricky mix of the majestic and the intimate that Gilbert Stuart's Athenaeum portrait accomplishes. Melville succeeded, in his own fashion: the novel that results is indeed like a kraken swimming in a bowl of milk, and it produces a fraught reading experience. As *Blithedale* was for Hawthorne, *Pierre* is for Melville an experiment in how, and how much, he wants his readers to see him. Like *Blithedale*, *Pierre* arrives at a version of shared spectatorship. The novel does not try to reproduce the sense of darkness revealed that we saw Melville's reviewer attain with Hawthorne. Instead, Melville arranges reader and author as spectators gazing together at the estranged self-portrait that is *Pierre*.

With characteristic irony, Melville uses the novel's fictionalized self-representation to make fun of his own will to stay out of sight. As noted above, Melville had refused in 1851 to have his daguerreotype made for a magazine. In the novel, we see Pierre do the same, with the narrator half-defending and half-abusing Pierre for that refusal. The novel is autobiographical in other ways; as Leon Howard notes, Pierre's backstory draws on Melville's family history, and the patriarchal portraits that figure so crucially in the novel's plot "closely resembled those of Melville's own father" (368). Even before Melville scholars had combed through such parallels, *Pierre* the novel was received as a revelation of its author—an unwelcome one. When it was published in 1852 the review headline in the New York *Day Book* declared its author crazy.[46] A more sympathetic reading in the *Literary World* regrets the loss of Melville's manly comradeship: "The author of *Pierre* . . . is certainly but a spectre of the substantial author of *Omoo* and *Typee,* the jovial and hearty narrator of the traveller's tale of incident and adventure. . . . We would rejoice to meet Mr. Melville again in the hale company of sturdy sailors, men of flesh and blood."[47]

Where that contemporaneous reviewer misses the familiarity and accessibility we might now align with the sentimental, the twentieth-century critics who revived Melville's reputation found the troubled depths appropriate to romanticism. The critic H. M. Tomlinson's preface to a 1929 edition of *Pierre* (a vivid paean to the novel that I have already cited in chapter 1) warns that "the story . . . is sufficiently disturbing to scare all who shrink from great heights and deeps and vacant outer space."[48] The relationship Tomlinson describes with Pierre's author is antagonistic but so intensely felt that he proposes "the shade of Melville is of greater importance and potency than most of the living men we know" (ix). Later critics gained something of a diagnostic upper hand over the author they found revealed in *Pierre*. Michael Paul Rogin in 1983 sees Melville losing control of the boundary between himself and his fictional protagonist.[49] In 1993, James Creech reads *Pierre* as representing Melville's deeply closeted homosexual desire.[50] Samuel Otter writes in 1999 that "[Pierre's] story is in many ways Melville's own."[51] Where Otter departs from the earlier critics is in his rightly identifying *Pierre* as "a sentimental text taken to the *n*th degree" (209). Otter sees how adopting sentimentality makes Melville "amused, horrified, moved, disgusted, disgusted that he is moved" (250). The self-alienation that Melville achieves by telling his story sentimentally is what generates the intimacy of shared spectatorship with his readers. Insofar as *Pierre* enables us to participate in Melville's reactions to this real yet unreal image of himself, and insofar as it moves us to register our own reactions alongside his, the novel offers a version of communion.

Read as a deliberately hypersentimental work, *Pierre* offers neither comfortable masculine companionship nor the unrequited longing of promised and withheld revelation. The novel critiques our wish to see Melville revealed as it critiques the drive for revelation generally. Pierre's self-destruction is the result of his dogged commitment to a depth drive that is both Protestant and romantic. Pierre the character reminds Jenny Franchot of the real-life Isaac Hecker, a convert to Catholicism who went on to found the Paulist Fathers and the *Catholic World*. Both Pierre and Hecker, for Franchot, find themselves burdened by "the culture's various Protestant versions of the unmediated spirit and the invisible church." Hecker sees Catholicism as "an ideological break" from that program (324). Invisibility and immediacy, however, are the powers Pierre longs for as an author. As Melville shows, that longing destroys him, and needlessly. Those are not goals worth dying for, and not the only viable routes to artistic prowess. As in *Blithedale*, in *Pierre* an attractive woman offers a different model of artistry. Isabel, like Zenobia, represents the creative repudiation of depth by her self-avowed performance. But, like Miles with Zenobia, Pierre is only interested in Isabel's hidden depths, not in the self she projects.

Isabel first comes onto the scene as the romantic bearer of mystery who contrasts Lucy's sentimental surfaces. The distinction between Lucy's shallowness and Isabel's depth collapses by the novel's end. But *Pierre* introduces Lucy as pure confection. The first pages present Pierre and Lucy in a sentimentally sweet Romeo-and-Juliet balcony tableau. We meet Lucy through that traditional verbal portrait of a woman as objet d'art, the blazon, that makes her hypervisible. She has cheeks of white and red; her eyes were "brought down from heaven" by "some god"; "her teeth," though of this earth, were things costly and rare, "dived for in the Persian Sea" (24). The Lucy love story could have developed into a kind of communion, like that between Eva and Tom, wherein two people encounter each other as piles of tropes and join in interpreting a shared text. Like Eva, Lucy has no depth. In an early scene, when Lucy sends Pierre to her room to bring her portfolio to her, he is sorely tempted to unroll a "mystic vellum" he finds on her bed. He restrains himself, but she counters: "Read me through and through. I am entirely thine" (40). She opens the portfolio and tosses out "all manner of rosy things," lightweight enough to float (40). Lucy's total visibility leaves no mystery for Pierre to desire. Her sentimental brightness is eclipsed by Isabel's romantic darkness, which seizes Pierre's appetite for withheld revelation.

The narrator's handling of Isabel's darkness does play on predictable gothic conventions. For us readers, she could be cousin to Poe's Annabel Lee or Ligeia. But to Pierre, Isabel exerts all the allure of unsuspected depth. As she tells her life story, Pierre sees in her face "one infinite, dumb, beseeching countenance of mystery, underlying all the surfaces of visible time and space" (52). Isabel becomes his white whale. As many readers have done in reading the novel *Pierre* against Melville's life, the hero Pierre tries to cross-reference Isabel's strange tale with the known biographical facts. He comes to believe she is his illegitimate half-sister and decides he must renounce his family name to protect her. But that certainty does not dispel her mystery. For Pierre she still "possessed all the bewitchingness of the mysterious vault of night, whose very darkness evokes the witchery" (142). That bewitching mystery enables Pierre to find, briefly, with Isabel the same erotic intimacy that Melville's Virginia tourist found in reading

Hawthorne. We see Isabel combine the invisible mystery that an iconoclast demands of God with the melting closeness that Beecher wanted with a picture of Jesus. Their passion generates some of the most stunning images in the novel, as in the embrace they share after Pierre has decided to faux-marry Isabel: "They changed; they coiled together, and entangledly stood mute" (192).

Such moments show the appeal of depth for Melville as writer. Melville also sympathizes with Pierre's depth drive more broadly. The novel is not the story of a callow young idealist getting his comeuppance. Hawthorne does not simply jeer at Miles, and Melville does not just scoff at Pierre; otherwise we would never feel as if Pierre might genuinely be Melville himself, and the only intimacy between reader and author would be that of being in on a joke at someone else's expense. Of course readers can, as many have, reject the novel's version of communion. It might be easier to accept the novel if it were just a bid for the in-group belonging of a shared smirk. But Melville's self-portrait is more complicated than that. The alienation *Pierre* achieves through its sentimentality does not settle into parody, but neither does the novel's adaptation of communion eliminate its faith in revelation.

Like Pierre, the narrator has boundless admiration for Dante and Shakespeare, fathomless authors who can only be understood by readers who dive deep. When Pierre sits for hours in the shabby writers' retreat of the Apostles, trying through cold and hunger to produce a work of genius, Melville roots for him and mourns for him. Pierre learns "very bitterly" that "the world worship Mediocrity and Common Place, yet hath . . . fire and sword for all contemporary Grandeur" (264). Melville half-admires Pierre's ascetic efforts to discipline his flesh toward the vanishing point as a means of concentrating his power.

Melville, however, does not endorse this program of self-immolation. Pierre is shown to be one of a colony of hungry young men all pitifully striving to think the deepest thoughts, and the narrator lampoons the romantic logic that an author needs invisibility to protect his power. In a scene that, as noted above, echoes Melville's experience, we see Pierre refuse when a magazine editor demands Pierre's likeness for his pages, claiming that Pierre's face is "public property" (254). The narrator takes the chance here to point out the prestige economy of portraiture. Where an oil painting can "immortalize" "the moneyed, or mental aristocrats," a cheap daguerreotype "only *dayalized* a dunce" (254). Because Pierre, un-like Melville, grew up a moneyed aristocrat, he has a painted portrait of himself that could have been loaned to the publisher for engraving. But the "most melancholy consideration" stops Pierre: the painting is no good because it presents him as smooth-faced, and he wants to have a beard, the "noble corporeal badge of the man," for his frontispiece image (253). This narrative aside belies Pierre's righteous claim that his image is not for sale. That is not to say the narrator scorns the wish to shape one's public image. What is scorned is the dressing up of a desire to look manly by casting it as the integrity of romantic genius.

Perhaps the novel's last word on authorship is that "the only original author [is] God" (259). Even Milton, the narrator says, was derivative. This standard of originality recalls Rev. Cumming's rejection of any portrait of God other than the Bible's. By that anti-Catholic rationale, man can produce only poor copies of the words God spoke. The narrator of *Pierre* is weary of a "world [that] is forever babbling of originality" (259), a pop-ulace continually announcing that it has found the first and best when it has found neither. Yet the novel does not collapse in despair at its own inevitable secondhand status. Accepting man's lot as a copyist is more a liberation than a surrender.

We see that point in the counsel Melville's narrator gives to Pierre to free himself from a fruitless standard of originality. Starving and isolation do not make great art: "Many a consumptive dietarian has but produced the merest literary flatulencies to the world; convivial authors have . . . given utterance to the sublimest wisdom" (299). It is better to eat oysters and champagne. The narrator ends his description of Pierre pining away at his desk by commanding "Civilization, Philosophy, Ideal Virtue" to "behold your victim!" One page later, an excerpt from Pierre's own man-uscript commands its reader to "cast thy eye" on its struggling author-hero, Vivia, and asks, "Is this the end of philosophy?" (302, 303). Both the author of *Pierre* and the hero Pierre are given to bombastic commands to see the writer as a martyr. The difference is that Pierre's autobiograph-ical work, embedded in Melville's, is a copy that does not realize it is a copy. Emory Elliott points out that whereas "Melville . . . writes a very funny book in *Pierre*," Pierre's own "autobiographical novel," the work he hopes will bring him literary immortality, is unfunny because Pierre takes himself too seriously. He is a "humorless Puritan, locked in an either/ or, saint/sinner" binary that prevents him from achieving the productive self-alienation that Melville himself achieves in this novel.[52] Melville's adaptation of communion in *Pierre,* suggested here by the play of copies, helps distance him from that Puritan faith. It testifies to this novel's at least partial faith in a Catholicized view of mediation as enabling, not falsifying, our apprehension of what is truly other.

The novel makes Pierre's insistence on unmediated truth look disastrous as a guide to authorship. Pierre's depth drive looks equally disastrous as a guide to love. The narrator points up the perversity of Pierre's sense of isolation: "On either hand clung to by a girl who would have laid down her life for him," Pierre still feels that "in his deepest, highest part [he was] utterly without sympathy from any thing" (338). That which is beyond others' sympathy—hidden from their understanding or identification— defines what is deepest and highest for the Protestant logic of invisibility. But as Pierre's conventional sentimental love with Lucy was hyperbolized and ironized, so, in its turn, is the gothic-romantic love with Isabel. In the end, Isabel's promise of deep love turns out to be no deeper than Lucy's, and the only revelation is that there is no revelation. The novel's climactic scene takes place in a picture gallery where Isabel and Pierre look together at a portrait of a "Stranger's Head by an Unknown Hand" (350). This random picture resembles the purportedly revelatory chair portrait of his father, the one that had proved for Pierre that he and Isabel shared the same father. In the gallery, Pierre sees what looks like the very portrait that had been private (only on view in Pierre's closet), made public, and put up for sale; he sees the familiarity of his father's face made strange. The effect is to collapse the boundaries Pierre relied on for his values: the boundary between private depth and public appearance, between original and fake. Pierre realizes then that Isabel's story, and the deep love founded on it, might be a performance, all mediation and no transcendence. That, for him, is a deal-breaker.

Melville suggests a different approach to Isabel's character—one that could solve Pierre's problems both as a lover and as a writer. Rather than alternately trying to authenticate her identity or worshiping her deep mystery, Pierre might have considered Isabel a model author. A storyteller herself, Isabel is endowed with what Peter Brooks called the "melodramatic imagination."[53] According to Brooks, the grandiose rhetoric of melodrama is a signal of its urge to make cosmic truth legible. For Pierre, anything legible to a wide audience cannot be true. But melodrama, like the sentimental as we saw it deployed by Stowe and Phelps, puts into play signs that "have a depth of symbolic meaning"; instead of asking us "to plumb" these depths, however, melodrama uses the "interplay" of those signs to make "the struggle of moral entities . . . visible to the spectator" (28).

In line with this artistic program, Isabel performs her autobiography, coupling language with gesture and music to make her story an emotional spectacle. Whereas Pierre hopes through solitude and fasting to become a prophet, Isabel's use of performance makes her a priestess. Emory Elliott sees her leading Pierre toward a catechism for the skeptical (343–44). But, following Brooks's lead, I propose that Isabel's melodrama points toward a more performative Christianity, akin to Catholicism, that Melville neither endorses nor condemns. The narrator hints at this by describing Isabel, with her hair falling down as she kneels over her guitar, as resembling a "Limeean girl, at dim mass in St. Dominic's cathedral" (149). Isabel's hair shroud, by which she turns a window alcove into the "vestibule of some awful shrine" (149), is a self-aware exhibition of mystery. She "[flings]" a "spell" over Pierre, as the narrator says (150), with a gesture calibrated to her audience's vision. She "dart[s] one swift glance at Pierre," making sure he is watching, before "toss[ing]" her hair down to create the shrine effect.

The passages that describe Isabel's performances for Pierre show the narrator inhabiting Isabel's melodramatic model of performance. If Isabel's music is a "[swarm]" of "unintelligible but delicious sounds" (126), the narrator seconds her performance with his own production of unintelligible, but delicious, sibilant mouthfuls of prose. This language renders Isabel's music thing-like, visible and tangible to the reader: "The sounds seemed waltzing in the room; the sounds hung pendulous like glittering icicles from the corner of the room; and fell upon [Pierre] with a ringing silveryness" (126). Isabel's storytelling performance accords with sentimental visibility, and what she is offering Pierre is the intimacy of communion.

So too with the narrator's description of Isabel's performance: that description resists positing a hidden significance for the melody and instead evokes a fantastic synesthesia that bombards its audience with sounds that have become shiny objects. Pierre believes the song amounts to a declaration of mystery and determines to penetrate that mystery. He wants revelation, potential if not actually fulfilled. The narrative suggests the mystery may be nothing more or less than the effect of Isabel's performance. Pierre could pursue a different kind of authorship by imitating her, as Melville's narrator does. Moreover (especially when we read it with Miles and Zenobia in mind) the novel suggests that Pierre could likewise achieve a different kind of intimacy—not by digging into Isabel, but by admiring and responding to her style.

The possibility the novel stages of a dramatically self-conscious authorship prevents *Pierre* from being a tour de force of negativity. True, its experiment in sentimentality versus romanticism seems to hollow out both possibilities. Sentimentality can be amplified for fun, but its lack of depth can disappoint. Romantic grandeur is alluring, but to insist on it looks silly. In a brief moment that cuts through that representational dilemma, the novel gives us an image of a couple looking and feeling together. In the scene where Isabel and Pierre stare at the "Stranger's Head" in the portrait gallery, Melville's narrator pauses to comment on their unshared spectatorship:

> Whether or not these considerations touching Isabel's ideas occurred to Pierre at this moment is very improbable. . . . For, indeed, [Pierre] was too much riveted by his own far-interior emotions to analyze now the cotemporary ones of Isabel. So that there here came to pass a not unremarkable thing: for though both were intensely excited by one object, yet their two minds and memories were thereby directed to entirely different contemplations; while still each, for the time—however unreasonably—might have vaguely supposed the other occupied by one and the same contemplation. (353)

This model of two unmatched minds responding to one portrait is what the novel offers to counter the romantic ideal of one-to-one revelation. To be sure, this is a moment of deep personal turmoil; the narrator notes Pierre's "far-interior emotions." But the bureaucratic verbosity ("however unreasonably"; "not unremarkable"; "cotemporary") prevents it from coming off as a tragic declaration of the failure of one deep soul to merge with another. The scene is not exactly warm, but it is not bitter or satirical, either. The togetherness Melville pictures here is structured like that of Eva and Tom, who, reading the same bible, share their different associations with the Gospel. As we will see, it also resembles the "intercourse by misunderstanding" Henry James describes between Bob and Fanny Assingham. The trouble is that Pierre and Isabel do not talk to each other. In their silence, each spectator assumes they share the same mind, and we can be certain that Pierre at least would be gravely disappointed to learn that Isabel was not on his wavelength.

What this image of two spectators suggests for reader-author intimacy is that we readers might look, along with Melville, at *Pierre* the novel as if at a picture of a stranger's head. Our mistake would be to think that we are looking through a window into Melville's head, or—if we construe the novel as a mirror—that we know what Melville sees in his reflected image. It would be a mistake, too, to feel that we must see the same thing he sees. The intimacy offered by *Pierre* does not merge the contents of one mind with another. As with *Blithedale,* this communion of spectators is generated by two minds reacting differently to the same work, a work that does not need to be original, true, or deep in order to keep both viewers intimately bound by its imaginative power.

In an earlier moment, Melville's narrator compares his own writing to "pleasant . . . chat" that "passes the time ere we go to our beds," and he compares himself to the "strolling improvisatores of Italy" who earn their keep by entertaining an easily bored audience (259). This passage could read as a self-loathing condemnation of writing for a public at all. But in light of the moment of unshared spectatorship between Pierre and Isabel—and in light of the narrator's own appreciation for and imitation of Isabel—we should not read *Pierre* as condemning such passing entertainment. It is possible that the "pleasant[ness]" of small talk redeems its smallness. That possibility gains support from the narrator's charge, later in the picture gallery scene, that Pierre fails to appreciate the fine execution of the "smaller and humbler pictures, representing little familiar things," because he is intent on finding a picture that will "[awake] dormant majesties in his soul" (350). This note of appreciation for what is familiar and small points back toward Stowe, who celebrates rocking chairs and kitchen gadgets redeemed by Christian love, and points forward to James, for whom small things are fine things.

As I noted in the introduction, when Melville responds privately to Hawthorne's appreciation of *Moby-Dick,* he writes to him in terms that idealize mutual revelation: "Your heart beat in my ribs and mine in yours, and both in God's." That image grows more complex as the letter continues. Melville asks "by what right" Hawthorne drinks from the same "flagon of life" as Melville; in that shared drinking he cannot tell whose "lips" are whose, and self and other dissolve into an "infinite fraternity of feeling."[54] That seems proof of Melville's wish—not just the wish of his Virginia tourist persona—to maintain the possibility of mutual transparency. But Melville's language in this letter imagines his connection to Hawthorne in terms of communion rather than as a mystery either revealed or withheld.

Their two hearts merged in God, the indeterminacy of lips on the flagon, become an image of shared sacramental participation: "I feel that the Godhead is broken up like the bread at the Supper, and that we are the pieces" (43). This is not the bond forged by one self unpeeling the other to its depths; this togetherness is made possible by a ritual routed through the third term of God. Melville speaks of the enduring flux of that relationship: "When shall we be done growing?" and "When shall we be done changing?" he asks (43, 44). Toward the end of the letter, he and Hawthorne are not merged into one, but passengers together on a "long stage, and no inn in sight"; it is cold and dark, "but with you for a passenger, I am content and can be happy" (44). Melville's description is characteristic of communion in that it imagines intimacy across time rather than as breaking through time. Unlike revelation, communion does not posit a grand finale but an ongoing flux sustained by the self's relation to the other. Melville's postscript envisions an "endless riband of foolscap" on which he would write a letter to Hawthorne forever (44).

Adopting the love story of communion enables *Blithedale* and *Pierre* to show the wrongheadedness of the view, shared by both Protestant iconophobia and romantic authorship, that becoming visible means losing power. It is true that the novels arrive at communion less by positive embrace than by reacting against the overvaluing of revelation. But by experimenting with the sentimental mode, both *Blithedale* and *Pierre* realize the potential for communion: a parallel looking-at that maintains real intimacy because it does not stop with a final revelation. This is an unromantic conceptualization of the aim of a self-portrait. It still provides the pleasure of being close to an author.

Four

Realistic Intercourse
Arranging Oneself for Another in
The Morgesons and *The Golden Bowl*

ELIZABETH STODDARD'S *The Morgesons* was first published in 1862, forty-two years before Henry James published *The Golden Bowl* in 1904. *The Morgesons* did have a turn-of-the-century afterlife, in its 1889 and 1901 reissues, when Stoddard's friends in the New York publishing world encouraged the reprintings, but it never gained widespread or sustained attention. Good reviews and bad sales figures greeted it both early and late. Henry Beers, assessing the state of American fiction in the *Atlantic* in 1901, finds Stoddard has suffered bad timing. The Civil War muffled her novel's initial reception, he surmises, and now it is too late; there is "a new school of fiction in possession of the field. . . . The spirit of the former age was lyrical . . . and its expression was eloquence and poetry. The spirit of the present age is observant, social, dramatic, and its expression is the novel of real life, the short story, the dialect sketch."[1] Beers cites Henry James's work as inaugurating this new "attitude toward life, cool, dispassionate, analytic, sensitive to the subtler shadings not only of character, but of manners and speech" (750). He sees in James traces of a prewar writer like Hawthorne, but says that, whereas Hawthorne's characters are almost allegorical and his plots "engaged in working out some problem of the conscience in an ideal world," James's characters sound like real people (750).

Beers's analysis not only assesses the literary scene but constructs it. His essay helps build the now-familiar literary-historical narrative that makes the Civil War vanquish romance and usher in clear-eyed realism. As a narrative of shifting tastes, it may indeed help account for why Stoddard never entered the American literary canon, whereas James dominated it from the start. But Beers's polarization of romance and realism keeps us from seeing how Stoddard and James neutralize that polarity. Stoddard is both lyrical and analytic. To deny Stoddard's skills as a realist who captures the subtleties of manner and speech misses as much as denying that James pursues problems of conscience in an idealized world. If we drop the urge to define a post- versus an antebellum literary style, we can see how James and Stoddard both develop a version of the love story of communion. Both texts find ways to portray selves and others making real contact without the benefit of revelation. To see that shared project helps us account for both the romance and the realism in their work.

The category of communion helps overcome the persistent binary between romance and realism because that binary itself is partly underwritten by the Protestant ideal of revelation. To divide literature between romance and realism is to define a text by its degree of faith in revelation: romance wants to break through the veil of appearance to the truth beyond while realism denies such a breakthrough is possible. Beers ends his essay by observing that what he calls Puritan rhetoric marked the best literary commemorations of the Civil War. Such Protestant eloquence, he says, has been replaced by the cool analysis of current literature. The difference between the prewar and postwar writer, for Beers, comes down to a faintly regrettable maturing out of naïve faith, as the secularization thesis would predict.

But a literary text might offer other modes of access to truth, to an otherness decisively beyond the self, without either aspiring to or denying revelation. Revelation's promise of unmediated access to the truly other is the Protestant ideal. However, as we have seen, communion proposes that our access to otherness is always mediated, dependent on tangible props and public ritual. To see Stoddard and James as repurposing the ideal of communion is to see that both are committed to representing a truth that gets beyond the self, even though neither author invests much faith in revelation as a means to that end. The romance/realism binary is the wrong lens for their work because it forces a choice between seeing the world as either redeemed by its hidden alterity or as emptied of otherness. We have just seen how, on the register of the author-reader relation, Hawthorne and Melville resist the depth drive of revelation and ask us instead to take the performances of *Pierre* and *Blithedale* as worthy representations of alterity. Returning to the register of the story-world, we find in the love stories of *The Morgesons* and *The Golden Bowl* two closely linked variations on the Catholicized communion that locates spirit in the material world.

It is true that Stoddard and James both reject the overt evangelizing of authors like Stowe and Phelps, whom I credit with inaugurating the love story of communion in American literature. Neither Stoddard nor James had kind words for sentimental productions. For James an author like Rebecca Harding Davis "drenches the whole field beforehand with a flood of lachrymose sentimentalism, and riots in the murky vapors which rise in consequence of the act."[2] Stoddard, in an 1856 review of Caroline Chesebro's *Victoria, or the World Overcome*, writes, "After the title (for why should the world be 'overcome'?) Miss Chesebro's dogmatic and pious ideal of a woman assails me in reading her book."[3] The characters who people Stoddard's and James's fiction can certainly sound like secular realists. In *The Morgesons*, the narrator, Cassandra Morgeson, says to her father, Locke, "I am afraid that Love, like Theology, if examined, makes one skeptical" (137). The closest instantiation of God on earth is Cassy's Grand'ther Warren. He is "aboriginal," a "Puritan," and he dies off early in the novel, living just long enough to give Cassy a chance to size him up and reject him. In *The Golden Bowl*, God scarcely rates mentioning. Only the pious Maggie goes to church.

But, as Edwin Sill Fussell points out, there is "nothing more . . . welcome" among James scholars "than continuing validation of the Master's unquestioned secularity."[4] We should beware such validation. To conclude that these novels abandon faith is to commit the error that Ashley Reed identifies with "secularized" reading. Drawing on Charles Taylor's thesis in *A Secular Age*, Reed argues that secularized reading misses the fact that a secular age is not an irreligious age but an age in which multiple faiths compete as possible routes to access transcendence. For Reed, secularized reading narrowly defines religion as a masculinized Protestant orthodoxy; it assumes that when Calvinist faith withers, only faithlessness remains. What Reed calls a "secular" reading, on the other hand, "assumes the interpenetration of hermeneutic regimes rather than the replacement of one regime (superstition) with another (science)."[5] This secular reading, like what other critics have identified as postsecular reading, is requisite to seeing how these two novels imagine transcendent otherness.[6] We can better comprehend *The Morgesons* and *The Golden Bowl* if we see them as continuing, instead of breaking with, Christian preoccupations in American literature. They are part of, rather than outside of, the trajectory of the love story of communion that emerged with Stowe and Phelps and that Melville and Hawthorne deployed to critique revelation. What these works all share is faith in an intimacy that works not through a soul-to-soul encounter but through an ongoing collaboration between two selves interpreting their world together.

Both *The Golden Bowl* and *The Morgesons* do, however, entertain the possibility of a romantic revelation of transcendent otherness. Erotic love seems to offer the perfect transparency of the depths of another's soul that Stowe and Phelps deferred to heaven. Stoddard and James let us glimpse the kind of soul-merge that Melville and Hawthorne mock their fictional doppelgangers for idealizing. Miles and Pierre both yearned for and were terrified of the dissolution of the self-other boundary; *The Golden Bowl* and *The Morgesons* show that dissolution in breathless moments of union. Charlotte and Amerigo act on their identities of impulses and achieve virtual telepathy. Between Stoddard's Cassy and her married cousin Charles, we see "a blinding, intelligent light [flow] from" his eyes and fill her "veins with a torrent of fire" (86).

However, the revelatory love portrayed in these moments of self-other union fails. In neither novel do these passions actually deliver the paradigm-shifting, earth-shattering jolt to the plot that they seem to promise. In *The Golden Bowl*, Charlotte and Amerigo are parted. And though Maggie reclaims Amerigo as her own, James shadows any confident reading that they finally know and love each other. In the final scene, Maggie hides her face from Amerigo's in a way that might be joyous but might equally be defeated. In *The Morgesons*, Cassy's Charles dies midway through the novel. Cassy finds an equally fiery lover, Desmond, who in turn drops offstage for many of the novel's later chapters. Stoddard returns to Cassy's love affair with Desmond only in the last few pages of the novel. Even then their happy reunion is overcast by the final scene's focus on Veronica's widowhood.

In neither novel does this failure of erotic revelation constitute a defining tragedy. Instead, in both novels, the love that is most enduring and most genuinely intimate is communion, not the revelatory love that flashes between the sexiest couples. James and Stoddard each portray a quotidian love that relies not on ecstatic merging but on mutual appreciation and display. Cassy's fractious relationship with her family, especially with her sister Veronica, takes up a greater share of the novel than her love affairs with Charles and Desmond. In James, the marriage between Fanny and Bob—their "intercourse by misunderstanding"—shows how a couple lives with the kind of incomprehension that Stoddard portrays in the Morgeson family. Moreover, Fanny and Bob are not simply a comic subplot; their ongoing role as reader stand-ins makes them central to the story. What binds the sisters Cassandra and Veronica Morgeson, and what unites Fanny and Bob Assingham in matrimonial success, is a creative mutual admiration born of mutual incomprehension. The love these couples share, like the love that grew between Mary and Winifred or the love that might have been between Pierre and Isabel, thrives on shared interpretation and performance.

Stoddard and James show us characters who love each other by regarding each other as performers, editors, fashion models, and set designers. Especially in the world of commodity fetishism these novels portray, such regard might seem dehumanizing. But in *The Morgesons* and *The Golden Bowl*, to be intimate with otherness involves objectifying the other. In her work on literary ethics, C. Namwali Serpell locates an ethics of objecthood, surprisingly, in Martin Buber. Buber's *I and Thou* (appearing in English translation in 1937) might be thought of as a classic twentieth-century celebration of revelatory intimacy that deplores objectification. Indeed, Buber writes that it is "the sublime melancholy of our lot" that "every You in the world is compelled by its nature to become a thing for us or at least to enter again and again into thing-hood."[7] But, as Serpell reminds us, "Buber entertains the possibility of ethical encounters with things . . . even a fragment of mica" (74). On Serpell's reading, Buber shows that an oscillation between the status of a You and an It, a trading of subjecthood and objecthood that applies to both partners in a relationship, is requisite to sustain genuine intimacy. When an other that we have seen as an object revives and talks back, we discover that we do not in fact have the final power to objectify them, and we learn to recognize the It-quality in ourselves that lets us become objects in turn for those others.[8]

Such a theory may help explain the affectionate objectification we find in these two love stories, an objectification that I understand as a creative response by James and Stoddard to their historical context. I read *The Morgesons* and *The Golden Bowl*, as I have all the novels in this study, through the lens of ongoing tensions traceable to the contest between Protestant versus Catholic modes of accessing transcendence. What makes these two love stories different is that those tensions play out in the interpretive field of late Victorian material and consumer culture. James and Stoddard imagine a version of communion for a thoroughly commodified world. Stoddard was writing in the early years of what would be a decades-long rise of interest in exhibitions and display. From public events like London's Crystal Palace Exhibition in 1851 to Buffalo's Pan-American Exposition in 1901 (to name just one of many such American expositions), interest in display filtered from public life to private life in the form of guidebooks and magazines advising people how to make their homes into attractive showcases of personality. These sources promoted a growing cultural consensus that home decor and dress could express selfhood.

This archive of decorating discourse may seem far removed from the more overtly religious sources that were relevant to the narratives written by Stowe and Phelps and by Melville and Hawthorne. But we will see that questions about how to interact with the things one could wear or collect were discussed in ethical terms, as questions of how a self could know and be known by others. The lens of Protestant-Catholic competition helps us understand the stakes involved in the consumption and interpretation of material culture. Victorian excess, I propose, was motivated in part by liberal Protestants' wishes to reintegrate a materiality that had been rejected by anti-Catholicism.

As in my treatment of Stowe and Phelps and of Melville and Hawthorne, my argument here focuses not on the authors' personal faith, but on their novels' participation in a tradition that resists dominant conservative Protestant ideals. I do not claim that Stoddard and James themselves wanted to be Catholic. Edwin Sill Fussell sees James's "literary Catholicizing," a stylistic and thematic interest most apparent in James's 1895 play *Guy Domville* and in *The Golden Bowl,* motivated by James's sense of Catholicism as an alien and picturesque faith.[9] To think of Catholicity as a "tone" that can appear in prose, as Fussell does (28), helps to illuminate what is Protestant-resistant in the ontology and ethics we find in both James's and in Stoddard's fiction.

Stoddard's work offers little of the direct engagement with Catholicism that Fussell discovers in James's voluminous writing. There is no reason to think she shared James's aesthetic admiration for Catholic practice, but there is evidence that she sees it as a less punitive faith than Protestantism. In one of her regular columns for the San Francisco *Daily Alta,* Stoddard reports an exchange between a friend who asks a recent convert to Catholicism why he has become "fat"; he replies that "the Church gave such repose that there was no need of fretting the flesh." Stoddard says she wishes someone, "(not a priest.)," would relieve her of the burden of her conscience for the summer so that she could "come back sleek and well-conditioned."[10] Stoddard's backhanded acknowledgment of Catholicism as a faith that nourishes the body, not just the soul, is less overt than the nods to Catholicism that we saw in Stowe or Phelps. But her novel, like James's, tells the Catholic-inflected love story of communion by portraying the body and its quasi-theatrical display as productive of a happily mediated intimacy.

The rise of consumer culture, then, is not just backdrop in these novels. It is a key element in the telling of this version of the love story of communion. As Stoddard and James portray the task of decorating oneself and one's home, that task testifies to a faith in the visible and tangible not as blocks to true otherness but as necessary mediators of true otherness. We can see the interest in material culture thematized in Adam Verver's collecting and in Cassy's shopping and decorating. It comes through, too, in the way both authors practice a mode of characterization that privileges wardrobe and setting. To be known and loved in these novels, a person must be seen as part of a display that she has designed, or within the context of the objects she has collected for herself. By making materiality and display crucial to real intimacy, *The Morgesons* and *The Golden Bowl* continue the Protestant co-opting of Catholic practice that gives us the model of communion. Communion, like revelation, promises intimacy with radical alterity. Unlike revelation, it promises that understanding of the other comes not by rending the veil but by admiring its construction.

CONSUMER CULTURE AS PROTESTANT COUNTERREFORMATION

Accounts of the growth of consumer culture frequently equate commodification with secularization. By the logic of such accounts, consumer fetishism must displace, rather than potentially augment, real faith. William

Leach, for example, writes that as retailers developed more sophisticated display techniques for shop windows, such displays had the effect of "shift[ing] the improvising power of the imagination away from natural and religious things toward artificial and secular things."[11] This opposition of natural religion to the artificial secular is beholden to a Protestant assumption that religion becomes more real as it grows less material. I do not mean to deny the critique that Gilded Age Protestants may have been purchasing cheap grace, but we should consider the possibility that consumerism could operate as a counterreformation within Protestantism, a return of the repressed desire for a faith that comprehends both spirit and body.

Jackson Lears writes that one of the driving aims of the Reformation had been "to create an alternative to the method of constructing meaning through the assemblage and display of objects" by "insist[ing] that salvation lay . . . in inner being rather than outward form."[12] Communion, as I have been developing the term in this book, aims to recover outward forms as valid sources of meaning, as ways to apprehend the truth of both God and other persons. By the later nineteenth century, the sanctification of material objects by which Stowe and Phelps recruited Catholic practice for sentimentality had become mainstream. Lears writes that turn-of-the-century Protestant "enthusiasm for the decorative and theatrical," for "church embellishment" and "public ritual," marked an effort to combat what many Protestants had come to feel was their overrationalized faith.[13] If the first Protestants objected to Catholics' making meaning through assemblage and display, then the embrace of decoration and exhibition around the turn of the century would appear to mark the return of the prodigal to the mother church.

The lens of material culture can help trace that trajectory of Protestant reappropriation of Catholicism back to the antebellum moment. Colleen McDannell observes the paradox that the Gothic Revival and the Oxford Movement imported from Britain in the mid-nineteenth century coincided with the flourishing of anti-Catholicism in America. The British writer John Ruskin modeled this paradox for Americans, simultaneously holding Roman Catholic faith in contempt and praising its architecture.[14] But as anti-Catholicism relaxed after the war, as the threat of foreign Papists was eclipsed by the threat of freed black Americans, Protestants could more readily embrace materialism in their religious faith. McDannell writes, "After 1860 fashion encouraged stronger iconic expression of religious sentiment," and a Protestant "woman's . . . spiritual devotion came to be measured by her ability to decorate her home" (39). Appropriately for the Protestant faith in reading, such women often used sacred text as "the basis of their religious art," needlepointing Bible verses into artful *objets* (39).

We can see evidence of that shift in changing editions of Catherine Beecher's *Domestic Treatise,* a manual for good Protestant housekeeping.[15] In the original edition of 1841, Beecher scolds women for wasting money on "finical ornaments" (260). But the expanded version of the *Treatise, The American Woman's Home* (1869), devotes a full chapter to "Home Decoration." Whereas the *Treatise* recommends, without providing further details, a "light screen . . . covered with paper or chintz" to offer privacy in a shared bedroom, the *Woman's Home* describes step by step how such a screen might be given a faux "ornamental cornice" with "fresco-paper" and how to paste and varnish pictures into its panels (27).

The prie-dieu, a sort of personal altar for at-home prayer, offers a case study. For the first Protestant woman who had one made, it would have been a frank appropriation from Catholic worship habits. But it became, with the popularity of the Gothic Revival style, simply another pretty piece of furniture. *Godey's* offered patterns for embroidering cushions for them. A male character in a satirical story in *Putnam's* describes a woman's insistence on a prie-dieu as "a romantic, not a religious whim. She'll want a missal next; vellum, or no prayers. . . . You'll see religion made a part of the newest fashion in houses, as you already see literature and art, and with just as much reality and reason."[16] This character's confident separation of the romantic from the religious impulse speaks to the prevailing logic that segregates false (feminized) romance from true (manly) religion. That distinction rests on a Protestant bias that assumes props like altars and pretty missals are antithetical to real faith.

Another case study, one worth sustained attention, is the paper doll house. Paper doll houses are a variant of the scrapbooks and collage albums popular during the nineteenth century, a popularity fed by new technologies that made foil and tissue papers, stamped card stock, color lithographs, and the like cheap and abundant.[17] They are not expressions of Christian devotion, but the paper doll house demonstrates the structure of communion in that it uses a representational economy of display and assemblage—a collage aesthetic—to foster intimacy. Women made these houses for children to play with; they were intended as backdrops for dramas improvised with paper dolls.[18] Print clippings were arranged atop backdrops of decorative paper, embellished, and glued into the pages of a bound book (blank or repurposed, as in the example opposite, pasted into an 1871 *New York Observer* yearbook, one of several preserved at the Winterthur Library). "Every paper-dollhouse scrapbook was a self-contained, particularized world," Beverly Gordon writes, and each one generally tracked the conventional layout of a home from public to private space. A parlor would appear in the first pages, a bedroom near the back.[19]

I turn to this archive because it demonstrates how consumer culture could be used to mediate love in a way that resists an orthodox Protestant ideal of revelation. These paper doll houses are artifacts of a collaborative reinterpretation of a commodified world. They testify to a mother-daughter love that is itself a model of playful intimacy between self and other. The paper doll houses, in short, manifest the structure of the love I call communion, and so they serve an as analogue to the relationships we find in James's and Stoddard's fictional worlds. Moreover, as a literalized house of fiction, the paper doll house makes an especially apposite form for comparison with James's work, and it is an equally appropriate artifact to consider in tandem with Stoddard's *The Morgesons,* given how Cassy and Veronica read each other by decorating themselves and their rooms.

It is also significant that the paper doll house exemplifies what Ann Bermingham calls "women's work": "A category of aesthetic objects that were produced as domestic amusements rather than as grand artistic statements."[20] That point helps support my broader argument for the countertradition of the love story of communion. The love story of communion is a literary genre that, in this third stage of the literary history I am developing, explicitly yokes masculine art to domestic kitsch. I am not alone in finding in visual forms like collage a cross-gendered aesthetic that counters the sense of modernism as chiefly men's work. Bartholomew Brinkman, for example, argues for what he calls Marianne Moore's scrapbook poetics, in part to push back against "the long-held assumption that visual (and poetic) collage is the product of a masculinized avant-garde

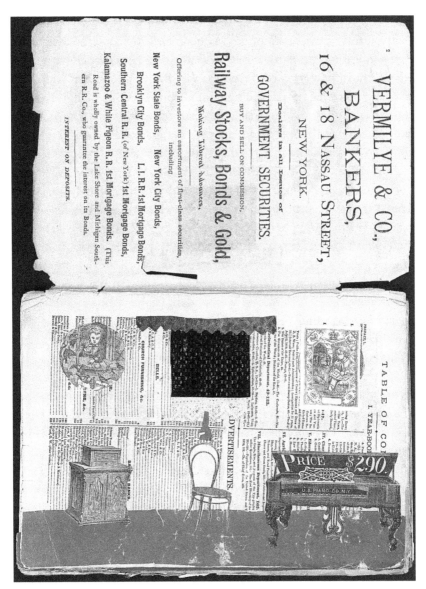

Paper doll house creators might repurpose a bound volume, such as this 1871 *New York Observer* yearbook, into a collaged domestic space. (Winterthur Library, Joseph Downs Collection of Manuscripts and Printed Ephemera)

that burst onto the scene in the first decades of the twentieth century."[21] By the terms of that assumption, when a male artist foregrounds mediation and artifice, his work is self-conscious and visionary, but a woman writer who, fifty years earlier, treated mediation and artifice as sources of aesthetic power had produced only middlebrow sentimentality. The love story of communion, which relies on a collage aesthetic in both Stoddard's and James's iterations, provides another example of a modern style that combines domestic intimacy with artistic experiment.

Thus, to read James and Stoddard in the context of these paper doll houses helps counter readings of the two authors that would divorce them from a trajectory that begins in the sentimental novel. To deny James's interest in feminized popular forms, or to focus on Stoddard's likeness to masculine high-art forms, have been reliable ways to amplify each author's prestige. Jessica Feldman, for instance, sees *The Morgesons* as a modernist work characterized by "jagged patterns of juxtaposition and dislocation."[22] In Stoddard's case, such moves have no doubt helped secure her status as an author worth studying. But focusing on such signifiers of prestige prevents us from seeing how both authors engaged with popular consumer culture in ways that make their work more, not less, powerful.

My argument that the same design principles animate both the prestige art and the domestic craft aims to demonstrate the homespun applications of the values of composition and theatricality. However, I do not mean to deny what feels weirdly dehumanized in either the paper doll houses or in James's and Stoddard's fiction. As in both novels, these paper doll houses offer abundant evidence that alienating materialism can coexist with cozy playfulness in the same formal structure. The paper doll houses can appear elaborate and spooky, eerily impersonal and overstuffed with commodities. The collage aesthetic, as it detaches and reorients images that are themselves familiar and often mass-produced, easily triggers such cognitive dissonance. Because of their disparate source material, even the most carefully arranged pages violate, if almost imperceptibly, rules of perspective and proportion. Some paper doll houses play freely with proportion, generating a sense of interiority that is claustrophobic and disorienting. Their creators may extravagantly upend realist illusionism, turning the image of a sweetly smiling infant into a colorful freak of disproportion. Despite its jarring enormity, the baby in one doll house (ca. 1885) reminds us that the audience for this work was a young girl, presumably one with a soft spot for infants, and that its aim was to delight that girl and to provoke her to play. So this image testifies to the both/and spirit that I find illuminating for James's and Stoddard's fiction, especially for their handling of the love story: both uncanny and affectionate. In their work, the material mediations of arrangement and display do not foreclose the possibility of domestic intimacy, even when the results verge on the surreal.

The collage aesthetic that is practiced in the paper doll house, like the broader model of communion, makes spectatorship productive of intimacy. The paper doll house composes the home as theater. Each page, each room, is a fixed backdrop for scenes to be played out by paper dolls. Some paper

This smiling infant (from a ca. 1885 example) is jarringly, even surreally, oversized, but it reminds us that the audience for such creations included children meant to play with them. (Winterthur Library, Joseph Downs Collection of Manuscripts and Printed Ephemera)

doll houses underscore the staginess of the form by framing their collaged interiors with theatrical curtains. The draperies of the four-poster bed in one doll house (ca. 1905–10), ostensibly shielding private space, are echoed and countered by the foil-starred metacurtains that render the whole scene a spectacle. A paper doll house like this makes such a theatrical structure something more homely—renders it susceptible, in fact, to child's play. It suggests that the mix of staginess and warmth readers find so striking in Stoddard's and James's fiction was not, after all, an elite cultural aberration. Registering the way the collage aesthetic animates the domestic playfulness of a paper doll house helps us register how it sparks the domestic playfulness between Cassy and Veronica and between Fanny and Bob.

The paper doll house can also teach us something about characterization in these novels, and about selfhood as it is conceived in the love

The framing curtains in this paper doll house (created ca. 1905–10) emphasize the theatricality of the form. (Winterthur Library, Joseph Downs Collection of Manuscripts and Printed Ephemera)

story of communion. The dolls themselves, the characters of the domestic drama, were usually catalog or magazine cut-outs, each one limited to one fixed fashion-plate gesture. But the dolls were not meant to stand alone, any more than James's or Stoddard's characters are meant to be abstracted from their well-designed settings. That James and Stoddard create oddly flat characters is a point often made by critics. Cassandra, as Feldman observes, is "a woman made of words that convey their autonomy," words that are not the "transparent windows" of realist fiction but units deliberately composed for effect (208). Bill Brown finds James's characters relying on "self-alienation" to turn their lives into material that can be "assemble[d] and exhibit[ed]."[23] For Leo Bersani, James's "fiction is . . . remarkably resistant to an interest in psychological depth," and James attains a "richly superficial art in which hidden depths would never ironically undermine the life inspired by his own and his characters' 'mere' ingenuities of design" (130, 132). This psychic flatness finds its archival correlative in the backless, depthless paper dolls that acted out their scenes within the pages of the paper doll house. Yet background is not just background for the collage aesthetic. In both the paper doll house and the novels, character is not an essence that can be abstracted from costume and setting. For the collage aesthetic, as for the love story of communion, both persons and things have the power to mean and to provoke real emotion by participating in a larger material context.

The creators of paper doll houses, like Stoddard and James, might well have absorbed this character-as-scenery logic from home decorating discourse, where it was repeatedly articulated. Writers advocated for decorating as the task of establishing an effective emotional circuit between oneself and one's things. The claim that good moral culture might be promoted through proper decor imparted to walls, rugs, and knickknacks a humanlike agency to form habits of perception and response. For Clarence Cook, writing in 1880, the question of what pictures to hang is tantamount, in its effects on heart and mind, to the question of the company we keep: "It is no trifling matter, whether we hang poor pictures on our walls or good ones, whether we select a fine cast or a second-rate one. We might almost as well say it makes no difference whether the people we live with are first-rate or second-rate."[24] This near-equivalence between pictures and friends blurs the line between animate and inanimate by granting

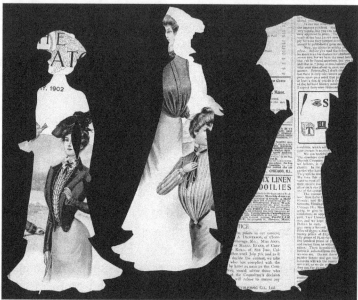

The paper dolls themselves (these examples are dated ca. 1905–10) are literally depthless, an archival correlative to the opaque characters portrayed by James and Stoddard. (Winterthur Library, Joseph Downs Collection of Manuscripts and Printed Ephemera)

both the power to shape dwellers' lives. The items gathered and arranged by a collector—who, like a collage artist, selects pieces and puts them on display—readily take on the nature of companions worthy of affection. Cook's contemporary, Herbert Byng Hall, who comes across as a real-life Ned Rosier, writes of his china collection, "I should be almost ashamed to confess how much pleasure these fragile treasures afford me. For hours I sit amidst my friends, pen or book in hand."[25] The near-shame registers a sense that an apology is needed, but Hall's tone is pleasurably confessional. He knows he can rely on his readers' shared experience. The friendliness of the things one has gathered need not be explained or defended.

The psychic economy of this theory of home decor recalls Stowe's image of the domestic utopia that Rachel Halliday oversees: love a rocking chair enough, and it starts to speak. In *Uncle Tom's Cabin,* only (white) owners had the power to redeem their possessions from the dehumanizing effects of capitalism, as Gillian Brown argues. But in these guides, as in Stoddard's and James's fiction, subjectivity circulates in both directions. Decor can enliven persons. As pictures and china *objets* are humanized, so the human itself becomes another *objet* to figure in the arrangement, but without necessarily being thereby dehumanized. Mrs. H. R. Haweis, author of multiple guides to decorating people and their dwellings (1889's *The Art of Decoration,* 1878's *The Art of Beauty,* 1879's *The Art of Dress,* and 1882's *Beautiful Houses*) explicitly treats furniture as "a kind of detached dress," assuring her readers that her advice on clothing oneself applies just as well to decorating one's room.[26] The best way to discover the right color for your living room, she writes, is to *"try it in a bonnet"* (365). In effect Haweis proposes thinking of a room as something one wears. When decorating a room becomes an extension of decorating oneself, though, things can go wrong: if the self depends for legibility and visibility on its setting, bad decoration becomes self-destructive. Haweis warns that, in a roomful of the wrong colors, a woman risks having her "personality . . . destroyed by the surroundings over-assimilating or absorbing her, so that she becomes a mere letter in an alphabet of violent colour" (22). The wrong backdrop can reduce a woman to unmeaning, truncated text; it takes the right backdrop to enable her to mean something.

Such a warning clarifies the stakes of making scenery and character mutually enhance each other, whether in collage or in prose. It shows us that, rather than claiming to reveal the soul of a character, as the face-to-face encounter of a portrait may do, the collage aesthetic claims only to intensify the qualities of a character by arranging the right scenery around her. Because its mode of characterization depends on a visible and shared setting, the collage aesthetic privileges the social understanding of communion rather than the private knowing that is revelation. Roger Cardinal's reflections on the purpose of collecting are useful here. He clarifies the sociability that motivates this way of engaging with material culture: "There is almost always an intention eventually to place the collage or the collection on display. Both ultimately exist to be *shown*, and implicitly to be shown to impress. We can say that both aspire to be noticed, inspected, admired, even envied" (71). The desire to impress, to be displayed, inspected, admired, and even envied also motivates the characters who populate *The Morgesons* and *The Golden Bowl*. These characters build their intimacy not, finally, through the transformative encounter of revelation, but through watching one another perform.

THE MORGESONS: LOVING INTEREST

When *The Morgesons* ends, Cassy and Desmond have been wedded for more than two years, but the novel does not show us their day-to-day life together. A short story published two years after the novel gives a sense of how Stoddard imagines married life between characters like them—a self-possessed woman, an intense husband—might play out. "The Prescription" portrays a couple, Caroline and Gérard, in crisis. Gérard's aggressive will-to-revelation renders his desire toxic and Caroline has become ill. Caroline, who narrates the story, recalls the healthiest moments in her marriage as those when she and her husband gazed not at each other but at other people onstage. She recalls good times "when [Gérard] took me to the opera, and forgot almost that I was his wife, or to the theatre, where we could not fail to have the same chord of appreciation struck" (798). Theatergoing prompts Gérard to forget his demand for revelatory knowledge of Caroline. Yet an intimacy is generated between them as both feel the same chord struck, the same strings vibrating, while they watch. As audience members, the two enjoy a temporary identification by sharing the same response to a spectacle. Like the reader-author relationship that

Hawthorne and Melville structure in *Blithedale* and *Pierre,* this shared spectatorship is a form of communion. It does not provide direct knowledge of the other; it forges a bond between self and other through shared appreciation of the same object.

Rather than privileging love that offers full disclosure, *The Morgesons* abides by Cassy's sense that the perfect transparency idealized by revelation is an unwelcome form of violence. As Hawthorne's Zenobia might have done, Cassy identifies the destruction that is latent in love's urge to know the depths of the other. About Veronica and Ben (the man who is Desmond's brother, Cassy's friend, and, later, Veronica's husband), Cassy says, "I think both would have annihilated my personality if possible, for the sake of comprehending me, for both loved me in their way" (156). Caroline in "The Prescription" might say the same. This is a matter-of-fact acknowledgment that the will to comprehend the love object may destroy it. We can find a similar warning in Cassy's observation of Ben, in a tense moment, picking up a book and "ben[ding] back" its "covers . . . till they cracked"; she accuses him of wanting to read her that way, an accusation he parries by saying that such is "rather [her] way of reading" (226). Whichever of them is more guilty of it, spine-cracking exposure is presented as a bad way to read books or persons. In resistance to that model, Carina Pasquesi argues, *The Morgesons* presents a series of "unconventional intimacies" fueled by the "conflict, interest, and engagement" that come from failing to know one's beloved.[27]

Cassy's remark on Ben's reading feels like a warning to readers of *The Morgesons* too. One way to heed that warning is to approach the novel as an instance of the collage aesthetic. Cassy's narrative gives us frequently impenetrable characters performing against the scenery of complexly decorated domestic spaces. But neither the scenery nor the characters can be peeled back to reveal hidden depths. And while Jessica Feldman sees an analogy to Cubism in Stoddard's abrupt transitions, the paper doll houses show that one need not wait for modernism, nor limit oneself to professional artists, to find practitioners who revel in artifice and discontinuity.[28] The pieced-together, slightly surreal collage albums of the Victorian era are evidence that such aesthetic effects were being produced before the twentieth century began. I too am comparing Stoddard to the modernism of the early-twentieth-century James, but I ground that comparison in the two authors' debts to the past, building the parallel on the basis of their shared adaptation of a model of love that begins in the sentimental novel.

On that view, Feldman's apt observation that Stoddard's characters "are, psychologically speaking, two-dimensional, stylized, abstracted" (224) should remind us of the knock against sentimentalism's flat characters, or against Hawthorne's allegorical persons. Deep characters are required by an ideal of revelation. But a resistance to depth does not dawn with literary modernism; it is there in antebellum sentimentality. Dorri Beam's identification of what she terms a "highly wrought" style helps us position Stoddard among her contemporaries. Beam identifies a group of nineteenth-century women writers, including Margaret Fuller, Harriet Prescott Spofford, and Pauline Hopkins, who produce prose that, like Stoddard's, "[indulges] in a sensual style that renders the world opaque and strange rather than assimilable and interpretable."[29] And while Stoddard's preference for "condensed and taut" prose makes her something other than a highly wrought practitioner for Beam (6), the point remains that Stoddard is a writer of her time. The novel's characters abide by the assumptions we see in the ambient discourse of fashion and decoration, assumptions that to be a person is to be, at least in part, a sociable consumer. That means we know each other by reading one another as displays; it means that knowledge of the other is mediated by a self-presentation that can be enhanced by shopping. The Morgesons thus participates in an embrace of mediation that stands as an alternative to the Calvinist austerity it shows as stunting human (especially women's) flourishing.

Stoddard's prose style shows an aptitude for arrangement that resonates with the burgeoning discourse of home decorating at midcentury. The guiding principle of the literary style of The Morgesons is that of the unexpected contrast. Taut condensation coexists with flourishes of romantic bombast. The two prose styles set each other off, each standing out more strongly against the foil of the other. Cassy, who reads Byron late into the night, is at times an unironic romantic. After her mother's death she walks by the sea as a storm comes up, staring at the water until "a strange tumult" overtakes her (214). She hears herself hailed by a "flying Spirit" and feels her "soul . . . brought in poise and quickened with the beauty before me" (214). She renders that beauty in a long and potent description of the sea as a sublime lover: "It gave tongue as its lips touched my feet, roaring in the caves, falling on the level beaches with a mad, boundless joy!" (214) Her description bears all the marks of a transcendental epiphany, a direct encounter with divinity that seems to let us readers see, too, into Cassy's soul.

The scene marks a turning point, but it does not end the chapter. The oceanic sublime is superseded by mundane domestic conflict. Cassy's encounter with the mad, tonguing ocean is followed by a one-line paragraph: "Aunt Merce was at the door" (215). We see Cassy vow to take on her mother's old position as head of the household. Right away the antagonism between Cassy and the Morgesons' servant Fanny resumes. There is a scene of clipped dialogue between Cassy and Fanny, and Cassy pulls the tablecloth off the table: "The dishes crashed, of course," she adds, underplaying the drama (215). The jarring stylistic shift from seaside transcendence to kitchen fractiousness prevents the development of anything that feels truly revelatory. Cassy records that she sat on the floor to eat from the crashed meal; she tells Fanny to clean up the mess; she asks where Veronica is; then she reflects on the prison of domesticity that she now realizes her mother had to endure. Heady moments of intimate self-awareness on Cassy's part alternate with rapid-fire conversation and seemingly melodramatic scenes deflated by minimal affect. Stoddard's principle of contrast generates an unpredictable relationship between the reader and the text.

Brief but heady moments of intimacy also feature in the courtships that punctuate Cassy's coming of age. Her relationships with Charles and Desmond include moments of sublime self-other transparency. In these erotic encounters, Cassy, like Pierre, seeks and finds a heated union with the object of her desire. Charles's eyes fill Cassy's veins with a torrent of fire, as noted above; the two are bound by an "intangible, silent, magnetic feeling" that follows "its own mysterious law" (74). "Charles read me," Cassy tells us of the moment before Charles declares his love for her in front of Ben. In the moment after that declaration, "his eyes softened, and mine filled with tears" (108–9). This is love as full legibility shared between two interiorities. Similar transactions occur years later, with Desmond. At a party, the way he says her name "set my pulses striking like a clock"; in a surprise encounter later that night, when Desmond hits his head on a fireplace mantel, she finds herself "involuntarily" expecting to feel the blow on her own body (184, 185). Later, Cassy likens her love for Desmond to "fire-tipped arrows" that once in a lifetime "pierce soul and sense, blood

and brain" (226). Such lines demonstrate the appeal, for Stoddard as novelist, of the possibility of a revelatory love that penetrates the senses.

These charged moments of revelation seem to me to resist Carina
Pasquesi's reading of Cassy as a cruel dominatrix who "experiences pleasure when her romantic love interests are symbolically castrated or killed
off," or as looking "ridiculous in her Byronic postures" (184, 198). This is
to overestimate the novel's negativity, a skewing that I would attribute to
Pasquesi's mode of reading the novel as "anticipat[ing]" queer theory's antisocial thesis (186). Like Pasquesi, I see Stoddard as ultimately "deflating
conventions of romanticism" (198). Yet moments like Cassy's oceanside
epiphany are not presented ironically. Rather than read Cassy's love affairs as late nineteenth-century antecedents to sadomasochism, reading
instead through the historicist lens of consumer culture suggests that Stoddard punctures the apparently mystic affinity between Cassy and Charles
and Desmond by letting us see that such intimacy actually depends on
arrangement. Introduced to Charles's home, Cassy takes stock of the red,
black, and bronze color scheme and is drawn to "the green and white sprays
of some delicate flower I had never before seen" (69). Her observation of
the contrast between the light flowers and the dark furniture leads to an
oblique exchange between her and Charles, whose face is also both "dark,
and delicate"; the effect of that contrast makes Cassy "shiver" (69). It requires such a setting to frame Charles as a brooding lover.

Similarly, Cassy's first glimpse of Desmond turns him into an arrangement of inharmonious elements: she views him as "an individual who
stood on a stone block, dressed in a loose velvet coat, a white felt hat, and
slippers down at the heel. He had a coach whip in his hand—the handsom-
est hand I ever saw, which he snapped at the dog, who growled with rage"
(163). The description identifies this person by coat, hat, shoes, whip, and,
finally, hand, an element that provides a focus for Cassy's attraction. That
hand, both handsome and hurtful, provokes her admiration as it elicits rage
from the dog. Desmond is a list of objects that in their totality produce both
attraction and repulsion. There is no face phrenologically mapped, no interior virtue or vice imputed to this figure, to account for the mixed affect.
This vision of Desmond as an arrangement of pieces develops into a love
that does not depend on revelation. Indeed, Cassy precedes her "fire-tipped
arrows" image with a more ambivalent line: "Desmond and I influence

each other to act alike" (226). "Influence" suggests something more indirect than the face-to-face unveiling of revelatory love. Their likeness manifests in the way they act in the world, not in the merging of invisible privacies.

But, on balance, heterosexual eros plays a secondary role among the novel's relationships. Cassy's erotic loves are more important for provoking her self-reflection and for prompting her to renegotiate her intimacy with her family. And within the Morgeson family, relationships thrive without revelation. For example, Cassy wishes she might know her mother Mary's deepest feelings. Sounding like Miles staring at Zenobia, Cassy laments that "it was not for me to know her heart. It is not ordained that these beautiful secrets of feeling should be revealed, where they might prove to be the sweetest knowledge we could have" (58). Yet despite the lack of that sweetest knowledge, Cassy builds a vivid portrait of her mother that details her self-presentation. Cassy recalls her mother's "long, lusterless, brown hair . . . threatening to fall out" of its comb; her "round-toed morocco shoes," minus their shoelaces; the "ruffle of fine lace [that] fell around her throat, and the sleeves of her short-waisted dress [that] were puffed at the shoulders" (17). At the end of this description of her mother's dress, Cassy confesses, "I make no attempt to analyze her character. I describe her as she appeared." But it is the scarcity of knowledge of her mother's depths that encourages Cassy's attachment: "I never understood her, and for that reason she attracted my attention" (17). Human opacity thus becomes a productive limitation. It prompts the lover to attend to the display and exhibition of the love object. Cassy's description of appearance yields a love based on attention without penetration. This is neither a merger of depths nor a painful incomprehension. Cassy's description testifies to a complex enjoyment of what is visible. Such uncomprehending but careful attention makes for a powerful love, a point borne out by the grief Cassy feels when her mother dies.

The most intense family relationship—and the leitmotif of the novel—is Cassy's bond with her sister Veronica. Sisterly love seems hereditary: late in The Morgesons, Cassy's Aunt Merce says she has finally learned that her sister Mary "was the love of my life" (237). The novel gives us a double-happiness heterosexual plot that marries off two sisters to two brothers. But instead of paralleling two tales of the progressive unveiling of man to woman that culminate in a march down the aisle, the novel focuses on the sisters' love. Fluctuating through fights and reconciliations, not aimed toward taking a vow that seals the deal, Cassy and Veronica's love forms the base of a triangle whose third point is one or the other man. Ben functions chiefly as a relay of feeling between the two sisters. "He tells me what I never knew—that I need you—that we need each other," Veronica says, reporting to Cassy on the contents of a letter that Ben has written to Veronica (223). Later on, just before Veronica marries Ben, she dreams of Desmond, a man she has never actually seen but nonetheless describes accurately. That dream leaves Veronica with a mark on her arm where the dream version of Desmond pricked her. What matters most about this eerie transaction is that, in watching Cassy react to the mark on her arm, Veronica now recognizes the power of Cassy's feelings: "My blindness is removed by a dream" (240). Even in this scene of paranormal emotional transmission, though, the sisterly epiphany is undercut by Cassy telling Veronica that "you are all wrong" and insisting that Veronica get up so Cassy can help her dress for the wedding (240).

Thinking back to their girlhood, Cassy reflects that "I did not love [Veronica]" because she was "so odd in her behavior" (13). Yet, twice, when she finds herself in a new town meeting new people, Cassy offers to be called by her sister's name (35, 90). What one sister feels, the other expresses. Veronica's piano playing makes audible Cassy's inner feelings; Veronica thinks she is crying, but it is Cassy whose eyes are full of tears (141). When their father Locke remarks that Cassy and Veronica "do not love each other, I suppose. What hatred there is between near relations!" Cassy contradicts his supposition. She says of Veronica, "I think I love her; at least she interests me" (100, 101). Interest may sound like a pale runner-up to love, but, as with Cassy's love for her mother, Mary, interest does not signify a failure of love; it is the basis of an extraordinarily fertile intimacy. When the two sisters "grasped hands, and stared mutely at each other" when Cassy returns from Rosville, Cassy records that "I felt a contraction in the region of my heart, as if a cord of steel were binding it" (128).

Such intense intimacy is, in the love story of communion, grounded on the theatrical self-presentation of costume and setting. In *The Golden Bowl*, characters are described with virtual scenery attached to them; in *The Morgesons*, rooms and dress are also crucial to characterization. This is a familiar mark of realism, but Stoddard's attention to details of contrast and arrangement loads such description with an attractive force that goes beyond verisimilitude. Veronica, who seems so otherworldly, is capable of catty judgments of other women's clothes—"She is an idiot in colors"— because she has "[made] a study of dress" herself. Veronica confesses that "it may be wicked, but what can I do? I love to look well" (151). Cassy goes on to describe Veronica's cream linen dress in admiring detail, with its "vivid yellow silk thread woven in stripes," each stripe with "a cinnamon-colored edge" (151). Cassy is herself a keen observer, and she questions the color scheme Veronica chooses for her room: "Green and blue together, Veronica?" (134). The decorating adviser Mrs. Haweis warns in *The Art of Decoration* that, when mixing the two colors, "care is required what blue and green" (364). But Cassy concedes that Veronica has, by taking her cues from heaven and earth, made a wholly "new atmosphere" there (134).

Rooms can work as mediators that help a self know and see itself. Cassy frequently identifies herself with her rooms. At Rosville, after a difficult scene with Charles and Ben, Cassy thinks that "in my room I shall find myself again," and indeed "it welcomed me with so friendly and silent an aspect, that I betrayed my grief, and it covered my misery as with a cloak" (110). Back home in Surrey after Charles's death, Cassy redecorates her room in blue chintz and damask. When it is finished, Cassy observes that "it already seemed to me that I was like the room," and when Veronica sees her in it, she says "I recognize you here" (143, 144). As she leaves Belem to return to Surrey, Cassy recognizes that individuality reposes in the arrangement of things in a room: looking back at her guest room in the home of Desmond and Ben, she thinks of the maid already tidying up after her: "The ghost of my individuality would lurk there no longer than the chairs I had placed, the books I had left, the shreds of paper flowers I had scattered, could be moved or swept away" (201).

Rooms, then, are scenery that is not dispensable. Draperies and carpet may seem like the mere trappings of an inner spirit, as the prie-dieu and vellum missal seem mere trumpery to the skeptic. But in the mode of communion, material context is what makes it possible to know and love one another. In Veronica's room, after accepting the unlikely combination of green and blue on the carpets and drapes, Cassy turns to the walls: "The paper on the wall was ash-colored, with penciled lines. She had cloudy days probably. A large-eyed Saint Cecilia, with white roses in her hair, was pasted on the wall. This frameless picture had a curious effect. Veronica, in some mysterious way, had contrived to dispose of the white margin of the picture, and the saint looked out from the soft ashy tint of the wallpaper" (134). This room overtly Catholicizes the spirituality the narrative has built around Veronica. Veronica is innocent, otherworldly, and given to self-mortification; she practices charity. These attributes make her recognizably saintly across the Christian spectrum. In her room, by putting a saint's picture on the wall, she highlights the specifically Catholic associations with her own name and with her miraculously sensitive musicianship. Veronica is the saint known for receiving the true image of Christ's face on her veil as he passed by carrying the cross.[30] It seems appropriate, then, that Veronica Morgeson, as decorator, has caused a mysterious visage to appear on her own wall. It feels appropriate, too, that she chooses Cecilia as the holy face to be pictured. Saint Cecilia is a virginal channel for heavenly music, one whose body was ultimately incorruptible despite the attacks that martyred her.

The point is not that Veronica is portrayed as an incorruptible saint herself, though Cassy is moved by a "holy pity" in watching the "virgin beauty" of her sister's body as she struggles through a spell of illness (147). Veronica is more complicated than that, and so is her room, which is not simply a saint's hermitage. There is a velvet-framed picture, across from Saint Cecilia, of a man with a face of "concentrated fury" (134). There are clothes and toiletries; Cassy admires the neatly organized "drawers and boxes for everything which pertained to a wardrobe" (135). Veronica keeps *The Arabian Nights* next to her bible. The point is that, for this relationship of communion, whatever is worth knowing about the other can only be known through the mediation of the material self, its body and costume and setting. Cassy says she feels no sympathy with Veronica, no magical currents of soul-to-soul contact, but she admires the "picture of Veronica" that her room's arrangement evokes (136). Veronica could not be so lovable without the decor to frame such pictures of her.

In *The Morgesons*, if all we have to know and love are the images we can provoke and admire in each other's minds—if there is no revelation of a deep and private self, stripped of its material and consumer decoration— this is sufficient. If they read each other through their rooms and triangulate their intimacy through men, Cassy and Veronica nonetheless genuinely love each other. The novel's moments of curious attention and of uncanny transmission add up to an intense bond whose power each sister acknowledges. When Fanny laughs at what she perceives as the sister's unloving relationship, Veronica erupts in a Cassy-like display of rage: she grabs Fanny, holds her against the wall, and lectures her about not knowing what real love looks like. "I admire her; you do, too. I *love* her, and I love you, you pitiful, ignorant brat" (145). Cassy, watching this dramatic expression of her sister's feeling, thinks to herself that "all declarations in my behalf are made to third persons" (145). That is a good description of how this version of communion functions. It does not culminate in a private transaction between two intimates. It requires a performance and a spectator.

THE GOLDEN BOWL: LOVING MISUNDERSTANDING

Love in James's last novel also adheres to communion's structure of spectatorial intimacy. Peter Brooks calls the late novels "James's most theatrical fiction": in these last works, "place is conceived as stage set, and within its confines a limited number of selected stage properties and gestures are made to bear the weight of an impassioned drama."[31] Given the long Protestant association of Catholicism with suspect theatricality, it is no surprise that James's one major attempt as a playwright, *Guy Domville,* tells the story of a young man grappling with a vocation in the priesthood. That play is "James' most purely Catholic work," in Edwin Sill Fussell's estimation, though Fussell calls *The Golden Bowl* "indisputably Henry James' Roman Catholic masterpiece" (120, 127).

One of James's earliest pleasures in the theater was his experience watching Uncle Tom shows. That point helps us see the place of *The Golden Bowl* in the American literary tradition I have been arguing for, the tradition of the Catholicized love story of communion that began with *Uncle Tom's Cabin.* As James recalls, Stowe's novel existed in the culture of his youth hardly as a book at all but as "a state of vision, of feeling and of consciousness" in which people "generally conducted themselves."[32] Its story transcended—"went gaily roundabout"—mere words on the page to "flutter down on every stage, literally without exception, in America and Europe," a feat that James is willing to count as a measure of its inexhaustible "amount of life" (160). James says that even as a boy he could see all the "loose patchwork" of the play and "could know we had all intellectually condescended" to believe Eliza crossed the river and Eva fell off a boat, while registering simultaneously "that we had yet had the thrill of an aesthetic adventure" (164). James's willingness to see theatrical artifice bonded with genuine aesthetic thrill begins, on this account, with the example of America's sentimental bestseller.[33]

As in the paper doll houses, and as in *The Morgesons,* the theatricality of communion means that the scenery of domestic space is crucial to making characters available for intimacy. Rooms are as important to Jamesian intimacy as they are to Cassy and Veronica's love. Decor is handled more abstractly; it is difficult to call up a vision of any one room in the novel. But if the interiors of Cadogan Place and Eaton Square are nearly invisible, each person in *The Golden Bowl* carries a virtual stage set around with himself, radiating a domestic space that makes him visible. The cut-and-paste backgrounds against which paper dolls could take on life translate, in James's prose, to incredibly vivid virtual impressions. Adam is described as having a face like "a small decent room, clean-swept and unencumbered with furniture" (137). Around Fanny, we are asked to see "hammocks and divans," "sherbets" and "slaves," a "mandolin" and a "pet gazelle" (64). Bob manages to project "strange straw-like textures, of the aspect of Chinese mats," and "a continual cane-bottomed chair" upon "wide verandahs" (86). Charlotte's hat and the color of her shoes emanate travel-guide clip art: "Winds and waves and custom-houses" (71). Seeing a person means seeing that layered collection of stuff, assimilated to the self. Extending Haweis's decorative principle, furniture in James's imagination becomes a character's attached (not detached) dress. His characters' presumed deep interiors are likewise only knowable as material artifacts. When we do enter a character's consciousness, James gives us that consciousness in terms of a pile of vivid things, not a list of general beliefs or propositions.

This is a change from his earlier handling of mental states. While Isabel Archer's meditations on her husband proceed through careful abstractions with only a few subdued images, Maggie's mind is a jumble of surfaces: bric-a-brac, pagodas, coaches. The narrative voice-overs in *The Golden Bowl* do not purport to reveal the truth deep within a character's heart or mind, nor do they give the sense that the deeper we get the truer we see; there is just more accumulated stuff. Such handling has given James a reputation for psychic flatness among some critics. H. G. Wells skewers James for his still-life fictions that amount to "a dead kitten, an egg-shell, a bit of string . . . very reverently placed" on a "high altar."[34] James as the sanctifier of soulless arrangement contends with James as the master of metaphysical subtlety. The latter is the version Carl Van Vechten helped establish in 1922 when he linked the late James to the late Melville.[35] James himself, however, wishes us to see mere stuff as productive of transcendence. He finds that the glow of "the Things, always the splendid Things" can suggest "the tempered light of some arching place of worship."[36]

The collage aesthetic manifests in James's work on the largest scale in the way he describes the job of producing the New York Edition. This undertaking prompts James to render his career as an intellectual collection arranged for sale in a prestige market. He encounters his work, as he says in the preface to *The Golden Bowl,* as a pile of "accumulated 'good stuff'" that needs choosing, polishing and arranging (31). Not that James thinks of his New York Edition as a curio cabinet; his resistance to the illustrations testifies to his wariness about any literal visualization. Revision for him is also the intellectual work of self-analysis, and the accumulated pile is also abstract, "the very record and mirror of the general adventure of one's intelligence" (31). But as the selection and arrangement that make a collage aim to produce a coherent whole from the pieces, so James wants his New York Edition to make of his works not just a haphazard sequence but a physically attractive collection that can be shown off and sold off.

James develops an intimate communion with his own works as he writes the prefaces for the New York Edition. Looking over his earlier texts, James echoes the filial tenderness of a collector like Herbert Byng Hall, viewing his stories and books not as inanimate objects but as persons. What makes revision "a living affair" is the unpredictability with which his old pieces respond now to his look and his touch. These fictional things are alienated by temporal distance, taking on the quality of found elements, but they come alive as he considers how to dispose them for the view of a new audience of possible readers. The "good stuff" actually "sit[s] up, in its myriad forms," and beseeches James to "'believe in us and then you'll see!'" (31). The anthropomorphized stuff inspires paternal pride, becoming James's "uncanny brood." He fondly enumerates that brood's flaws and charms. His early works strike him first as a batch of aged persons whose dusty clothes have to be "twitched" into place after so many years gone by; then, as he prolongs the metaphor, they shift into "awkward infants" who need their faces washed in the nursery before being put on display for visitors (27, 28). In either case revision has become the work of polishing and arranging, and thereby humanizing, one's gathered things for public display. Thinking of things with an eye toward arranging them into an exhibit, it turns out, is what makes them human-like objects of affection.

In the intimacy of communion, characters who read like bundles of scenery, like well-designed exhibits of detachable scraps, can enjoy an en-during happy marriage. Fanny and Bob are united in matrimonial good cheer, if not in ecstatic bliss. Fanny and Bob show, from the beginning to the end of *The Golden Bowl,* how the kind of incomprehension that reigns in the Morgeson family can be turned toward affectionate companionship. As critic John Bayley puts it, *The Golden Bowl* "consummat[es] [James's] idea that love . . . in the end meant intimacy without knowledge."[37] And yet this lack of knowledge is not elevated to a sublime mystery. It is simply a condition of human relationship as James sees it.

In *The Golden Bowl,* the ability to see the beloved as an exhibited col-lection is requisite to intimacy. This is as true for the more central couples as it is for Fanny and Bob. When Amerigo sees Charlotte at Fanny's, years after their affair has ended and just before he marries Maggie, she strikes him as a delectable collection, "a cluster of possessions of his own," a group of "relics" for him to relish: her hair and face and dress are "items in a full list, items recognized . . . as if . . . they had been 'stored'—wrapped up, num-bered, put away in a cabinet" (72). The collection that is, for Amerigo, Char-lotte comprises her "tawny" hair like that of a "huntress," her "rounded" arms like a "Florentine" statue made of "old silver" or "old bronze," her hands and fingernails, the "special beauty" of her back; her waist is both "the stem of an expanded flower" and gives her the look of a "long loose silk purse" whose coins he can just hear clinking in his ear as she turns toward him.[38] Amerigo is a collectible item himself, "a rarity, an object of beauty," a "curious and eminent" example of his kind, as Maggie tells him before their marriage (49). Amerigo seems to accept this equably enough, and while he might well be read as a victim of capitalist dehumanization, his view of Charlotte as a collection of *objets* suggests that his apparently quite real passion for her is equally informed by this ready conflation of person and thing.

Maggie is the heroic lover in the novel, but her loves, too, follow the structure of communion, and they depend on arrangement for their visibility. The development of her love, both for her father and for Amerigo, depends on seeing the desired man in a tableau that is the object of another's gaze. Early in the novel we learn that Maggie "never admired [Amerigo] so much, or so found him heart-breakingly handsome, clever, irresistible" as when she sees him desired by other women (157). It stands, in fact, as "one of the most comfortable things between the husband and the wife" that Maggie is capable of such jealousy. She jokes with Amerigo that "even should he some day get drunk and beat her, the spectacle of him with hated rivals" would make her forgive him, just for the "sovereign charm of it . . . as the exhibition of him that most deeply moved her" (157).

We cannot dismiss it as just a symptom of Maggie's immature infatuation that she is most moved by the spectacle of Amerigo on display. Her whole course of action in the novel's second part is determined by her finally seeing how Charlotte wants him. It takes her recognition of Charlotte's desire for Amerigo to rouse Maggie's desire and to prod her to take back her husband for herself. That Maggie is at least in part reenacting Charlotte's desire accounts for Maggie's ability to understand better than anyone else Charlotte's pain. Maggie is the one who can interpret Charlotte's "[frantic] tapping" "against the glass," the one who imagines Charlotte's message to Amerigo in a long unspoken address that begins, "You don't know what it is to have been loved and broken with" (552–53).

As for her love for her father, we should recall that it takes Maggie's witnessing Mrs. Rance's pursuit of Adam to realize how desirable he is to other women, how vulnerable her marriage has left him. Adam and Maggie's "decent little old-time union" (135) has placed Adam "too deep down" in her heart and in her life "to be disengaged, contrasted or opposed, in short objectively presented" (148–49). Maggie has not really seen Adam until now because he has not been set off properly by contrast, because she hasn't seen him on display.[39]

Adam's professional life as a museum builder depends on the work of collection and display that comprises the collage aesthetic. So does his emotional life. He decides to marry Charlotte when he can suddenly see how that move would arrange him and his daughter more felicitously. The decision comes to him as the making-visible of "an object that lay at his feet" that he had failed to see (186). Later he "held his vision" of the rightness of this new arrangement in the same way "he had . . . kept a glazed picture in its right relation to the light" (188). Making marriage the object of such an aestheticizing view may seem appropriate for what James portrays as the essentially economic conquest of Charlotte. As critics such as Martha Nussbaum and J. Hillis Miller have noted with disapproval, Adam does not distinguish between humans and objects in his judgments. He measures "old Persian carpets . . . and new human acquisitions" by the same "one little glass" of judgment, and he "[cares] for precious vases only less than for precious daughters" (172). He imagines Maggie as a statue, one whose "perfect felicity," whose balance of antique and modern touches, would be appropriately seen against the backdrop "of Vatican or Capitoline halls" (172).

Yet Adam's aestheticizing does not, in James's telling, hinder him from loving Maggie tenderly. His sense for Maggie's precious fineness is "kept sharp, year after year, by the . . . comparison of fine object with fine object, of one degree of finish, of one form of the exquisite with another" (172)— in short, by a sense for the art of arrangement and juxtaposition. The Adam-Maggie relation is presented as genuinely intimate (if anything, too genuinely intimate) throughout. Even Adam's acquisitive admiration for Charlotte looks warmer than Gilbert Osmond's—that earlier, poorer collector's—coldly possessive desire for Pansy or for Isabel. The disengagement, contrast, and opposition that help Maggie recognize Adam's value are the same moves by which James learns to appreciate his own work in assembling the New York Edition. In both cases such treatment does not dehumanize but amplifies an object's affectionate appeals.

Like Stoddard, James tests the appeal of communion by putting revelation into play as a privileged, if ephemeral, experience of transcendent intimacy. Revelation is premised on the superiority of an invisible deep truth, and so it runs against the grain of the novel's collage aesthetic, which privileges a self made visible through comparison and contrast. But revelation is what we see as the climax of the relation between Charlotte and Amerigo, who achieve a mutual transparency that allows them to arrange a rendezvous without having actually to speak about alibis and train schedules (282–83). When they kiss, boundaries dissolve, and the couple merges into an undifferentiated state of union: "Everything broke up, broke down, gave way, melted and mingled" (259). In this moment the distinction between subject and object disappears. Charlotte and Amerigo echo each other ("It's sacred"; "It's sacred"); they mirror each other as they stand "facing and faced . . . grasping and grasped . . . meeting and met" (259). It is a high point in the novel. Charlotte has achieved her desire for full identification with Amerigo, and she is proud to say to him that "you're not too different from *me*," as he has confessed he feels too different from his wife and her father.

Yet the novel shows this drive toward sameness may be Charlotte's biggest mistake. Being too close to actually see each other is a problem for the intimacy James imagines as enduring and creative. He casts an ironic shadow on the erotic telepathy that enables the pair to pull off their afternoon dalliance. His narrator notes that "if such unarranged but unerring encounters gave the measure of the degree in which people were, in the common phrase, meant for each other, no union in the world had ever been more sweetened with rightness" (290). This claim for the sweetest, rightest union in the world is too heavy a load for that "if" to bear. The idea of lovers being meant for each other is slighted as a "common phrase." James suggests that any love that aims toward the boundary-erasing soul-merge that Charlotte and Amerigo briefly enjoy is doomed to be, if not immoral as in their adulterous case, then at least fruitless. Those who pursue such love may pursue it heroically, or deceitfully, or pathetically, or all three at once, as Charlotte does. But, in a James novel, to believe that love is, at its very best, a matter of merging one's depths with another is a dead end. Tellingly, after Charlotte claims her full identity with him, Amerigo suggests in reply that perhaps if he and she were married they would "find some abyss of divergence" (258). The final image of Maggie and Amerigo's embrace is ambivalent because it is not clear that they will be able to acknowledge such divergence, or know how to turn it to creative purpose. This would look like ambivalence about marriage, period, if it were not for the strength of the counterexample James provides in Fanny and Bob. For James, what makes a marriage successful is not its possible moments of union but its never-ending work of textual play—play that works on the principle of arranging found elements in the most pleasing order.[40]

If the novel's more prominent lovers see each other as displayed collections, and if that is key to James's version of the love story, why isn't everyone as happy as Fanny and Bob? Fanny and Bob's love also works according to the principles of display and spectatorial admiration, but theirs is uniquely a relationship not in crisis. The difference is that they have given up trying to see deeply into each other in favor of looking at each other, and at others. They adapt the collage aesthetic toward telling stories about other people's lives, seeing others as objects to be arranged, much as James does. This is James's answer to the question of what married love can look like if seduction and adultery are off the table. Within-wedlock sex is not totally off the table. Bob at least imagines that the "fun" of storytelling will lead to fun in bed, though Fanny shuts down the one veiled come-on James depicts for us. "'Oh I don't mean,' she said from the threshold, 'the fun that you mean. Good–night.'" Bob registers that dismissal with "an odd short groan, almost a grunt. He *had* apparently meant some particular kind" of fun (101).

The activity we do see between the Assinghams is their partaking of the vicarious pleasures of matchmaking, of watching other, sexier lives. This vicariousness, though, proves to be a strength rather than a weakness. (We might recall that Dante's great lovers, Paolo and Francesca, also relied on other people's love stories to ignite their own connection.) Fanny and Bob's "intercourse by misunderstanding" (297) enables a happy marriage that proceeds by their collaborative composition and by their mutual enjoyment of each other's performances. They talk far into the night; they know how to push each other's buttons, but they seem always to relish the routine. James at times invites us to mock them, as when the narrator draws our attention to Bob's childish delight at hearing the same story repeated twenty times. But James's work shares too much with the Assinghams' storytelling—and their love shares too much, structurally, with the major characters' passions—for either him or us to dismiss them as comic relief.

We are told early on that Fanny and Bob have neither children nor wealth. Stories will substitute for both. Fanny gathers "social scraps" to fill those two voids, like an "old [lady]" collecting "morsels of silk" for a quilt, and rather like James (e.g., in the preface to *The Spoils of Poynton*), who speaks of "rescu[ing]" and "hoard[ing]" the "germ[s]" and "nugget[s]" of stories, though he does so with "the sublime economy of art" in mind.[41] As a narrative collage artist, Fanny "invent[s] combinations" (65) and creates "situations" (85); Bob listens and performs "masterpiece[s] of editing"

(87). The proof that such scrap collection and arrangement serve their purpose for Fanny is that she finds "sympathy and curiosity could render their objects practically filial" (65). The stories and their component elements are objects of desire for her and Bob. James's love for his collected narratives may be purely paternal, but Fanny and Bob have crushes on the objects of their narratives. Bob accuses Fanny of arranging Amerigo's marriage as a way of exercising (if not exorcising) her love for Amerigo: "You fell violently in love with the Prince yourself, and . . . as you couldn't get *me* out of the way you had to take some roundabout course," that of marrying him off to Maggie (96). Much later, Fanny coaches Bob to draw on his love for Maggie ("as I've given you so perfect an opportunity to fall in love with [her]," Fanny notes) to bear up under the burden of lying about Amerigo's affair with Charlotte (410). They are aware of each other's wandering eyes, but, in James's telling, this mental infidelity spices up rather than threatens the bond of their coauthorship.

In contrast to Charlotte and Amerigo's mutual transparency, what makes Fanny and Bob such a good team is their mutual opacity. They are spectacularly, comically divergent. Fanny loves excess; Bob's thinness routinely cuts down his wife's surplus, figured as overwriting: "[A] large proportion of [Fanny's] meanings he knew he could neglect. He edited for their general economy the play of her mind, just as he edited . . . her redundant telegrams" (87). Their misunderstanding enables them to continue seeing one another as objects, objects that are susceptible to arrangement and display and therefore to a crucial visibility. Fanny's endless hand-wringing over her friends' relationships reminds Bob of "the celebrated lady" at "the Aquarium" who "turned somersaults and did tricks in the tank of water" (85), and he comports himself as a spectator who wants to enjoy the show.

Bob helps Fanny become other to herself, too. We are told that generally Fanny's "thoughts . . . in her husband's company, pursued an independent course. He made her, when they were together, talk, but as if for some other person. . . . [S]he addressed herself with him as she could never have done without him" (235). He serves as her audience—an uncomprehending but appreciative one—without which she cannot be herself. But it is also "extraordinary for her always" how Bob, for all his obtuseness, "fell to speaking better for her than she could . . . speak for herself" (412–13). Neither one understands the other in what we would call a deep way, but the spectatorship and the contrasting juxtaposition they provide each other help them keep articulating themselves.

It also helps keep them writing and creating. James's narrator notes Fanny's "repeated practice" as storyteller, how she "enjoyed invariably" evoking her own risk of being implicated, the "anxious satisfaction" in which she can "[lose] herself each time" she retells the story with Bob (412–13); for his part, Bob "resemble[d] not a little the artless child who hears his favourite story told for the twentieth time and enjoys it exactly because he knows what is next to happen" (414). This is repetition, but not the sort that Lauren Berlant writes about as the means by which "intimates who repulse each other can remain coupled when it is no longer fun."[42] Fanny and Bob do have fun. Their aim is not to keep reenacting the wedding-vow promise of, as Berlant writes, "imminent mutual transparency, simultaneity, and completion" (15). They neither expect nor desire to be transparent to each other. What makes their marriage fun is their pleasure in each other's performances, the spectacle they each make for the other.

If there is any scene in the novel that seems poised to show us Fanny and Bob engaged in deep communion à la Charlotte and Amerigo, it would be their midnight conversation, after they leave the younger pair at Matcham. The conversation is figured from Bob's point of view as occurring by a "mystic lake." Their usual cheerful talking past each other has yielded to something more intense (297). But they never enter the "deep water" of the lake. Though Bob fears that Fanny's boat might falter, she "bump[s] . . . ashore" before the "sheet of dark water" is broken. Instead, their talk on this night is, as usual, a matter of piecing together a story.

They take the scraps Fanny's observation has gathered and play with them until they look right. Bob pushes Fanny to provide character motivation: "You mean then [Amerigo] doesn't care for Charlotte—?" And Fanny, after a dramatic pause, "simply said: 'No!'" (314). Together they work out how Maggie will behave in the coming chapters. Even when Fanny seems to conclude the story by asserting that Maggie's intention to keep her father in ignorance of the adultery "will be work cut out!" and says good night to Bob, he lures her back with a choice of adjectives. "Ah, but, you know, that's rather jolly!" he says, and she questions "jolly." "I mean it's rather charming," he amends. When she again questions "charming," he finally edits it to, "I mean it's rather beautiful" and reminds Fanny, "You just said yourself it would be" (311). This challenge provokes Fanny to cite one of James's cardinal rules of artistic creation, and a key element of the collage aesthetic: she says that Charlotte was otherwise doomed to be "a piece of waste," and that it was thus Fanny "[fell] in love with the beautiful symmetry of [her] plan" (313). "I see—I see," muses Bob, not seeing Fanny but the love story they are writing. They prove here that they, like their creator, are capable not just of repetition but also of revision.

Fanny and Bob do embrace, in a moment of lyrical beauty, by the mystic lake, and there is great tenderness in this scene. When Fanny begins to cry, reflecting that she has no idea how far Charlotte and Amerigo might go during their stay at Matcham, Bob hesitates but then "put his arm round her." Prefiguring the pose in which we leave Maggie and Amerigo, "he drew her head to his breast, where, while she gasped, she let it stay a little—all with a patience that presently stilled her" (305). For the moment, in the gasping and the stillness that follows, they make a "community of passion" that suggests a bond almost as revelatory and erotic as Charlotte and Amerigo's (282). There is "wonderment," "kindness," and "comfort" between them; James tells us they have together "entered . . . the region of the understood" (305).

Yet the "beauty" of this moment does not amount to the climactic merging of depths that revelation promises. The embrace ends neither the scene nor the conversation. James continues both in the next chapter. Their late-night conversation keeps moving onward as Fanny begins to invent the kind of character Maggie will become. They return to their rule of divergences and misunderstanding: the narrator tells us that "it had still to be their law, a little, that she was tragic when he was comic" (311). While Fanny explains how Maggie will have to learn about evil, Bob "nodded again almost cheerfully—as if he had been keeping the peace with a baby or a lunatic" (310). What matters is that in the end Fanny finds that "the amplitude of her exposition sustained and floated her," and for Bob "she had done perhaps even more to create than to extinguish in him the germ of a curiosity" (320). His narrative hunger and sexual appetite will, like hers, persist as long as mutual understanding is only a temporary slip from their law of contrast. Such is happily married love in James's last novel: the telling of the endless story of other people's love lives.

Bill Brown agrees with Carolyn Porter that the world of *The Golden Bowl* is one where reification has saturated human relations, so that everyone sees everyone else as some kind of object.[43] This objectification, though, must include the possibility we find in the paper doll houses for real intimacy to be facilitated by consumer excess. It must also include the possibility that materialism might enable contact with genuine alterity—the promise of communion as imagined by a Protestant imagination partly reclaiming Catholic practice. In *The Golden Bowl*, as in *The Morgesons*, even the dearly beloved is a shifting display of images clipped from the cultural consciousness. But if this amounts to dehumanization or objectification, then James seems to think dehumanization and objectification have their uses—uses that may not be dissociable from their abuses. Bob sees Fanny as a circus performer, all to the good of their relationship; that Maggie and Adam view Charlotte and Amerigo as human furniture seems rather more to the bad. What keeps Fanny and Bob's marriage praxis relatively innocent is that, as artist figures (like James, and like the creators of paper doll houses), they are not fiscally empowered, as Adam and Maggie are, actually to acquire and handle real things. They arrange only the images of things, their mental representations of them. The people the Assinghams set up are real, in the novel's story-world, but Fanny and Bob neither control them nor keep anyone for themselves.

Brown suggests that things and objects so predominate in James's fiction because it appears that loving an object is perhaps the only way that one can love, period. "Collecting thus appears as . . . [a] mode of keeping boredom at bay, of transforming abstract longing—the desire for *something*—into a desire for some (particular) things" (163). But if modernity hands us fragmentation and spectacle, then James seems to think, as Serpell's reading of Buber suggests, that those forces can be put to work serving the cause of intimacy.

The pages of the paper doll houses, made of the printed debris of commerce, do not testify to alienation. These artifacts, like the love stories in *The Golden Bowl* and *The Morgesons*, show how Victorian consumerism might foster self-other relationships. Fanny and Bob's union is not shown as thin, flat, cold, or superficial; neither is Cassy and Veronica's sibling love. In literature, the careful arrangement and perception of "the furniture of the world" has the power, as James puts it, to "address . . . the spiritual and the aesthetic vision," to lead the mind "captive by a charm and a spell, an incalculable art" (35). In human relations, too, James suggests that genuine intimacy can thrive as self and other appreciate each other's displays. In that case, as we also saw in Stoddard's work, modern consumer culture has not stripped love of its own possible charm and spell.

Five

Love and Depth Revisited
History and the Ethics of Reading American Literature Now

THE EXAMPLE OF FANNY AND BOB ASSINGHAM sets up my consideration of literary ethics now, which returns us to the opening argument that an anti-Catholic interpretive protocol has shaped American literary criticism. A conservative Protestant faith in the immediacy of reading, I have claimed, helped underwrite a canon of fiction whose signal power was to make the reader feel intimate with a transcendence just barely withheld. That privileging of revelation was inverted, though not extinguished, by the canon-breaking work of New Historicism and ideology critique. Such work largely aimed to reveal the truth of historical materialism behind a false veil of humanist pieties. More recently, the ideal of revelation withheld has been revived under the banner of what Dorothy Hale terms the "New Ethics."[1] My case for the Assinghams as exemplars of communion runs against the grain of most literary-ethical readings, which are committed both to an ideal of revelatory love and to an ahistorical interpretive approach. This final chapter examines the link between those two commitments and argues for an alternative set of linked commitments—to a model of love as communion, and to historicist reading—for literary ethics.

I pick up the story of American literary scholarship where I left it at the end of chapter 1, around the 1980s, with scholars like Eve Sedgwick and Jane Tompkins critiquing the biases of the initial American canon and contending for the value of sentimentalism. Such arguments worked; the canon expanded. But they left unfinished business, to my mind, insofar as those arguments abandoned the ideal of literary transcendence instead of proposing an equal and alternate version of such transcendence. The initial canon had designated withheld revelation as the mark of a great book. Rather than contest that designation directly, scholars like Tompkins swapped what had been an aesthetic and ethical payoff for interpretation (reading yields an encounter with radical otherness) for a sociopolitical one (reading yields an understanding of the cultural work that texts do).

Understanding a text's role in the power structure of its time is a worthy aim for readers. The kind of interpretive intimacy I am calling communion requires us to see a text as participating in its culture, and to reckon with the unequal distributions of power in that culture. But to substitute the sociopolitical for the ethical payoff is to concede that some texts are cultural workers while other texts present us with genuine alterity, and to accept having to choose between those two possibilities. Communion insists that we apprehend and enjoy alterity best when we see it framed by its time and place and claims access to an otherness just as radically other as that promised by revelation. Making that case has been the point of historicizing revelation and communion as competing routes to the same God in nineteenth-century America. That theological context grounds my claim that, as a model of literary criticism, communion offers contact with a book's alterity just as valuable as that promised by revelation—even when the book is a bestseller like *The Gates Ajar* or when it is read alongside an archive of paper doll houses.

This final chapter considers the evolution of literary ethics since the 1990s, detailing its model of reader-text intimacy and its allergy to historicist methods. In chapter 1, I argued for the adoption by literary scholars of an emotional and interpretive protocol from conservative Protestantism, an import of neo-orthodox principles that shaped New Critical antisentimentalism. This chapter traces the continuing influence of the revelatory ideal in literary ethics while also querying the sometimes reflexive disavowal of a theology of close reading as a gesture by which scholars assert their intellectual freedom.[2] Such claims can operate as a professional self-defense that obscures a critic's own commitment to some version of textual alterity. As Tracy Fessenden observes, "An in-house account of retreat from religion, both as institutional history and as professional credo, remains the one progress narrative" literary studies still puts faith in.[3]

Literary ethics is not the special domain of American literary studies. The ethicist methods I examine below were, however, developed by critics in the American academy. Those critics have taken on the task of resuscitating a kind of literary transcendence in the late twentieth and early twenty-first century. Whether it focuses on surface, form, or affect, literary ethics theorizes the work of interpretation as an encounter with alterity. Familiar concepts like the voice of the text, or authorial intention, shift to a claim for the text as a proxy for otherness in general. Literary ethics asks how the text positions its readers, accommodating or baffling them. In effect, I will argue, literary ethics imagines reading as a love story that can produce either a happy or a sad ending. Whether it is consummated or unrequited, the reader's desire to know the text's otherness is what makes reading an ethical activity. The reader-text love story is an interpretive template that literary ethics uses to define what we talk about when we talk about the love of literature.

There is nothing in this basic approach that would seem to deny the value of historical context. Why, then, has literary ethics been so suspicious of historicism? I will consider that question in detail below. In brief, much like Protestant anti-Catholicism, literary ethics imagines history as an unwanted mediator between reader and text. On this view, historicism robs the text of its power, a power that derives from a perception of the text as existing beyond time, and it is the reader's desire to know such power—the balking or fulfillment of that desire—that makes reading an ethical occasion. Literary ethics constructs its reader-text love story around this desire for the revelation of an eternal, essential difference.

The love story I have argued for between Fanny and Bob Assingham, however, is not the same love story that literary ethicists find in Henry James or enact in their own practice as scholars of fiction generally. The Assinghams will serve as a specific example before I turn to the broader scene of literary ethics versus literary historicism. To see Fanny and Bob as in love because they perform for each other, and to read *The Golden Bowl* in the context of turn-of-the-century commodity culture, is to take an approach different from other ethicist readers of James before me. Martha Nussbaum's *Love's Knowledge,* published in 1990, still stands as a key text for literary ethics, if only as an example of humanist confidence that is useful to define oneself against. For Nussbaum, Henry James offers proof that literature can guide us to better moral perception. Nussbaum's version of revelatory reading is not an all-at-once rending of the veil; she rejects the Stoic concept of catalepsis, in which sudden pain constitutes certain truth, as a route to solipsism (263–84). She argues that love, like reading, is a cumulative process that culminates in a stable mutual understanding. At its best, reading is a slow road to revelation.

Nussbaum's reading of *The Golden Bowl* focuses on the maturation of Maggie's love for Amerigo, a love that ends with Maggie "see[ing] in her husband the genuine, unredeemed . . . 'hero'" who understands that true passion means making hard choices (137). Nussbaum's ideal of love as successful mutual revelation carries over to her treatment of Fanny and Bob. Rather than emphasize their misunderstanding, as I do, Nussbaum sees them joined in a neatly matched understanding. Their marriage is a union of Bob's "rules and [Fanny's] perceptions" (160). Their complementary union is virtuous too: their "mystic lake" conversation makes Fanny and Bob moral exemplars. Yet I tend to agree with Joshua Landy that "if, as Nussbaum correctly states, Fanny stands as a model for the reader, this is because her interest is just as amoral as ours, not because ours is just as moral as hers."[4] My claim for the genuineness of Fanny and Bob's love is not a claim that they are virtuous as much as it is a claim that they really do apprehend each other's alterity, despite the failure of revelation between them. Communion's intimacy need not discover or embody timeless moral norms, a point that holds as well for the reader-text communion that can develop through historicist interpretive methods, as I will explain below. Philosophizing, however, is Nussbaum's route to revelation, and it fixes the Assinghams' marriage as a universal example of good love.

An adjacent variety of literary ethics defines intimacy as revelation not granted but withheld. This version more closely replicates the emotional structure of immediacy claimed by anti-Catholicism and by neo-orthodoxy, and it more explicitly rejects the mediation and tradition valued by communion. Many ethicists of this bent have cited the theology of Emanuel Levinas as inspiration. In their adoption of Levinas, literary ethicists have stressed that aspect of Levinas's work that, as Dominick LaCapra observes, shares the commitments of both "a certain Judaism and a certain Protestantism" to "the radical transcendence of a totally other Hidden God."[5] It is the invisible presence of that God in our fellow creatures, and the responsibility we therefore owe to them, that calls us forth into being. The unstable ontology of selfhood Levinas describes is attractive to literary ethicists who wish to jettison Nussbaum's confident humanism. For Levinas, "it is this responsibility for the creature," the other that we confront, "that constitutes the self."[6] On this basis Levinas can affirm that "the Other (*Autrui*) is the end, and me, I am a hostage" (94). Translated to the scene of reading, this structure confers on the text an unknowable difference, and on the reader an unanswerable obligation to that text.

My account of *The Golden Bowl* aligns with this Levinasian ethic insofar as Fanny and Bob seem to me admirably nonpossessive, trying neither to master one another nor to dissolve into each other. They are not held hostage by their obligations to one another. My sense that they enjoy each other's company runs counter to the usual austerity of such readings. J. Hillis Miller, for instance, argues in *Literature as Conduct,* a study of James's major novels, that readers are to be held infinitely accountable for their readings.[7] Miller bolsters his argument with the final assertion of *The Golden Bowl*'s preface: James's claim that "to 'put' things is very exactly and responsibly and interminably to do them" (James, 36). The author's great responsibility becomes the reader's great burden.

Reading *The Golden Bowl* in the context of paper doll houses, however, brings into focus James's prefatory promises of pleasure. Rereading his own novel prompts James to extend in the preface "an earnest invitation to the reader to dream again in my company" (34). And though he feels the heavy responsibility as author that Miller claims for the reader—James writes that "there is then absolutely no release to [the author's] pledged honour on the question of repaying [the reader's] confidence"—James plans to fulfill that responsibility through enjoyment. The author repays the reader's trust by "multiply[ing] in any given connexion all the possible sources of entertainment" and by "intensify[ing] his whole chance of pleasure" (34–35). James underscores that pleasure in a parenthetical aside: "(It all comes back to that, to my and your 'fun'—if we but allow the term its full extension)" (35). To test whether it is fun enough, James advises us to read a work out loud—in effect, to perform it. It is hard to imagine applying that "*vivâ-voce* treatment" to a novel as dense as *The Golden Bowl* (35). But James's emphasis on play and entertainment is missing in both Nussbaum's and Miller's accounts. Literary ethics knows James as a theorist of ethics and aesthetics, not as the historical James who was mesmerized by Uncle Tom shows as a child, who tried and failed to make a hit on stage, whose fiction struck some of his peers as empty artifice. Bracketing James's affinity for arrangement and display makes it easier for Miller to claim that James views it as "reprehensible" to "treat a person like a thing" (57). That seems true in the case of the villainous Gilbert Osmond, on whom Miller is commenting there, but not in the case of *The Golden Bowl*.

The relative lack of moral outrage in James's last novel brings me to a third iteration of literary ethics that might apply to Fanny and Bob. This is the kind of surface reading that is avowedly friendly to the idea of persons as things. I have said that the collage aesthetic grounds the vision of intimacy we get in James's last novel, and that it means seeing people as arrangements of cultural debris. I paralleled James's fictional practice to the storytelling habits of Fanny and Bob. My argument, then, may qualify the couple as exemplars and practitioners of the kind of "close but not deep" reading that Heather Love proposes for literary interpretation. Love gives a reading of Toni Morrison's *Beloved* in order to demonstrate "an alternative ethics" that rejects such humanist ideals as "empathy and witness" (375). She follows Erving Goffman's lead in denying any difference between "authentic action and . . . conventional behavior" (381). Her interest in finding a post- or antihumanist selfhood that is thin and flat would seem to meet its literalization in the form of the paper doll. If James's version of marriage relies on the same principles of composition and theatricality as the paper doll house, then I would appear to have argued that the Assinghams are surface lovers, an exemplary posthumanist couple.

However, my claim is that the Assinghams, and the paper doll houses, do embody humanist values—for instance, the value of an enduring shared creativity. More specifically, the Assinghams embody a particular version of the transcendent intimacy imagined by a Catholicized Protestant faith that developed in later nineteenth-century America. They exemplify that intimacy because and not in spite of their practice of mutual performance and mutual spectatorship. Spectatorship and performance are usually allied with surface, rather than with the depth that a religion of close reading is supposed to worship. But critics who want to resist close reading as too theological have conflated surfaces with antireligion and depth with religion because they have identified religion with conservative Protestantism. That identification is not strange, given that American literary studies came into its own on the strength of a mode of thought with roots in anti-Catholicism. An account that takes Protestant orthodoxy as a stand-in for all theology, though, or even for all American Christian theology, fails to consider other models of accessing transcendence, and it fails to see that while Fanny and Bob's union does thrive on theatricality, it is not therefore portrayed as merely conventional, artificial, or superficial. They play spectator and spectacle to each other, but they play together, avoiding either solitary masturbatory pleasure or the heroic suffering of the lone artist. With the Assinghams' marriage of communion, James makes intimacy and creativity persist in an apparently posthumanist relationship, giving the lie to the "post."

As a literary ethicist myself, I have been asking what kind of self-other encounter a given text portrays and provokes. As an Americanist who wishes to reform literary ethics from within, though, I have been answering those questions by applying historicist methods. As with all the novels in this study, I have read *The Golden Bowl* as illuminated by the cultural context in which it was imagined. That basic historicizing move—juxtaposing the literary text with contemporaneous extraliterary textual or material archives—is mostly foreign to literary ethicists. But the historicist method is what makes visible the love story of communion that James tells about Fanny and Bob. Their love story, built on an endlessly shared play, is not legible to literary ethicists who idealize intimacy as a transformative revelation.

LITERARY ETHICS AND THE READER-TEXT LOVE STORY

Literary ethicists agree on the revelatory power of reading, but differ on whether that revelation should or should not be granted within an ethical interpretation. That divide has been widely observed. Robert Eaglestone splits the field between "epi-readers" who confidently grasp the text's content and "graphi-readers" who attend to the off-putting qualities of the text's form.[8] C. Namwali Serpell finds ethicists shuttling between empathy and alterity as the two possibilities for the act of interpretation.[9] Dorothy Hale divides literary ethics between humanist and poststructuralist strands.[10] The humanists, who believe in empathy and engage with content, generally rely on an Aristotelian view of literature as the rhetorical act made by a knowable other who aims to communicate with an audience. The poststructuralists, who focus on the alterity of form, generally rely on a Levinasian claim that the self is constituted by its responsibility to the other. This polarization maps on to the opposition between a happy or unhappy ending to the reader-text love story constructed by literary ethics. James is a crossover favorite for both. James's fiction presents the off-putting ambiguity that poststructuralists like; his prefatory essays offer a portable theory, useful for humanists, of how ambiguous fiction promotes finer perception.

Hale's analyses demonstrate the persistence of a love story model of reading across the spectrum. As Hale sees it, terminology may be the chief difference between Nussbaum and her successors, since "the name given by poststructuralists to their valorization of readerly experience is anything but 'love'" ("Aesthetics," 902). But, as Hale argues, poststructuralist accounts of the ethics of reading are themselves more or less marked by "erotic overtones," talk of vulnerability, surrender, and bondage: "'The web of the other,' the seduction of the implied author, the call of the text, the anxiety from estrangement: in all these new ethical paradigms 'sharing' is made possible only by the reader's willingness to submit" ("Fiction," 201). For a humanist like Nussbaum or Wayne Booth, the knowledge that comes from love of the text satisfies the reader both rationally and emotionally. By contrast, in Judith Butler's reading of James's *Washington Square*—as in J. Hillis Miller's or Derek Attridge's work—reading is ethical because it positions us as yearning lovers who can never truly know the beloved. Whether the story ends with a reciprocal marriage of reader and text or in unrequited longing depends on the relative agency granted to the reader versus the text. Happy or sad, this love story is enacted between a reader and a text who face each other in an elemental space of desire, where cultural and historical specificity has dropped away.

The basic structure of the revelatory reader-text love story that literary ethics imagines is the same across the spectrum. It can be outlined in a few moves. The first step is to grant the text the status of an other, a stand-in for a friend or a stranger. The text's otherness is enhanced by literary ethics' insistence on privacy for the reader and the text. Literary ethics ensures such privacy and enhances the power of the text-as-other by eliminating the distractions of the extraliterary documents that historicist approaches rely on. With reader and text positioned together in a decontextualized encounter, the middle of the love story can unfold as the reader's moment-to-moment emotional response to the text's provocations. The love story concludes with the text either yielding a reciprocal and emotionally satisfying relationship to the reader, or withholding its true meaning and leaving the reader to suffer unrequited love.

Nussbaum is a good representative for the humanist happy-ending side. She draws on Wayne Booth to build her case for ethical reading. Booth theorizes the text-as-other as the implied author: the product of a real author's particular values and quirks as they answer the demands of a particular artistic project. The implied author comprises "the core of norms and choices" represented in a given work; the other that we meet in reading is thus the cumulative personality that accrues through authorial choices.[11] Nussbaum, borrowing Booth's idea, finds that a well-written novel instantiates an author's "sense of life" so thoroughly that reading a novel necessarily takes on the character of meeting the person who holds those values (5). Novels—at least the good ones—thus have the power to "lure [the reader] with more mysterious and romantic charms. . . . into a more shadowy passionate world, asking her to assent, to succumb" (238).

Nussbaum also follows Booth in self-consciously adopting such language as a counter to what both feel is the aridity of poststructuralist approaches. She writes, "After reading Derrida . . . I feel a certain hunger for blood: for, that is, writing about literature that talks of human lives and choices as if they matter to us all" (171). Booth prefers the language of meeting and making friends to the vocabulary of structuralist and deconstructive accounts, with their "more mechanized pictures of texts / webs / prison houses / mazes / codes / rule systems / speech acts / semantic structures."[12] Personification—the knowing projection of human traits onto a bound stack of pages—fights the bloodlessness of such approaches to the text. By excising webs of cultural influence and the cultural code systems that historicists routinely examine, humanist literary ethics turns reading into a one-on-one encounter. The aim is to revive the text-as-other within a scene of reading that can be claimed as timeless. But to a historicist this scene might look as lifeless as the reading prescribed by the heirs of structuralism that Booth and Nussbaum are critiquing.

A poststructuralist literary ethicist like Derek Attridge will insist on revelation withheld. For this more avant-garde camp of literary ethics, the text is a stranger, not a friend. Here the model of interpersonal relations is informed by Levinas's idea that the self only becomes itself through its encounter with the infinite obligation it faces in the other. Attridge justifies thinking of a text as an other because of its power to utterly change the reader who encounters it. A text remakes both its writer in the process of its being written, and its reader in the process of its being read. Such power comes through the newness and uniqueness of the written creation. Literary otherness "implies a wholly new existent that cannot be apprehended by the old modes of understanding and could not have been predicted by means of them; its singularity"—even if just a matter of revision or adaptation—"is absolute."[13] This insistence on the singularity of the text vaults it to the status of a one and only, setting up a reading that produces unrequited love.

Both the poststructuralist and humanist literary ethicists insist on privacy for the encounter between reader and text. Literary ethics positions the reader standing alone before the text-as-other. Miller's reading of *The Awkward Age* makes explicit this demand. "I as reader feel myself to be to some degree alone with the text," Miller writes. This is true of *The Awkward Age* specifically because it has received relatively little critical attention, but Miller understands this loneliness to extend to reading generally: "Reading is, for the most part, a lonely, silent business. How could one know what happens when another person reads a book I have read or am reading?"(99) Like Booth's and Nussbaum's happier version of revelatory reading, the poststructuralist story views both reader and text as islands, each possessed of a hidden interiority. The difference is that in Miller's argument the text remains fundamentally unknowable.

Such privacy for the reader and text entails decontextualized, ahistorical close reading. Literary ethicists across the spectrum make the case that close reading is the only ethical way of encountering a text. "Literal reading," as Attridge calls the kind of reading he endorses, "defers the many interpretive moves that we are accustomed to making in our dealings with literature, whether historical, biographical, psychological, moral, or political" (60). This call for deference—and I shift the verb to the noun advisedly, since it captures the attitude narrative ethicists generally call for—finds an echo in more recent calls for surface reading, reparative reading, and postcritique, as we will shortly see. The reader must face the text vulnerably, without the aid of any overt political, psychological, or ideological apparatus. Attridge calls politicized interpretations "allegorical," insofar as they render the literary text a mere code for some more salient master narrative. Such politicized readings threaten the text's integrity and self-sufficiency as the other. On this view, close reading allows the text freedom to speak without having to prove a reader's politics right.

Once the text has been established as an other, and once the reader and text have been established in decontextualized privacy by the method of close reading, the getting-to-know-you that provides the middle of the reading love story can begin. For both poststructuralist and humanist narrative ethics, interpretation is an event that unfolds between the reader and the text. As with Attridge, for Miller the ongoing relationship with the text really makes us readers anew, so that the moment that most matters is happening now: "A rhetorical reading"—a close reading that attends to nothing but the text—"may actively liberate a past text for present uses. . . . The reading is constitutive of the 'I' that enunciates it" (29). By carefully attending to the text's rhetoric, the reader lifts it from its historical moment; shedding that historicity is figured here as liberating. In return, the text reconstitutes the reader. Attridge, too, ties the concept of the text as the other to the event quality of reading. Reading at its best is like an ongoing effort to get to know someone. The text's "Otherness, that is, is produced in an active or eventlike relation—we might call it a *relating*" (22). Reading thus becomes a love story, one in which, as Attridge says, "I affirm, cherish, sustain the other" that is the text (27).

For a humanist like Booth, ethical criticism must proceed by showing how the time spent with a novel affects a reader's sense of the world; one of his grounding claims is that "each work of art or artifice . . . determines to some degree *how at least this one moment will be lived*. The quality of life in the moment of our 'listening' is not what it would have been if we had not listened" (*Company*, 17). For instance, he isolates the various steps in understanding Jonathan Swift's satire, showing how our moment-by-moment testing of possibilities yields "an inferred total reciprocity and intimacy" with Swift: "His mind works, I infer, much as mine does—only better" (189). For Nussbaum, reading itself can become a love story because the activity of reading so closely mirrors the process of falling in love. The reader must be patient and trusting, focused keenly on the text's every nuance but emotionally open to it, not aggressive or "controlling"

(282). Nussbaum endorses a love that occurs slowly, accumulating data and responding to that data over time, just as reading does. In reading a story about a woman who reluctantly opens herself to a relationship, Nussbaum says that, "like her, we have learned to fall. Reading a story is like that. Like her love, it takes time" (280). The humanists among literary ethicists think of revelation less as a shattering event and more as the final payoff of a longer getting-to-know-you process.

Booth recognizes multiple kinds of encounters between reader and text, but his ideal relationship envisions mutual transparency as the happy ending of the reader-text love story. Friendship with a book means that both sides "offer each other not only pleasures or utilities but shared aspirations and loves of a kind that make life together worth having as an end in itself," a relationship whose consummation is found in "the quality of the life" the two friends "live during their time together" (*Company*, 174). Still, Booth's reader, like Nussbaum's, must be willing to become vulnerable. Having to follow difficult language, such as surprising metaphors, intensifies our sense of being occupied, made to think thoughts that would otherwise never have occurred to us. Booth calls this "figurative bonding" (190). But for Booth such figurative bonding really grants us an experience of, say, Shakespeare's otherness, rather than chiefly making us feel its inaccessibility. For Booth, while "any ironic or metaphoric shaping required of me as I play the role of implied reader will become *mine*"—Booth's emphasis, and a reminder of the reader's power—"insofar as I genuinely engage with the text," it is still the case that "I may repudiate it later" (190). Surrender does not block the reader from being objective enough to process and digest the reading, to judge the values that the reading offers or the kind of friend the text might become. Like Booth's, Nussbaum's version of reading involves a degree of self-surrender compensated by an increase in knowledge. The reader is always aware of her own life projects and goals and can choose to read, and to love, texts that further such goals. The emotional charge of falling in love yields knowledge rather than unhinging the reader.

For poststructuralist critics influenced by the Levinasian notion of the self as hostage before the other's infinite alterity, the reader-text love story ends in unrequited longing. Miller and Attridge tip the happy reciprocity of Booth's and Nussbaum's reader-text relationship into an asymmetry that insists on risk, challenge, and uncertainty. Where Booth imagines that figurative bonding really allows us for a moment to think with Shakespeare or Swift, Miller stresses the off-putting nature of figures of speech. Miller turns necessity into virtue by making the failure of understanding a condition of ethical reading. The aporias of the text— for example, the "blank place in the narration" of *The Portrait of a Lady* where Isabel Archer's decision to marry Osborne should be filled in and described—rule the act of reading and give it its ethical charge (74). We readers can try to understand the text-as-other; in fact, says Miller, we are "enjoined" to do so, "but . . . the bridge between the performative speech act, sealed with a kiss that silences speech, and the knowledge the performative gives is missing. It is a blank place in the language. Whereof one cannot speak one perhaps should remain silent" (80). The reader is ethical insofar as she keeps trying to know and love a text that by nature refuses to be known or loved.

Rather than imagine the reader's vulnerability as rewarded by a union with or an understanding of the text-as-other, poststructuralists emphasize the reader's endless responsibility to the text. Such responsibility, for Attridge, "involves assuming the other's needs, being willing to be called to account for the other, surrendering [our] goals and desires in deference to the other's" (27). It puts "my emotional and sometimes my physical self . . . at stake" (28). Miller, for his part, writes that "certainly I have fallen in love with" Isabel, and he imagines that anyone, whether reader or writer, might do the same. On Miller's reading, Ralph Touchett serves as a proxy both for James and for us readers, doomed to love Isabel without consummation. Such is the case for poststructuralist ethics generally. At the end of its reader-text love story, readers are left to love the texts they read without ever really understanding them. But they are made ethical by that love.

It is true that literary ethicists have voiced admiration for historicist critics. Booth observes that "the best new Marxists"—he cites Raymond Williams, Fredric Jameson, and Terry Eagleton—are pursuing their own version of ethical criticism (*Company*, 6). Furthermore, he argues that "a serious ethical criticism cannot be divorced finally from political criticism" (12). Similarly, though Derrida leaves her hungering for blood, Nussbaum notes that feminist and Marxist critics do provide interpretations that bear on real-life ethical questions (171n6). Attridge specifically excludes from his critique of allegorical reading a humble historicism that simply gathers data without any guiding agenda. Such "estimable effort[s]" have "enrich[ed] the reading of literary works by illuminating the relevant historical and cultural contexts." Attridge goes further: ethical interpretation "fails if the reader is not possessed of the necessary contextual information. Literal reading needs all the history—literary history, social history, political history, cultural history, intellectual history—it can get" (60). Still, if he approves such historicism, Attridge does not figure it as part of the reader's falling in love with a text. Literary ethicists may admire historicist criticism, but they generally do so as nonpractitioners.

David Haney clarifies the stakes of the ethicist rejection of historicism. For Haney, historicist approaches are incompatible with literary ethics because they suppress the agency both of the artwork and of the reader. Haney is willing to personify the text enough to argue for the likeness of the relationship of reader and text to the relationship of self and other. Drawing on Coleridge, he proposes "the poetic text's resemblance to a human other" based on "its resistance to incorporation into subjectively controlled concepts."[14] Haney rejects, however, the ontological slide in the other direction, from person to product, that he finds in the Marxist-inflected critiques of Stephen Greenblatt or of Gilles Deleuze and Felix Guattari. He cites "Greenblatt's emphasis on 'the whole structure of production and consumption' within which the work of art 'is itself the product of a series of manipulations'" (34). If art becomes such a product, so does the reading self. For the same reason, Haney objects to Deleuze and Guattari's claim that (in Haney's words) "even desire is only production," and "selves are products rather than agents of" the systems of production in a given society (35). Like Attridge, and like Felski after him, Haney approves of the data-gathering function of historicism, "because part of a past text's resistance to conceptual appropriation is its historical otherness," but he objects to the historicist tendency to make texts (like persons) into mere things, passive relays in a capitalist system.

It is not surprising, then, that the recent arguments recirculating literary-ethical concerns have emerged from a weariness with, or hostility to, the habits of literary historicism. Eve Sedgwick's reparative reading, Stephen Best and Sharon Marcus's surface reading, Heather Love's close-but-not-deep reading, and Rita Felski's postcritique have all helped disseminate the ideals that motivate literary ethics. Their arguments have cast the reader-text love story in less moralizing terms than Nussbaum or Booth did, but they maintain (as do I) the baseline ethicist vision of reading as an encounter whose emotional and interpersonal component must be taken into account. Sedgwick, for instance, describes reparative reading as aiming for a productive intimacy with the object of study. The reparative reader "wants to assemble and confer plenitude on an object that will then have resources to offer to an inchoate self" (*Touching*, 149). And Sedgwick identifies New Historicist approaches as a vector of what she calls "paranoid reading." Like a historicist, however, Sedgwick retains a stake in the political effects of interpretation; she wants reading to offer both personal pleasure and social reform. Insofar as these ethicist pro-grams accommodate historicism, they resemble the interpretive model of communion that I have been describing. Sedgwick is not antihistoricist; nor is Heather Love. But both make their arguments for how to read by applying sociological and psychological theories that tend to essentialize human behavior and development, rather than by examining specific his-torical contexts.

The brief against historicism comes into sharper focus in the case for surface reading. Fredric Jameson's program for seeking the historical un-conscious that drives fiction is identified by Best and Marcus as a habit worth dropping. Best and Marcus do identify a version of surface read-ing that "plac[es] a text in its discursive contexts," but only so as to "illu-minate textual features that are obvious," not hidden.[15] This is historicism minus the urge to uncover false consciousness, and it does align with the historicized reader-text communion I am imagining. But surface reading more generally casts readerly desire in opposition to historicist attention, an attention seen as dominating and exposing. As "an affective and ethical stance," surface reading calls for an interpretation that "replace[s] suspicion and critical mastery with a susceptibility that could undo the dichotomy between subject and object" (8, 9). To develop that susceptibility entails giving up the historicist task of unmasking ideology, and, with that task, the critic will also give up the faith that either art or criticism produces freedom. It is enough that surface reading offer pleasure in the moment; that pleasure principle aligns with the model of communion. As a model of interpretive intimacy, however, communion relies on seeing the text in its time and place, a view that will include some account of how that text participates in the sociopolitical landscape. On the model of communion, the text's participation in historical conflict is what makes it a powerful other.

Rita Felski, perhaps the leading current proponent of literary ethics, is also explicit in her suspicion of historicist methods. Those methods, as Felski surveys the field, have encouraged an abusive relationship between the critic and the text. Felski sees historicism deployed as a tool of domination, "rendering" an artwork a "puny, enfeebled, impoverished thing" with no power to change us.[16] Historicist methods give the critic an unfair advantage because that critic knows now, as her objects of study did not know then, how things turned out. That present-tense perch allows the historicist to judge whether the text was on the right or wrong side of history and to prove her own progressivism by disapproving of the text's backwardness. That judgmental attitude is what Felski has in mind when she identifies the historicist smugness that assumes "we know more than the texts that precede us" (579).

Just as Franco Moretti and Heather Love distanced themselves from theological reading, Felski's postcritical literary ethics wants to avoid "a retrograde religion of art" (583). To avoid deifying the text, Felski aims to acknowledge its historicity, adopting Bruno Latour's actor-network theory for that purpose. Casting the text as a networked actor allows us, Felski argues, to reckon with the text's power without denying that the text exists in a specific time and place. Actor-network theory enables a power-sharing ontology where no one and nothing is "a self-authorizing subject"; the power to do things is dispersed among "mediators and translators linked in extended constellations of cause and effect" (583). This describes a historical embeddedness that chimes with the self-other intimacy we find in communion.

But this constellation of actors, as Felski describes it, produces a weirdly conflict-free picture of history. The actor network is a space where all voices have a chance to be heard, provided they are "sociable" enough (584). Felski asks us to imagine an "unrepentant avantgardist" whose work succeeds by angering conservatives and pleasing progressives (584). Such an artist proves that "a work's dexterity . . . in soliciting and sustaining attachments" is "far more salient to a text's survival than matters of ideological agreement" (584). Felski acknowledges that politics can influence a work's prestige. But this is a glancing acknowledgment. As Bruce Robbins observes, in Felski's argument actor-network theory "makes all causes seem equal, thereby erasing the differentials of power that determine in any given case who or what is in fact the major cause and who or what suffers the most significant effects."[17] In Robbins's view, this view of history is wrong, and it promotes a false critical modesty.

I do not see the problem as false modesty; Felski's wish for critics to be vulnerable to art reads as genuine. But we can see here an unintended consequence of trying to defend art's agency from history without sounding religious. An ethicist who wants to protect art from historical determinism without accidentally describing art as a transcendent well-wrought urn is in a tight spot. Such a critic can find herself evacuating both the text and its reader of agency. This consequence becomes visible in Felski's statement that "history is not moving forward and none of us are leading the way" (579). Such a view rejects a vision of progress that we might legitimately critique as illusory. Yet it also rejects a vision of historical conflict that is anything but illusory.

That unintended consequence appears, too, in Caroline Levine's *Forms*. Levine does not make overt calls to recoup the emotional power of artworks. Her argument does, though, charge historicism with confining texts to periods and reducing art to an effect of social reality. To counter that reduction, Levine adopts the concept of "affordances": "a term used to describe the potential uses or actions latent in materials and designs."[18] Like Latour's actor-network theory, the concept of affordance resists historicist determinism by denaturing ideas of cause and effect, subject and object, and allows Levine to argue for relationships between persons and texts and contexts as a give-and-take, productive not just of oppression or subversion but of random collisions and contradictions.[19] By Levine's account, historicists, wedded to a winners-and-losers view of power, fail to notice such possibilities and thereby shortchange the power of forms.

Yet in Levine's readings, as in Felski's, it seems as if power has become so diffuse as to vanish. As Marijeta Bozovic argues, citing Levine's example of the tension between tenure clocks and female PhDs' biological clocks (*Forms*, 8), it appears that "university administrations are innocent of patriarchal or exploitative intentions here, but women 'opt for' life in the academic precariate. No one is to blame—only unplanned collisions between forms."[20] In the effort to grant art the power to do transhistorical and surprising things, Levine, like Felski, pictures a world where it is finally hard to see that power does anything at all.

HISTORICISTS IN AND OUT OF LOVE WITH THE TEXT

The apparent incompatibility of literary ethics and literary historicism comes down to a disagreement over what constitutes the power that makes a text desirable. The model of revelatory love that structures ethicist interpretation indexes reader desire to textual power. The same is true of communion. But power, by the ethicist's revelatory standard, is a quality the text manifests by rising above the time and place in which it appeared. To the literary ethicist, literary historicism would make that time and place the determining source of all the unique qualities of the text-as-other. If historical circumstances can claim to have shaped the text's particular otherness, then the text loses the desirability that compels the reader's love, and the reader's love for the text-as-other is what makes interpretation an ethical encounter.

Literary ethics' equation of power with timelessness manifests in its objects of study. Historicists read what is ephemeral and popular, while ethicists prefer the enduring and challenging. If the link this book makes between James and Stowe seemed at first counterintuitive, that dissonance is a measure of how little crossover there is in the work done by the two camps. James is a foundational source for literary ethics; Stowe is a regular touchstone for historicist scholars. But what could be more ethically efficacious than a novel like *Uncle Tom's Cabin,* credited by Abraham Lincoln, as legend has it, with starting the Civil War? Why should literary ethics ignore a novel that seems to have succeeded in producing ethical effects in its readers?

Sentimentalism offers a uniquely functional hinge between the interests of literary ethics and historicism. That is because sentimentalism is both emotionally intimate and context-bound. A novel like Stowe's or Phelps's assumes that its power to command a reader's desire is based on its speaking to those readers' immediate concerns, on its proliferating that desire through material artifacts like spin-offs and sequels. Such a novel wants to win the reader's love. But to the ethicist critic who seeks revelation withheld, sentimentality's means of courting the reader are too obvious, too conventional, too easily indexed as of-the-moment. Sentimentality is objectionable to literary ethics because it makes visible the way the emotions we take as proof of our private freedom are in fact social and conventional. It crosses the decisive line from autonomy to heteronomy, as Elizabeth Dillon (following Jacques Rancière) describes it.[21] By materializing and ritualizing emotion, it turns human beings from sovereign individuals into creatures of society.

Put another way, the sentimental mode, as June Howard writes, blurs the line between "public and private, proclaiming their separation and at the same time demonstrating their inseparability," thereby "mark[ing] a moment when the discursive processes that construct emotion become visible" (76–77). Where literary ethics conceives love as a private matter between the reader and the text, the sentimental form makes such love widely sharable and so vitiates the intimacy that is key to good interpretation. Sentimentality affronts the literary-ethical ideal of revelation because it has nothing to hide. It performs itself; it turns otherness into a spectacle; it instrumentalizes its own potential emotional and aesthetic power to achieve an immediate end, like freeing slaves (or boosting the prestige of white homemakers). Is a feeling really love, is it really ethical, if it has the quality of public spectatorship, if it does not longingly await the revelation of truth? All of the novels considered in this study have proposed that the answer is yes.

However, Stowe's novel is not legible as the kind of other that literary ethics recognizes. If it did help mobilize an army, that proves its publicness. If it seems to offer a private reading encounter, in fact the novel reproduces that encounter hundreds of thousands of times. It can replicate that intimacy because any reader (or nonreaders, watching the show) can follow its directions to feel special feelings. That directness makes it fail, for literary ethicists, as a source of potential revelation. Adam Zachary Newton speaks for a poststructuralist literary-ethical position when he notes that, while Tolstoy may have loved *Uncle Tom's Cabin,* the novel fails to offer an ethical reading experience because it urges "its readers . . . to imitate and inculcate" good morals by way of "a chain of mimetic and performative substitutions." This "exemplary" modus operandi is at odds with Newton's preference for "confrontation" with the text.[22] Such confrontation can only occur when the text is felt to possess unrevealed depths that challenge the reader's desire.

The preference for confrontation over imaginary substitution is motivated by the legitimate ethical wish to avoid colonizing the radical difference of a text, or of another person. But it leaves literary ethics open to be charged with the same modernist elitism that Jane Tompkins invokes in her defense of sentimentality. Tompkins reads the formation of the canon of American literature as "a struggle to supplant the tradition of evangelical piety and moral commitment" by elevating the modernist attributes of "psychological complexity, moral ambiguity, epistemological sophistication, stylistic density, formal economy."[23] All of these attributes are the qualities that make the ethicist text-as-other desirable. Elizabeth Dillon likewise notes the "disdain in high modernist thought for both mass culture and the sentimental," a split she finds reproduced in the methodological divide between cultural studies and close reading (496). That divide aligns with the historicist-versus-ethicist split I have been examining.

A humanist like Wayne Booth, though, argues that modernist works are not the only source for literary ethics. For him, the idea that the text must offer the promise of overwhelming revelation can be carried too far. Booth complains that "for some ethical critics, no fictions are worth bothering about if they do not stagger us, shatter our complacencies, open up new worlds, change us from what we were, teach us new (and often dark) truths, shock our technical expectations: Make it new!" (*Company*, 194). Booth's ironic citation of the modernist credo finds its sincere echo in Derek Attridge's claim for the exemplary ethics of J. M. Coetzee's work. For Attridge, Coetzee's work places the reader in an ethical relation because Coetzee's "foregrounding of language and other discursive and generic codes" challenges reigning discourses. Sentimentalism, by this reasoning, only recirculates the discursive codes of its time. Coetzee's metafictional techniques provoke "the testing and unsettling of deeply held assumptions of transparency, instrumentality, and direct referentiality" and thereby "[open] a space for the apprehension of the otherness which those assumptions had silently excluded" (30). Coetzee also wins praise from Gayatri Spivak, who sees his work as exemplary of the kind of difficult fiction that can provoke the reader to feel, fleetingly, what it might be like to be objectified.[24] The point here is still an empathic intimacy with the other. But where Coetzee indirectly provokes such intimacy, or prompts us to feel the absence of intimacy, Stowe's instructions to imitate Tom and Eva are too direct.

Attridge and the poststructuralist ethicists offer compelling descriptions of the ethical power of revelation withheld. I do not deny the moral or the aesthetic value of such a reader-text encounter. But unrequited love cannot be the only model for ethical reading. It is not that literary ethicists are wrong to imagine a love story between the reader and a text like *The Golden Bowl*; where literary ethics goes wrong is in excluding the possibility of a reader-text love story that acknowledges time and space—for example, one that sees James's last novel as a descendent of sentimentalism and frames it within the context of turn-of-the-century materialism. Literary ethics would have a better account of otherness if it did not overlook the historical factors that helped canonize the ambiguity that it deems the enduring sign of otherness.

Again, it is not that ethicists actually deny that a novel's historical context could be a useful thing to know about. Ethicist critics, however, do see historicism as liable to make a complex literary other serve a critic's political agenda, and they see politics as deflating complexity, denying the timelessness of a textual other by tying it to a local power struggle. Miller rejects what he views as the indoctrination in "anthropology, political science, cultural studies, and the study of gender, race, and class" that goes by the name of "literary teaching" (44). Henry James's characters are "not representatives of social types or classes," so, for instance, it would be wrong to insist that *The Portrait of a Lady* "reflect[s] the conditions of women and marriage conventions at the time the novel was written" (62). Isabel makes her own choices, Miller emphasizes; like the novel she appears in, she is not determined by society or historical circumstances. Notwithstanding the note of grumpy conservatism Miller sounds here, his argument parallels Attridge's attack on allegorical reading and more recent critiques of symptomatic reading. On this view, to recall Miller's argument about Gilbert Osmond's immorality, historicists commit the reprehensible mistake of treating an other (the text as a willful free agent) as a mere thing (the text as a product of social and historical forces).

There are historicists who would gladly plead guilty to Miller's charges. For Nancy Armstrong, the idea of falling in love with a novel is a symptom

of our capitulation to anticommunitarian liberal ideology and our acceptance of its psychic consolations. According to Armstrong, the domestic
novel in Britain was a stealthy public policy tool that helped "[ensure]
the ubiquity of middle-class power" by turning desire from a public and
political act into a private emotion (5, 9). H. Aram Veeser's account of historicism admires its practitioners for their ability to see literary works as
expressions of capitalism. Stephen Greenblatt, for instance, is a great critic
because he shows how "all aesthetic representation anticipates or embodies market relations."[25] In this formulation, market relations become the
explanatory key to all reading, just the opposite of the agenda-free, literal
close reading of the text that Attridge and Miller call for. Instead of the rich
offers of friendship or the baffling but alluring aporias that literary ethicists find in the text-as-other, Veeser writes that New Historicists "all agree
that contemporary life at its best embodies mobility and impersonality,"
and that they further "agree that capitalism requires hollow, empty per-
sonalities that resemble money itself" (4). For New Historicism, though,
Veeser says, this emptiness is not an outrage; instead, such criticism "ac-
cepts the inevitability of emptiness" (19). The text's agency, as feared by the
literary ethicist, has been cheerfully evacuated.

In the scholarship on the American sentimental novel that flourished in
the 1990s, such aggressive historicism has been prominent. Many critics
have persuasively used historical context, just as Attridge or Felski would
have predicted, to read authors like Stowe and Phelps not as offering a
powerful encounter with otherness but as manifesting the bigger story
of the march of capitalism. Lori Merish, for instance, reads sentimental
novels along with the autobiography of a Methodist preacher, Stowe's
House and Home Papers, and the works of Scottish Common Sense phi-
losophers (among other documents) in order to trace the development of
what she calls "sentimental ownership" as a justification for consuming
luxury goods. For Merish, sympathy amounts to an "affectional equivalent
of the money form," and she argues that although it is "constructed as an
autonomous emotional response, sentimental ownership is a fantasy of
intimate possession that is in fact—like the 'free market' itself—produced
and sustained by laws and economic policies."[26] Her work follows Gillian
Brown's argument that sentimental possession offered women the fantasy
that they could remove commodities, whether furniture or slaves, from

the marketplace and humanize them.[27] Like Merish, Brown also takes a broad contextual view of the text-as-other—for instance, by reading *Uncle Tom's Cabin* in concert with Catherine Beecher's domestic manuals. Both authors employ such textual juxtaposition to help expose the apparently private and emotional space created by the sentimental novel as a smoke-screen for capitalist enterprise.

These unsympathetic, if incisive, accounts of the complicity of the sentimental in turn would come under fire, not just from ethicists but from other historicists. June Howard argues that "it is time for American literary historians to vacate, once and for all, the discourse of judgment that has characterized so much work on sentimentality" (63). Glenn Hendler charges critics like Merish and Brown with an "uncharacteristic literalism" that ignores sentimental authors' intentions and suggests approaching the sentimental as an instance of what Raymond Williams terms a "structure of feeling" in order "to avoid reducing sentimentalism to a form of false consciousness or a merely strategic use of rhetoric."[28] Samuel Otter urges that when we read a work like the sentimental bestseller *Ruth Hall*, we should see its deployment of sentimental clichés as offering "a set of forms saturated with affect and rife with possibilities," functioning as an instance of Roland Barthes's "notion of 'écriture'": "the historically inflected patterns of syntax, diction, and logic that elicit recognition with but an allusion or a gesture."[29] Such critics, in pushing for better interpretations of sentimental fiction, argue that historical context might enhance rather than erase the possible emotional potency of the text.

Critiques of reductive historicism by other historicists should demonstrate to literary ethics that, indeed, historicists may be earnestly devoted to reading for otherness, not just to proving their own can't-be-fooled perspicacity. Historicism, though, in contrast to literary ethics, and in line with the model of communion, imputes the power of alterity precisely to a text's activity in its time and place. For some New Historicists, this has meant that the desired textual other is culture very broadly construed, not the novel or the poem itself. Stephen Greenblatt and Catherine Gallagher, introducing their volume *Practicing New Historicism*, note that "the linguistic turn in the social and humanistic disciplines" has made it possible to understand "cultures as texts" and thus to apply close reading to an entire way of life in a given time and place.[30] The same German theorists who inspired biblical historicism—Herder, for example—are cited by New Historicists to justify "treating all of the written and visual traces of a particular culture as a mutually intelligible network of signs" (7). New Historicism can interpret objects that in themselves offer none of the challenge and ambiguity that literary ethics requires, because New Historicism does not require one single text to represent alterity; its objects may be artistically negligible or commercially marginal, flat or superficial. When historicists do begin with a Hawthorne or a Melville, they read such canonical authors through their surrounding social and cultural milieu, such as phrenological charts, accounts of South Seas exploration, or popular gift books celebrating scenic America.[31]

Along these lines, Jane Tompkins's work would seem to exemplify the model I am seeking. She claims that "in order to understand the appeal of their [the sentimental novelists'] project one has to have some familiarity with the cultural discourse of the age for which they spoke."[32] Further, "it is only by attempting to see that reality from within the assumptions that founded it that one can arrive at a notion of what gave sentimental fiction its tremendous original force" (36). We can only fall in love with these novels, in other words, if we drop our expectation that they will reveal some transformative depth and see them instead as creatively repurposing the contexts of their time and place.

The difference is that Tompkins is not trying to read a novel like *The Wide, Wide World* to enter the kind of relationship—whether in its revelatory form, or on the model of communion that I am proposing—that literary ethics imagines. For Tompkins, the readerly intimacy offered by Stowe is less important than the novel's demonstrable cultural activism. She argues for a redemptive value for the sentimental granted by its sociopolitical potency in a particular historical moment. Communion, by contrast, maintains that the payoff of interpretation is creative intimacy with the text, a new understanding of past and present that reader and text generate together. But, as with the reading Tompkins describes, communion achieves that intimacy by paying attention to the text as a social actor.

If they are not quite practicing literary ethics, historicists like Tompkins are theorizing a desirable otherness that is available only in the historically contextualized text. That theory of the text as a social creature, as Dorothy Hale points out, ultimately aligns with Henry James's account of the novel form. Literary critics who read the novel form as a privileged window onto historical formations of social life, a practice Hale calls social formalism, may disavow the humanist ideal of free agency. However, social formalists do share an "enduring desire to imagine that even de-essentialized identity can have stability, that the 'characters' of both people and literary genres can be recognized through their material manifestations in language."[33] Such scholars find justification for imagining the novel as embodying a personality, for "transfer[ring] . . . social identity from persons to texts" (17), in Bakhtin's argument that the novelist's special use of language makes the best representation of the social. But this "belief that the novel instantiates social identity through its form" is also in fact "at the heart of the Jamesian tradition of novel theory" ("Aesthetic," 904). Jamesian novel theory, with its celebration of formal achievement and its disregard for historical context, is as likely to be disavowed by historicists as to be cited by literary ethicists. Yet the sociality of the novel as James imagines it can provide an account of a text-as-other that is desirable to both ethicists and historicists.

That desire is made explicit by some historicists in terms as emotionally saturated as any literary ethicist would use. Greenblatt and Gallagher write that good interpretation "depends . . . on an encounter with the singular, the specific, and the individual" (6). Veeser argues that New Historicism is better than old historicism because the literary critic's close reading of a cultural document "get[s] an inside look at something also beneath most historians' notice—a single *human subject*" (5). For New Historicists, the privileged form—the kind of text that embodies the power and desirability of the other—is not the novel but the anecdote. As Greenblatt and Gallagher explain, it is through the anecdote (a ship's log, a broadside, a popular song) that historicists seek "real bodies and living voices, and if we knew that we could not find these—the bodies having long moldered away and the voices fallen silent—we could at least seize upon those traces that seemed to be close to actual experience" (30). Veeser recognizes that the liberal humanist ethos of New Historicism is a "scandal," given the Marxism generally avowed by its practitioners (13). He observes an "oscillating effect" in New Historicism's "contradictory valuation and debasement of the human individual." By way of example he cites a Catherine Gallagher essay about Dickens characters who are, as Gallagher says, "equally garbage and treasure to each other; indeed, they are treasure because they are garbage."[34] On this view, if the human subject is as fungible as money, even trashy, it is all the more worth cherishing.

We might, then, describe the difference between ethicists and historicists by saying that the former pursue an aspirational love while the latter nurture the outcast. Nurturing is one possible kind of intimacy with a historicized textual other, and the project of recovering forgotten texts is one of the most valuable contributions historicists have made to literary study. But there is potential for patronizing here. Nurturing is not the collaborative relationship of shared recreation that characterizes communion. Indeed, the image of the critic as rescue artist has brought historicists their share of criticism. Alan Liu calls New Historicism a "profoundly narcissistic method," given to "stud[ying] itself in the anxious pose of reaching for the other."[35]

For Liu, New Historicists, by lavishing their attention on the single anecdote, ignore the bigger picture of historical struggle and thus replicate an antihistoricist formalism. Liu finds in New Historicism the same false model of history as static, and the same false critical humility, that Bruce Robbins finds in actor-network theory. In a world made of anecdotes, Liu says, no one has any real power, and nothing ever happens. The only kind of historical action a New Historicist can imagine, says Liu, amounts to the action of "insects chew[ing] in a gigantic, too-quiet house" (734). Liu argues that, to combat this disempowerment, historicist critics need to recognize the conflict and coercion through which historical actors work to change the future. Only with that recognition can historicists actually break through their narcissism to reckon with the powerful historical others they wish to access.

Carolyn Porter's critique of New Historicism furthers Liu's argument by analyzing what she sees as New Historicism's perverse notion of power as existing outside of time. Porter's analysis, which I referenced in the introduction to this book, is valuable for clarifying the role that historical context plays in the interpretive model of communion. Porter argues that the idea of literature as transcendent, far from recognizing the power of literature to change us or the world, makes it impossible to see how literature could change us or the world.[36] To get around the problem of the false equivalence of power with timelessness, and the false opposition between transcendence and history, Porter sketches a model of history as a "continuously heterogeneous discursive field in which dominant and subjugated voices occupy the same plane" (265). Not unlike Best and Marcus, Porter favors this flat model for its ability to block our privileging of depth and transcendence. This model also shares Felski's preference for a horizontal network.

But the horizontal playing field, as Porter envisions it, acknowledges struggle among actors exercising different degrees of power. Reading with this model of the past lets the reader understand marginalized voices not as "neutralized by the ideologies they must speak through in order to be heard, but rather as inflecting, distorting, even appropriating such ideologies, genres, values so as to alter their configuration" (268). Likewise, the dominant voices—the canonical works—also show the signs of their struggle to repress the opposition. Most important for Porter (and for any literary ethicist), on this historical model, the others that speak in historical texts "cannot be denied agency," because they are seen as operating on "the same heterogeneous discursive field as their dominant opponents" (269). Porter's argument calls out as an error the idea that the most powerful kind of power is beyond history. Porter argues, in effect, that the only kind of power worth talking about, the kind that would allow a reader to engage the text as an other, is the power to act within history.

The problem with literary ethics is not that revelation is a faulty model of intimacy; the problem is that literary ethics fails to imagine that real power can exist in history. A model of interpretive intimacy based on revelation defines the only desirable object as one that has escaped from time. In adopting that model, literary ethics excludes other possible models of transcendence and intimacy. One such model is offered by Catholic practice, as it developed in tension with nineteenth-century American Protestant prejudice: abused by anti-Catholic Protestants, defended by Catholic apologists, and appropriated by Catholic-friendly (or at least Catholic-curious) Protestant novelists. That practice provides the model of communion I have tracked across this study. It is an interpretive intimacy that is not spontaneous, but mediated by ritual; not interior, but dependent on material and visual aids; not autonomous, but determined by historical institutions and traditions.

If literary ethics wants to understand all the versions of love that Henry James depicts in his late fiction, it must read that fiction as participating in a larger world beyond James's own theorizing. Indeed, if we are to understand James's theories, we need to consider his own experience living in a culture of capitalist spectacle. Doing so lets us understand the kind of otherness that his fiction—or anyone's fiction—offers us: not as singular and timeless, but as responsive to its own time and place. To reach that understanding requires considering texts diachronically and synchronically.

This is why it is helpful to read novels like *The Golden Bowl* or like *The Gates Ajar* in tandem with a particular archive that opens on to the cultural scene in effect when the fiction was produced and also to read them in the broader historical trajectory of, in this case, a widening Protestant embrace of what had been seen as a Catholic materiality. Reading in that broader context prevents us from making the distinctly Protestant assumptions that material mediations impoverish true faith, or that performance must be at odds with genuine feeling.

In this way, communion expands literary ethics' account of what it means to love literature. It is a love story that provides a different interpretive template for literary ethics, one that accommodates historicism. Unlike revelation, communion models a self-other interaction that apprehends the object of love as mediated by its ambient culture, not in isolation from that culture. That principle of mediated love translates to the stories we have encountered here. Mediation appears in the way the beloved carries around his or her own scenery, costume, and decor, which can be literal (like Veronica's collaged bedroom wall) or a projection (like Fanny's gazelles and sherbets). Revelation, by contrast, strips self and other of their publicly visible context, illuminating a hidden truth (as when Pierre sees and loves Isabel as his secret sister).

The intimacy of communion also assumes, like historicist reading, that both self and other are temporal creatures. In fiction, the timebound quality of communion might be portrayed as ongoing change (Cassy and Veronica growing up together, watching each other mature) or as ongoing ritual (Fanny and Bob telling each other the same stories, with small alterations). Either way, communion is an intimacy that exists in time. The intimacy of revelation is experienced as the irruption of a force beyond time.

Finally, the difference between communion and revelation comes down to the difference between a mediated and an unmediated experience of something decisively beyond oneself. Revelation may be felt as a once-and-for-all joining of self to other or as a transformative shattering of the self by a glimpse of the true other. Even when those moments never arrive, revelation's withholding is felt as a trembling anticipation of such joining or shattering. Whatever the outcome, revelation promises transparent understanding of the object of interpretation.

In communion, self and other do not exactly understand each other and do not really expect to. What binds two partners in communion is the work they do with a third term, a shared text they recreate together. In a love story, that third term might be theological works or the Bible; it might be one's room and wardrobe or one's friends' affairs. On the register of the author and reader, as Melville and Hawthorne imagine it, the third term is the spectacle of the author's own performance, which is not a revelation but partakes of both fact and fancy.

For the critic reading a text in pursuit of communion, that third term is historical context. Communion is not a dyadic reader-text encounter. The critic aiming for communion with a text will examine how the text adapts the materials of its world and will project a vision of that world in tandem with the text. That interpretive work requires the vision of the text itself; it requires the vision of the critic who lets the text guide his attention into the sociohistorical world around the text; and it draws those visions together in an interpretation of the text in that world. The interpretation produced through the intimacy of communion is a provisional recreation of the meaning of a past world newly made by the critic and the text, and that interpretation in turn may participate in a potentially endless interpretive ritual that never arrives at a fully disclosed meaning. Both critic and text face each other not as lone eternal souls but as actors whose desires are mediated by the time and place they find themselves in. It is their shared interpretive action, within history, that makes communion's intimacy endure.

NOTES

Introduction

1. Phelps, "The Great Hope," 36.
2. James, "Is There a Life after Death?," 228.
3. Letter to Hawthorne, November [17?], 1851, in Bryant, ed., *Herman Melville*, 43.
4. Buell, "In Pursuit of Ethics," 13.
5. Felski, *The Limits of Critique*, 154.
6. Hale, "Fiction as Restriction," 190.
7. Lynch, *Loving Literature*, 3.
8. Serpell, *Seven Modes of Uncertainty*, 17.
9. Levinson writes that the critic who wants to understand "the unique way that each artwork tries to make symbolic what experience has suggested as actual," who wants "to respond . . . to the work's cognitive regrouping" of "the elements of empirical reality," "must first grasp the presence of 'empirical reality' . . . both inside and in tension with the formal design of the work." Levinson, "What Is New Formalism?" 565, 567.
10. Sedgwick, *Touching Feeling*, 131. Sedgwick identifies this as a quote from her own earlier work, an essay she wrote in 1986.
11. Porter, "After the New Historicism," 263.
12. LaPorte and Lecourt, "Introduction," 151. The authors cite the scholarship of Timothy Fitzgerald, Talal Asad, and Brent Nongbri.
13. Taylor writes that "the change I want to define and trace is one which takes us from a society in which it was virtually impossible not to believe in God, to one in which faith, even for the staunchest believer, is one human possibility among others." Taylor speaks later of those possible faiths, or routes to a sense of fullness, as "itineraries" (*A Secular Age*, 3, 745).
14. Fessenden, *Culture and Redemption*, 4.
15. Reed, "'I Have No Disbelief,'" 155–56.
16. Sarah Rivett, "Early American Religion in a Postsecular Age," 991.
17. Lynch, *Loving Literature*, 156.

18. Kaufmann, "The Religious, the Secular, and Literary Studies," 614, 613.

19. Moretti, *Distant Reading*, 48. Quoted in Wickman, "Theology Still?," 674.

20. Love, "Close but Not Deep," 374, 371.

21. Franchot, "Invisible Domain," 836.

22. Fessenden, "The Problem of the Postsecular," 16.

23. Here I cite Coviello and Hickman, "Introduction," 648.

24. See Hale, "Fiction as Restriction," 190, 197. In "Discourse in the Novel," Bakhtin writes that poetic language tends toward a hermetically-sealed expression of its "author's intention," "a unitary and singular Ptolemaic world outside of which nothing else exists and nothing else is needed" (*The Dialogic Imagination*, 286).

25. Thoreau, *Walden*, 99.

26. Coviello, *Intimacy in America*, 150, 155.

27. Bersani, *A Future for Astyanax*, 55.

28. Lynch, *The Economy of Character*, 131.

29. Tanner, *Adultery in the Novel*, 15.

30. In Hale, *The Novel*, 349.

31. Hale, 437.

32. Armstrong, *Desire and Domestic Fiction*, 5.

33. Posnock, "Innocents at Home," n.p.

34. I have in mind those critics that Baym identifies as establishing the best American fiction as the least realistic, by claiming, for instance, that "the classic American writers try through style temporarily to free the hero (and the reader) . . . from the pressures of time, biology, economics, and from the social forces which are ultimately the undoing of American heroes" (Richard Poirier, *A World Elsewhere*, 1966) or that our best fiction veers from "the broadly novelistic mainstream of English writing" in its "adherence to a tradition of non-realistic romance" (Joel Porte, *The Romance in America*, 1969). Quoted in Baym, "Melodramas of Beset Manhood," 137, 127.

35. Fiedler at first cites Denis Diderot commenting on Samuel Richardson's *Clarissa* as the source for this metaphor: "It is he who carries the torch to the back of the cave. . . . He blows upon the glorious phantom who presents himself at the entrance of the cave; and the hideous Moor whom he was masking reveals himself" (quoted in Fiedler, 40). Fiedler later reuses that image himself (e.g., 64, 73, 105, 141).

36. Fiedler, *Love and Death in the American Novel*, 56.

37. Wiegman, "Fiedler and Sons," 52.

38. Silverman, *Bodies and Books*, 2.

39. See Coviello, *Intimacy in America*.

40. Douglas, *The Feminization of American Culture* (1977); Tompkins, *Sensational Designs* (1985).

ONE. Love and Depth Canonized

1. *"The Gates Ajar," Christian Union,* February 12, 1870, quoted in Smith, "From the Seminary to the Parlor," 106.

2. Best and Marcus offer a précis of such sources in their appraisal of symptomatic reading. See "Surface Reading," 2.

3. For an account of this genealogy, see Chai, *The Romantic Foundations of the American Renaissance.*

4. Brookes, *Is the Bible Inspired?* 17.

5. Faber, *The Blessed Sacrament,* 6. See also reference in Taves, "Context and Meaning," 486.

6. Zboray and Zboray, *Everyday Ideas,* 283–84.

7. Thoreau, *A Week on the Concord and Merrimack Rivers,* 72.

8. Marty, "America's Iconic Book," 22.

9. Gutjahr, *An American Bible,* 44.

10. Nord, *Faith in Reading,* 147–149.

11. Taves, "Context and Meaning," 482–95.

12. Kelley, "Pen and Ink Communion," 557.

13. Parker, "A Discourse of the Transient and Permanent in Christianity," in Myerson, ed., *Transcendentalism,* 354.

14. Fessenden, *Culture and Redemption,* 5.

15. Griffin, *Anti-Catholicism and Nineteenth-Century Fiction,* 6.

16. Holland, *Sacred Borders,* 26–27.

17. Hatch, "Sola Scriptura and Novus Ordo Seclorum," 61.

18. Bushnell, *God in Christ,* 70.

19. Ahlstrom, *A Religious History of the American People,* 527, 542.

20. Gutjahr, *An American Bible,* 116–17.

21. Quoted in Noll, *America's God,* 243.

22. Quoted in Noll, 397.

23. Stokes, *The Altar at Home,* 15–16.

24. Fenton, *Religious Liberties,* 6–7.

25. Quoted in Noll, *America's God,* 380.

26. Quoted in Franchot, *Roads to Rome,* 239.

27. Channing, "Likeness to God," 9.

28. Emerson, "Sermon CLXII [The Lord's Supper]," 75.

29. See Prickett, *Words,* 45, and Noll, *America's God,* 321.

30. "A Heretic of Yesterday," 79, 514. Ahlstrom observes that Bushnell worked for the "founding of the Evangelical Alliance in 1846" "chiefly on anti-Catholic grounds, and he expressed his disgust when it adopted more positively evangelical aims" (*A Religious History of the American People,* 559).

204 · NOTES TO PAGES 36–44

31. Quoted in Fogarty, *Nova et Vetera*, 3.

32. "Protestantism versus the Church," 4.

33. Holifield, *Theology in America*, 424–25.

34. Prickett identifies "the revolution in biblical studies" as being initiated by Robert "Lowth's *Sacred Poetry of the Hebrews* in the middle of the eighteen century"; Lowth helped "fuel the German critical revolution," particularly influencing Johann Herder's "seminal work, *The Spirit of Hebrew Poetry*." In *Words and* The Word, 33, 50.

35. Noll, "Nineteenth-Century American Biblical Interpretation," 3.

36. See Gutjahr, *An American Bible*, 63–64.

37. "Radical Higher Criticism in the Confessional," 1.

38. Beecher, *Reasonable Biblical Criticism*, 75.

39. Moore-Jumonville cites W. H. Jones and T. DeWitt Talmage as exemplary anticritics. See *The Hermeneutics of Historical Distance*, 23.

40. Marsden, *Fundamentalism and American Culture*, 46.

41. Quoted in Moore-Jumonville, *The Hermeneutics of Historical Distance*, 53.

42. Pierson, *The Bible and Spiritual Criticism*, 16.

43. See Moore-Jumonville, *The Hermeneutics of Historical Distance*, 63.

44. Clarke, *Sixty Years with the Bible*, 30, 69.

45. Hutchison, *The Modernist Impulse in American Protestantism*, 77.

46. For his indictment of Protestant bibliolatry, see Briggs, "The Authority of Holy Scripture," 30. As Marsden notes, Union Theological Seminary, which had promoted Briggs to an endowed professorship, "severed its ties with" the Presbyterian Church after its trial of Briggs (*Fundamentalism*, 117). See also Massa, "'Mediating Modernism.'"

47. Terry, *Biblical Hermeneutics*, 232.

48. Gray, *How to Master the English Bible*, 49.

49. Weber, "The Two-Edged Sword," 112–13.

50. Graff, *Professing Literature*, 171.

51. Schweitzer, *The Quest of the Historical Jesus*, 398, 399. As Ahlstrom pungently summarizes Schweitzer's conclusion, nineteenth-century historicist theologians had "peer[ed] down the 2,000-year-long shaft of history and see[n] their own bourgeois faces reflected from the bottom of the well" (*A Religious History of the American People*, 935).

52. See Marsden, *Fundamentalism in American Culture*, 113–14.

53. Poland, "The New Criticism," 466.

54. On Hulme's critique of Romanticism as carelessly "spilt religion," see Poland, "The New Criticism," 463.

55. Brightman, "The Neo-Orthodox Trend," 130.

56. Barth, *The Epistle to the Romans*, 10.

57. Kierkegaard, *Philosophical Fragments / Johannes Climacus*, 49, 47.

58. Tillich, *Dynamics of Faith,* 13.

59. Douglas, *The Feminization of American Culture,* 328.

60. From *The Kingdom of God in America* (1937), quoted in Ahlstrom, *A Religious History of the American People,* 940.

61. Miller, *Jonathan Edwards,* 50–51.

62. Tomlinson, *Pierre,* ix.

63. Percival, *A Reading of* Moby-Dick, 16.

64. Lee, "Emerson Through Kierkegaard," 229–48.

65. Domestico, "Editing Modernism," 21.

66. Quoted in Domestico, 31.

67. Hutner, "Reviewing America," 102.

68. Gallagher, "The History of Literary Criticism," 136–38.

69. Ransom, "Criticism, Inc.," 601.

70. Ransom, *God without Thunder,* 328 (italics in original), 315.

71. Lauter, "Melville Climbs the Canon," 5.

72. Quoted in Lauter, 19.

73. "General Introduction," *An Approach to Literature,* 6.

74. Sedgwick, *Epistemology of the Closet,* 115.

75. The review essay Sedgwick cites is by J. M. Cameron, titled "The Historical Jesus," in *New York Review of Books* 33 (February 13, 1986): 21. Discussed in *Epistemology of the Closet,* 141–42.

TWO. Sentimental Communion

1. Stowe, *Uncle Tom's Cabin,* 266.

2. Quoted in Rossi, "Uncle Tom's Cabin and Protestantism in Italy," 422–23.

3. Quoted in Rossi, 423.

4. For recent instances of such work, see, for instance, Coleman, who argues for Stowe's narrative voice as homiletic ("The Unsentimental Woman Preacher," 266–67), and Farrell ("Dying Instruction," 245–46), who shows the influence of Puritan primers on her prose. Smith catalogs Phelps's "personal exposure to currents in biblical hermeneutics" ("From the Seminary to the Parlor," 108).

5. Critics have observed this tendency in Stowe's other work. Franchot argues that in *Agnes of Sorrento,* published ten years after *Uncle Tom's Cabin,* Stowe "Catholicize[s] her narrative" on the rhetorical level "by imitating the liturgical practices celebrated by the plot" (*Roads to Rome,* 250). Szczesiul finds that in her religious poetry "Stowe openly expresses a desire for the 'imagistic' tradition of Catholicism—the sights, smells, and sounds of Catholic ritual," and argues for Stowe's portraying Eva and Tom according to specifically Catholic conventions of sainthood ("The Canonization of Tom and Eva," 62).

6. Phelps, *Chapters from a Life*, 45.

7. Phelps, *The Gates Ajar*, 62.

8. "Review 1—no Title," 248.

9. Lears, *No Place of Grace*, 192. The citation from Lyman Abbott comes from Abbott's *Impressions of a Careless Traveler*.

10. Quoted in Lear, 192.

11. See Girard, *Deceit, Desire, and the Novel*, chapter 1; Sedgwick cites Girard in *Epistemology of the Closet*, 151–52.

12. Noble, "The Ecstasies of Sentimental Wounding in *Uncle Tom's Cabin*," 296.

13. Warner, *The Wide, Wide World*; see, for example, 312–13, 407–8, 476–82. In that latter section, Ellen proves to John that she has successfully learned to translate the flower of a white camellia into the Biblical "lesson" of "those that have not defiled their garments" (479).

14. Halttunen, *Confidence Men and Painted Women*, 40.

15. For an illuminating full discussion, see Colbert, *A Measure of Perfection*, particularly chapter 5.

16. "To Gamaliel Bailey, March 9, 1851," 66.

17. Brodhead, *Cultures of Letters*, 53.

18. Phelps, *Chapters*, 114. Discussed in Frank, "'Bought with a Price.'"

19. Dillon, "Sentimental Aesthetics," 498.

20. See Kete, *Sentimental Collaborations*; Hendler, *Public Sentiments*; and Tompkins, *Sensational Designs*.

21. Frank, "'Bought With a Price,'" 180.

22. Quoted in Frank, 179. The source is Sanchez-Eppler's "Then When We Clutch Hardest."

23. Angus, *Bible Hand-book*, 2.

24. Massachusetts Sabbath School Society, *The Interpretation of the Bible*, 41, 52.

25. Wheeler, *Our Master's Footsteps*, 311.

26. Watson and Lee, *The Bible and the Closet and Secret Prayer Successfully Managed*, 24.

27. Möhler, *Symbolism*, 367.

28. "Protestantism versus the Church," 10.

29. See Howard, "What Is Sentimentality?" for a thorough discussion of sentimental epistemology in these terms. I return to this argument and to Howard's essay in chapter 5.

30. Reprinted in the Norton Critical Edition of *Uncle Tom's Cabin*, 498.

31. Spillers, "Changing the Letter," 192.

32. "First Little Eva Meets Uncle Tom."

33. Barnes, "The Epistemology of the 'Real,'" 325.

34. Barnes, *Love's Whipping Boy*, 11–12.

35. Gilmore, "*Uncle Tom's Cabin* and the American Renaissance," 58–76.

36. Stowe, *Agnes of Sorrento*, 20, 21.

37. As Franchot notes, Catholicism was very broadly assigned the role of "the weaker femininity to [Protestantism's] superior masculinity," a role propagated by texts that "enabled parallel processes of masculine mystification of the bodily interiors of Catholicism and women, mirrored structures of exterior allure and recessed corruption" (*Roads to Rome*, 14, 121).

38. Cited in Noble, "Sentimental Ecstasies," 311. Noble's source is Gossett, *Uncle Tom's Cabin and American Culture.*

39. "*Uncle Tom's Cabin,*" *Littell's Living Age*, 15.

40. "*Uncle Tom's Cabin,*" *Mercersburg Review*, n.p.

41. Fisher, *Hard Facts*, 14.

42. Brown, *Domestic Individualism*, 41–42.

43. Morgan, *Uncle Tom's Cabin as Visual Culture*, 27.

44. Phelps, *Beyond the Gates*, 226.

45. "*The Gates Ajar,*" *Ladies' Repository*, 272.

46. Smith, "From the Seminary to the Parlor."

47. Weinstein, "Heaven's Tense," 65.

48. That is Jenny Franchot's gloss on Brownson's theory of communion (*Roads to Rome*, 339).

49. In *The Works of Thomas Chalmers*, 413.

THREE. Romantic Spectatorship

1. Melville, "Hawthorne and His Mosses," 2308.

2. Reed, "Self-Portraiture in the Work of Nathaniel Hawthorne," 53.

3. Rogin, *Subversive Genealogy*, 160–83.

4. Franchot, *Roads to Rome*, 190, 191.

5. These two quotes appear in two letters—the first to William Ticknor in 1855, the second to Sophia Hawthorne in 1856—cited in the introduction to Myerson, ed., *Selected Letters of Nathaniel Hawthorne*, xiv–xv.

6. Melville, *Pierre*, 353.

7. See Harris, *The Artist in American Society.*

8. See Smith, *American Archives*, 13.

9. Novak, *American Painting of the Nineteenth Century*, 51. See also Harris, *The Artist in American Society*, 88.

10. "Art. XI," 249.

11. In Dillenberger, *The Visual Arts and Christianity in America from the Colonial Period to the Present*, 142.

12. Quoted in Dillenberger, 143.

13. "The Fine Arts," 510.

14. "Our Artists.—No. IX. Benjamin West," 64.

15. Beecher, *The Incarnation*, viii.

16. Cumming, *Lectures on Romanism*, 461.

17. Beecher, *Star Papers*, 80.

18. Peale's 1824 *Patriae Pater* depicted Washington with a miniature of Jupiter above his face; Greenough's 1840 sculpture posed Washington in a toga, arm raised in a godlike gesture of command.

19. Quoted in Colbert, *A Measure of Perfection*, 238.

20. "Gilbert Stuart," 324.

21. Yarmolinsky, *Picturesque United States*, 34. These lines are also cited in Harris, *The Artist in American Society*, 87–88.

22. "Original Portraits of Washington," 346.

23. This account comes from the recollection of Washington's grandson George Washington Parke Custis. In "Portraiture of Washington," 389.

24. Quoted in Verheyen, "'The Most Exact Representation of the Original,'" 128.

25. Quoted in Verheyen, 132.

26. Evans, *The Genius of Gilbert Stuart*, 67.

27. As Greenhalgh notes, Stuart never delivered the canvas to Martha Washington, who had commissioned it ("'Not a Man but a God,'" 275). Keeping it unfinished may have been a strategy to keep the portrait under his control. Stuart himself was reported to refer to the Athenaeum portrait as his "hundred-dollar bill," because by keeping the portrait in his studio, he could easily paint copies for sale. That report appears in Yarmolinksy, *Picturesque United States*, 34.

28. Lukasik, *Discerning Characters*, 32.

29. Excerpted in Gutjahr, ed., *Popular American Literature of the Nineteenth Century*, 435–72. The headnote tells us that the Fowlers' guide was "one of the century's most popular self-instruction manuals, going through more than twenty editions in the next fifty years" after its initial publication in 1849 (435).

30. "Original Portraits," *Putnam's*, 346.

31. For a helpful analysis of this context, see Williams, *Confounding Images*, especially 31–34.

32. Howard, "Historical Note," 376.

33. See Davis, *Hawthorne's Shyness*, 2–3.

34. Hawthorne, *The Marble Faun*, 3.

35. Hawthorne, *The Blithedale Romance*, 37–39.

36. Hawthorne, *The Scarlet Letter*, 7–8.

37. Howe, *Politics and the Novel*, 170.

38. Siogvolk, "Nathaniel Hawthorne," 383.

39. Reed, "Self-Portraiture," 47–48.

40. Quoted in Reed, 47–48.

41. For more on Hawthorne's voyeurism, see Martin, "'I saw a concourse of strange figures.'"

42. Stein, "*The Blithedale Romance*'s Queer Style," 225.

43. As Mitchell notes, contemporaneous reviews took Hawthorne's fictional Zenobia as a far more truthful portrait of Fuller than the purportedly authentic biography of her that had been recently published ("Julian Hawthorne and the 'Scandal' of Margaret Fuller").

44. Quoted in Howard, "Historical Note," 366.

45. Quoted in Howard, 366.

46. "HERMAN MELVILLE CRAZY," September 5, 1852, cited in Parker's "Historical Note," 380.

47. August 21, 1852, 118.

48. H. M. Tomlinson, preface to *Pierre*, ix.

49. Rogin, *Subversive Genealogy*, 178.

50. Creech, *Closet Writing/Gay Reading*, 122–23.

51. Otter, *Melville's Anatomies*, 250.

52. Elliott, "Art, Religion, and the Problem of Authority in *Pierre*," 346. As Elliott points out, we learn early in the novel that Pierre "seemed to have inherited" the "docile homage to a venerable Faith, which the first Glendinning had brought over sea" (*Pierre* 7).

53. Brooks, *The Melodramatic Imagination*, 28.

54. "Letter to Nathaniel Hawthorne, [17?] November 1851, Pittsfield," 43.

FOUR. Realistic Intercourse

1. Beers, "Literature and the Civil War," 749.

2. Quoted in Howard, "What Is Sentimentality?," 74.

3. Quoted in Stoddard, *The Morgesons and Other Writings*, 325.

4. Fussell, *The Catholic Side of Henry James*, 33.

5. Reed, "'I Have No Disbelief,'" 155.

6. Coviello and Hickman, for instance, define one version of postsecular reading as an approach that does not "presume . . . the decline of religion" as the basic condition of modernity. "Introduction," 649.

7. Quoted in Serpell, *Seven Modes of Uncertainty*, 73, 75.

8. Serpell develops this point further in discussing Barbara Johnson's essay "Using People: Kant with Winnicott," in *Seven Modes*, 224–26.

9. Fussell, *The Catholic Side of Henry James*, ix, 29.

10. Stoddard, letter dated June 5, 1857, in the *Daily Alta*, 1857.

11. Leach, "Strategists of Display," 100.

12. Lears, "Beyond Veblen," 76.

13. Lears, *No Place of Grace*, 193.

14. McDannell, *The Christian Home in Victorian America*, 14–18. McDannell wryly notes that "in order to create a Protestant Gothic style it became necessary to ignore certain facts, such as the existence of Gothic cathedrals at the center of major European cities" (35).

15. According to Gutjahr, the *Treatise* was "so popular and influential that it was reprinted annually for the next fifteen years" (from his headnote to the selection reprinted in *Popular American Literature*, 255).

16. "A Meditation by Paul Potiphar, Esq.," 660–61.

17. For a helpful summary of the scrapbook's history, see the editors' introduction to *The Scrapbook in American Life*. Beverly Gordon's essay in that volume identifies the particular form of the paper doll house as having been "popular in the United States between approximately 1875 and 1920" (116).

18. Gordon cites an 1880 how-to column in *Godey's Lady's Book* calling the paper doll house a "help to mother." In other cases, she finds, women from art clubs or art schools had a hand in designing the paper doll houses, but they were always made as gifts to young girls (188, 122–23).

19. They vary widely in detail and in scope; some, writes Gordon, "expanded to more than forty separate spaces, including dressing rooms, pantries, backyard gardens, and even outdoor cottages" (117). The degree of care and polish varies widely, too, from haphazard to precise, presumably depending on the time or skill or interest of the maker.

20. Bermingham, "Women's Work: Albums and Their Makers."

21. Brinkman, "Scrapping Modernism," 46.

22. Feldman, "'A Talent for the Disagreeable,'" 202.

23. Brown, *A Sense of Things*, 166.

24. Cook, *What Shall We Do with Our Walls?*, 49.

25. Hall, *The Bric-a-Brac Hunter*, 19–20.

26. Haweis, *The Art of Decoration*, 363.

27. Pasquesi, "*The Morgesons*," 187.

28. Feldman, "A Talent for the Disagreeable," 221n25.

29. Beam, *Style, Gender, and Fantasy in Nineteenth Century American Women's Writing*, 7.

30. My thanks to Ashley Reed for suggesting this connection.

31. Brooks, *The Melodramatic Imagination*, 162.

32. James, *A Small Boy and Others*, 159.

33. See also O'Loughlin on the cultural portability of *Uncle Tom's Cabin*, which cites this passage from James ("Articulating Uncle Tom's Cabin," 573–97).

34. Wells, *Boon, The Mind of the Race, The Wild Asses of the Devil, and the Last Trump.*

35. See above, in chapter 1, for further detail. Van Vechten, "The Later Works of HM," 12; quoted in Lauter, "Melville Climbs the Canon," 19. See also Matthiessen's appreciation, albeit qualified, of James's mastery of symbolism and ambiguity in *The American Renaissance* (294, 476).

36. Preface to *The Spoils of Poynton*, in *The Art of the Novel*, 126, 127.

37. Bayley, "Cracking *The Golden Bowl*.".

38. See also Otten's reading of Amerigo's appreciation of the metaphorical pieces of Charlotte in *A Superficial Reading of Henry James*, 16–17.

39. See Nussbaum's argument that this moment of visualization shows us that "moral objectivity about the value of a person . . . requires, evidently, the ability to see that item as distinct from other items" and "as a value that can be contrasted or opposed to others" (*Love's Knowledge*, 131).

40. Liebowitz observes that in *The Spoils of Poynton*, Fleda's "model of love"—one that James discredits as naive in that novel—"postulates two individuals, inscrutable to the world but thoroughly legible to one another, such that each resembles an author generating text for an ideal reader who values the other's refusal to 'make any show'" ("Legible Reticence," 18). The fact that the adulterous Charlotte and Amerigo seem to match Fleda's vision, as Liebowitz notes (25), suggests that it is not for James a sound ideal. Ultimately, Liebowitz argues, "the most radical consequence of James's practice" is "his revalorization of artifice as an intrinsic good" (24).

41. James, *The Spoils of Poynton*, xxxix–xl.

42. Berlant, *The Female Complaint*, 15.

43. Brown, *Sense*, 122, referencing Porter's *Seeing and Being*.

FIVE. Love and Depth Revisited

1. See Hale, "Aesthetics and the New Ethics."

2. As noted in the introduction, Moretti and Love, for example, have designated close reading as a religious practice they do not follow. We will see Felski make a similar gesture in the discussion below.

3. Fessenden, "The Problem of the Postsecular," 155.

4. Landy, *How to Do Things with Fictions*, 34.

5. LaCapra, *History, Literature, Critical Theory*, 132.

6. Levinas, "Substitution," 94.

7. Miller, *Literature as Conduct*, 256.

8. Eaglestone, *Ethical Criticism*, 4.

9. See Serpell, "Mutual Exclusion," 245.

10. See Hale, "Aesthetics" and "Fiction."

11. Booth, "Rhetoric," 161.

12. Booth, *Company*, 170.

13. Attridge, "Innovation," 22.

14. Haney, "Aesthetics and Ethics," 37.

15. Best and Marcus, "Surface Reading," 7. This was a special issue of *Representations*, the journal that put New Historicism on the map in the early 1990s (see Hamilton, *Historicism*, 163).

16. Felski, "Context Stinks!" 582. The argument of this article reappears in chapter 5 of Felski's *The Limits of Critique* (2015).

17. Robbins, "Not So Well Attached," 375.

18. Levine, *Forms*, 6.

19. Levine sounds this note of the "aleatory and sometimes contradictory" (*Forms*, 7) work of forms interacting with each other throughout the book. See also, for example, 17–18, 107–109.

20. Bozovic, "Whose Forms?", 1185.

21. See Dillon, "Sentimental Aesthetics."

22. Newton, *Narrative Ethics*, 66.

23. Tompkins, *Sensational Designs*, 123, xvii.

24. Spivak, "Ethics and Politics," 18.

25. Veeser, *The New Historicism Reader*, 3.

26. Merish, *Sentimental Materialism*, 51, 4.

27. See Brown, *Domestic Individualism*, 41–42.

28. Hendler, *Public Sentiments*, 9, 10.

29. Otter, *Melville's Anatomies*, 235.

30. Greenblatt and Gallagher, *Practicing New Historicism*, 7.

31. These are some of the many sources that Otter uses to read Melville in *Melville's Anatomies*.

32. Tompkins, "Other," 35–36.

33. Hale, *Social Formalism*, 18.

34. Quoted in Veeser, *The New Historicism Reader*, 13.

35. Liu, "The Power of Formalism," 746.

36. I cited this point in the introduction. Porter writes: "'Transcendence' . . . is not equivalent to, but in fact—historically speaking—is an ideological defense against, literature's potential as a discursive site of subversion, resistance, or antagonism." But literature's powers of subversion, resistance, and antagonism, "once stripped of [their] ideological function as transcendent," still maintain their "active force within the discursive field" ("After the New Historicism," 263).

BIBLIOGRAPHY

Ahlstrom, Sydney. *A Religious History of the American People.* 2nd ed. New Haven,
CT: Yale University Press, 2004.

Altieri, Charles. "Lyrical Ethics and Literary Experience." In *Mapping the Ethical
Turn,* edited by Todd Davis and Kenneth Womack, 30–58. Charlottesville: University of Virginia Press, 2001.

———. "What Differences Can Contemporary Poetry Make in Our Moral Thinking?" In *Renegotiating Ethics in Literature, Philosophy, and Theory,* edited by Jane
Adamson, Richard Freadman, and David Parker, 113–33. New York: Cambridge
University Press, 1998.

Angus, Joseph. *The Bible Hand-book: An Introduction to the Study of Sacred Scripture.* London: Religious Tract Society, 1869.

Armstrong, Nancy. *Desire and Domestic Fiction: A Political History of the Novel.*
New York: Oxford University Press, 1987.

"Art. XI." Rev. of George Gilfillan, *Bards of the Bible. North American Review* 73
(July 1851): 238–67.

Attridge, Derek. "Innovation, Literature, Ethics: Relating to the Other." *PMLA* 114,
no. 1, Special Topic: Ethics and Literary Study (1999): 20–31.

"Authority in Matters of Faith." *Catholic World,* November 1871, 145–57.

Aynsley, Jeremy, and Charlotte Grant, eds., with assistance from Harriet McKay.
Imagined Interiors: Representing the Domestic Interior since the Renaissance.
London: V&A, 2006.

Barnes, Elizabeth. "The Epistemology of the 'Real': A Response to Marianne
Noble." *Yale Journal of Criticism* 10, no. 2 (1997): 321–26.

———. *Love's Whipping Boy.* Chapel Hill: University of North Carolina Press,
2011.

Barth, Karl. Preface to *The Epistle to the Romans,* 2nd ed. Translated by Edwyn C.
Hoskyns. New York: Oxford University Press, 1968.

Bayley, John. "Cracking *The Golden Bowl.*" *New York Review of Books,* March 1,
1984, https://www-nybooks-com.proxy.libraries.smu.edu/articles/1984/03/01
/cracking-the-golden-bowl/ (accessed October 14, 2019).

Baym, Nina. "Melodramas of Beset Manhood: How Theories of American Fiction Exclude Women Authors." *American Quarterly* 33, no. 2 (1981): 123–39.

Beam, Dorri. *Style, Gender, and Fantasy in Nineteenth-Century American Women's Writing.* New York: Cambridge University Press, 2010.

Beecher, Catherine. "A Treatise on Domestic Economy for the Use of Young Ladies at Home and at School" (excerpt from *A Treatise on Domestic Economy,* 1841). In *Popular American Literature of the 19th Century,* edited by Paul C. Gutjahr, 255–86. New York: Oxford University Press, 2001.

———, and Harriet Beecher Stowe. *The American Woman's Home.* New York: J. B. Ford, 1869.

Beecher, Charles. *The Incarnation; Or, Pictures of the Virgin and Her Son.* New York: Harper & Brothers, 1849.

Beecher, Henry Ward. *Star Papers, or, Experiences of Art and Nature.* New York: J. C. Derby, 1855.

Beecher, Willis. *Reasonable Biblical Criticism.* New York: Harper, 1911.

Beers, Henry. "Literature and the Civil War." *Atlantic Monthly* 88 (1901): 749–60.

Berlant, Lauren. *The Female Complaint.* Durham, NC: Duke University Press, 2008.

Bermingham, Ann. "Women's Work: Albums and Their Makers: The Art of Victorian Photocollage." Metropolitan Museum of Art, June 2011, https://www.metmuseum.org/metmedia/video/collections/ph/victorian-photocollage-1 (accessed October 14, 2019).

Bersani, Leo. *A Future for Astyanax.* Boston: Little, Brown, 1976.

Bérubé, Michael. "What's the Matter with Cultural Studies?" *Chronicle of Higher Education,* September 14, 2009, n.p.

Best, Stephen, and Sharon Marcus. "Surface Reading: An Introduction." *Representations* 108 (2009): 1–21.

"Bookbinding as a Fine Art." *Curio* 1, no. 1 (September 1887): 25–30.

Booth, Wayne. *The Company We Keep: An Ethics of Fiction.* Berkeley: University of California Press, 1988.

———. "The Rhetoric of Fiction." In *The Novel: An Anthology of Criticism and Theory, 1900–2000,* edited by Dorothy Hale, 154–83. Malden, MA: Blackwell, 2006.

Bozovic, Marijeta. "Whose Forms? Missing Russians in Caroline Levine's *Forms.*" *PMLA* 132, no. 5 (2017): 1181–86.

Briggs, Charles Augustus. "The Authority of Holy Scripture: An Inaugural Address." New York: Charles Scribner's Sons, 1891.

Brightman, Edgar Sheffield. "The Neo-Orthodox Trend." *Journal of Bible and Religion* 14, no. 3 (1946): 129–30.

Brinkman, Bartholomew. "Scrapping Modernism: Marianne Moore and the Making of the Modern Collage Poem." *Modernism/Modernity* 18, no. 1 (2011): 43–66.

Brodhead, Richard. *Hawthorne, Melville, and the Novel.* Chicago: University of Chicago Press, [1973] 1976.

———. *The School of Hawthorne.* New York: Oxford University Press, 1986.

Brookes, James Hall. *Is the Bible Inspired?* Reprint ed. St. Louis: Gospel Book & Tract Depository, 1902.

Brooks, Cleanth, John Thibault Purser, and Robert Penn Warren, eds. "General Introduction." In *An Approach to Literature,* 1–8. New York: Appleton-Century-Crofts, 1964.

Brooks, Peter. *The Melodramatic Imagination: Balzac, Henry James, Melodrama, and the Mode of Excess.* New Haven, CT: Yale University Press, 1976.

Brown, Bill. *A Sense of Things: The Object Matter of American Literature.* Chicago: University of Chicago Press, 2003.

Brown, Candy Gunther. *The Word in the World: Evangelical Writing, Publishing, and Reading in America, 1789–1880.* Chapel Hill: University of North Carolina Press, 2004.

Brown, Gillian. *Domestic Individualism: Imagining Self in Nineteenth-Century America.* Berkeley: University of California Press, 1990.

Buell, Lawrence. "In Pursuit of Ethics." *PMLA* 114, no. 1, Special Topic: Ethics and Literary Study (1999): 7–19.

Bushnell, Horace. *God in Christ.* Hartford, CT: Brown & Parsons, 1849.

———. *The Vicarious Sacrifice.* New York: Charles Scribner, 1866.

Cameron, Sharon. *Thinking in Henry James.* Chicago: University of Chicago Press, 1989.

Cardinal, Roger. "Collecting and Collage-making: The Case of Kurt Schwitters." In *The Cultures of Collecting,* edited by John Elsner and Roger Cardinal, 68–96. Cambridge, MA: Harvard University Press, 1994.

Chai, Leon. *The Romantic Foundations of the American Renaissance.* Ithaca, NY: Cornell University Press, 1987.

Chalmers, Thomas. "On the New Heavens and the New Earth." In *The Works of Thomas Chalmers: Complete in One Volume,* 411–17. Philadelphia: A. Towar, Hogan & Thompson, 1833.

Channing, William Ellery. "Likeness to God" (1828). Reprinted in *Transcendentalism: A Reader,* ed. Joel Myerson, 3–20. New York: Oxford University Press, 2000.

Clarke, William Newton. *Sixty Years with the Bible: A Record of Experience.* New York: Charles Scribner's Sons, 1912.

Clarkson, Lida, and M. J. Clarkson. *Household Decoration: The Home Made Attractive in Simple and Inexpensive Ways.* Lynn, MA: J. F. Ingalls, 1887.

Colbert, Charles. *A Measure of Perfection: Phrenology and the Fine Arts in America.* Chapel Hill: University of North Carolina Press, 1997.

Coleman, Dawn. "The Unsentimental Woman Preacher of *Uncle Tom's Cabin*." *American Literature* 80, no. 2 (2008): 265–92.

Cook, Clarence. *The House Beautiful: Essays on Beds and Tables, Stools and Candlesticks*. New York: Scribner, Armstrong, 1878.

———. *What Shall We Do with Our Walls?* New York: Warren, Fuller, 1880.

Coviello, Peter. *Intimacy in America: Dreams of Affiliation in Antebellum Literature*. Minneapolis: University of Minnesota Press, 2005.

———, and Jared Hickman. "Introduction: After the Postsecular." *American Literature* 86, no. 4 (December 2014): 645–54.

Creech, James. *Closet Writing/Gay Reading: The Case of Melville's Pierre*. Chicago: University of Chicago Press, 1993.

Cumming, John. *Lectures on Romanism, Being Illustrations and Refutations of the Errors of Romanism and Tractarianism*. Cleveland: Jewett, Proctor & Worthington, 1854.

Davis, Clark. *Hawthorne's Shyness: Ethics, Politics, and the Question of Engagement*. Baltimore, MD: Johns Hopkins University Press, 2005.

Davis, Theo. "'Just apply a weight': Thoreau and the Aesthetics of Ornament." *ELH* 77, no. 3 (Fall 2010): 561–87.

Didron, Adolphe Napoléon. *Christian Iconography: The History of Christian Art in the Middle Ages*. Translated by E. J. Millington. London: Henry G. Bohn, 1851.

Dillenberger, John. *The Visual Arts and Christianity in America from the Colonial Period to the Present*. New York: Crossroad, 1989.

Dillon, Elizabeth. "Sentimental Aesthetics." *American Literature* 76, no. 3 (2004): 495–523.

Dobson, Joanne. "Reclaiming Sentimental Literature." *American Literature* 69, no. 2 (1997): 263–88.

Domestico, Anthony. "Editing Modernism, Editing Theology: T. S. Eliot, Karl Barth, and the *Criterion*." *Journal of Modern Periodical Studies* 3, no. 1 (2012): 19–38.

Douglas, Ann. *The Feminization of American Culture*. New York: Alfred A. Knopf, 1977.

Eaglestone, Robert. *Ethical Criticism: Reading After Levinas*. Edinburgh: Edinburgh University Press, 1997.

Earle, Alice Morse. *China Collecting in America*. 1st ed. New York: Charles Scribner's Sons, 1892.

Eastlake, Charles Locke. *Hints on Household Taste in Furniture, Upholstery, and Other Details*. Edited by Charles Perkins. Boston: James R. Osgood, 1874.

"Editor's Literary Record." *Harper's Monthly* 56, no. 332 (January 1878): 307–11.

Ellicott, Charles J., ed. *Prayers and Meditations for the Holy Communion*. London: Rivingtons, 1870.

Elliott, "Art, Religion, and the Problem of Authority in *Pierre*." In *Ideology and Classic American Literature*, edited by Sacvan Bercovitch and Myra Jehlen, 337–51. New York: Cambridge University Press, 1986.

Emerson, Ralph Waldo. "Sermon CLXII [The Lord's Supper]" (September 9, 1832). In *Transcendentalism: A Reader*, edited by Joel Myerson, 68–78. New York: Oxford University Press, 2000.

Evans, Dorinda. *The Genius of Gilbert Stuart*. Princeton, NJ: Princeton University Press, 1999.

Faber, Frederick William. *The Blessed Sacrament*. London: James Toovey, 1879.

Farrell, Molly. "Dying Instruction: Puritan Pedagogy in *Uncle Tom's Cabin*." *American Literature* 82, no. 2 (2010): 243–69.

Feldman, Jessica. "'A Talent for the Disagreeable': Elizabeth Stoddard Writes *The Morgesons*." *Nineteenth-Century Literature* 58, no. 2 (2003): 202–29.

Felski, Rita. "Context Stinks!" *New Literary History* 42, no. 4 (2011): 573–91.

———. *The Limits of Critique*. Chicago: University of Chicago Press, 2015.

Fenton, Elizabeth. *Religious Liberties*. New York: Oxford University Press, 2011.

Fessenden, Tracy. *Culture and Redemption*. Princeton, NJ: Princeton University Press, 2007.

———. "The Problem of the Postsecular." *American Literary History* 26, no. 1 (2014): 154–67.

Fiedler, Leslie. *Love and Death in the American Novel*. Normal, IL: Dalkey Archive, 1960.

"The Fine Arts." *Literary World* 2, no. 47 (December 25, 1847): 510.

"First Little Eva Meets Uncle Tom." *Hartford Times*, October 11, 1933.

Fisher, Philip. *Hard Facts: Setting and Form in the American Novel*. New York: Oxford University Press, 1985.

Fluck, Winfried. "'The American Romance' and the Changing Functions of the Imaginary." *New Literary History* 27, no. 3 (1996): 415–57.

Fogarty, Gerald. *Nova et Vetera: The Theology of Tradition in American Catholicism*. Milwaukee, WI: Marquette University Press, 1987.

Franchot, Jenny. "Invisible Domain: Religion and American Literary Studies." *American Literature* 67, no. 4 (1995): 833–42.

———. *Roads to Rome: The Antebellum Protestant Encounter with Catholicism*. Berkeley: University of California Press, 1994.

Frank, Lucy. "'Bought with a Price': Elizabeth Stuart Phelps and the Commodification of Heaven in Postbellum America." *ESQ: A Journal of the American Renaissance* 55, no. 2 (2009): 165–92.

French, Lillie Hamilton. *Homes and Their Decoration*. New York: Dodd, Mead, 1903.

Fussell, Edwin Sills. *The Catholic Side of Henry James*. New York: Cambridge University Press, 1993.

Gallagher, Catherine, and Stephen Greenblatt. *Practicing New Historicism.* Chicago: University of Chicago Press, 2000.

"The Gates Ajar." *Christian Union,* February 12, 1870.

"The Gates Ajar." *Ladies' Repository* 32, no. 4 (1872): 272–78.

"Gilbert Stuart." In *The Treasury of Knowledge and Library of Reference,* 324–28. Vol. 3. New York: C. C. Childs, 1850.

Gilmore, Michael. "*Uncle Tom's Cabin* and the American Renaissance: The Sacramental Aesthetic of Harriet Beecher Stowe." In *The Cambridge Companion to Harriet Beecher Stowe,* edited by Cindy Weinstein, 58–76. Cambridge: Cambridge University Press, 2004.

Gordon, Beverly. "Scrapbook Houses for Paper Dolls: Creative Expression, Aesthetic Elaboration, and Bonding in the Female World." In *The Scrapbook in American Life,* edited by Susan Tucker, Katherine Ott, and Patricia Buckler, 116–34. Philadelphia: Temple University Press, 2006.

Gossett, Thomas. *Uncle Tom's Cabin and American Culture.* Dallas, TX: Southern Methodist University Press, 1985.

Graff, Gerald. "How 'bout That Wordsworth!" *MLA Newsletter* 40, no. 4 (Winter 2008): 3–4.

———. *Professing Literature: An Institutional History.* Chicago: University of Chicago Press, 1987.

Granniss, Mary C. "The True Charm of Home." *Arthur's Illustrated Home Magazine* 11 (January–June 1858): 284.

Gray, James. *How to Master the English Bible.* Chicago: Winona, 1906.

Greenhalgh, Adam. "'Not a Man but a God': The Apotheosis of Gilbert Stuart's Athenaeum Portrait of George Washington." *Winterthur Portfolio* 41, no. 4 (2007): 269–304.

Griffin, Susan. *Anti-Catholicism and Nineteenth-Century Fiction.* New York: Cambridge University Press, 2004.

Gutjahr, Paul C. *An American Bible: A History of the Good Book in the United States, 1777–1880.* Stanford, CA: Stanford University Press, 1999.

———, ed. *Popular American Literature of the Nineteenth Century.* New York: Oxford University Press, 2001.

Hale, Dorothy. "Aesthetics and the New Ethics: Theorizing the Novel in the Twenty-First Century." *PMLA* 124, no. 3 (2009): 896–905.

———. "Fiction as Restriction: Self-Binding in New Ethical Theories of the Novel." *Narrative* 15, no. 2 (2007): 187–206.

———. *The Novel: An Anthology of Criticism and Theory 1900–2000.* Malden, MA: Blackwell, 2006.

———. *Social Formalism: The Novel in Theory from Henry James to the Present.* Stanford, CA: Stanford University Press, 1998.

Hall, Herbert Byng. *The Bric-a-Brac Hunter; Or, Chapters in Chinamania*. London: Chatto & Windus, 1875.

Halttunen, Karen. *Confidence Men and Painted Women: A Study of Middle-Class Culture in America, 1830–1870*. New Haven, CT: Yale University Press, 1982.

Hamilton, Paul. *Historicism*. New Critical Idiom Series. New York: Routledge, 1996.

Haney, David. "Aesthetics and Ethics in Gadamer, Levinas, and Romanticism: Problems of Phronesis and Techne." *PMLA* 114, no. 1, Special Topic: Ethics and Literary Study (January 1999): 32–45.

Harris, Neil. *The Artist in American Society: The Formative Years, 1790–1860*. New York: George Braziller, 1966.

Hatch, Nathan. "Sola Scriptura and Novus Ordo Seclorum." In *The Bible in America: Essays in Cultural History*, edited by Nathan Hatch and Mark Noll, 59–78. Oxford: Oxford University Press, 1982), 61.

Hatch, Nathan, and Mark Noll, eds. *The Bible in America: Essays in Cultural History*. New York: Oxford University Press, 1982.

Haweis, Mrs. H. R. *The Art of Decoration*. London: Chatto & Windus, 1889.

Hawthorne, Julian. "Novelistic Habits and *The Morgesons*." *Lippincott's Monthly Magazine*, December 1889, 868–71.

Hawthorne, Nathaniel. *The Blithedale Romance* (1852). Boston: Bedford Books of St. Martin's, 1996.

———. *The Scarlet Letter* (1850). Introduction by William Charvat. Boston: Houghton Mifflin, 1963.

Hendler, Glenn. *Public Sentiments: Structures of Feeling in Nineteenth-Century American Literature*. Chapel Hill: University of North Carolina Press, 2001.

"A Heretic of Yesterday." *Congregationalist* (Boston), April 12, 1894, 79.

Holifield, E. Brooks. *Theology in America: Christian Thought from the Age of the Puritans to the Civil War*. New Haven, CT: Yale University Press, 2003.

Holland, David. *Sacred Borders: Continuing Revelation and Canonical Restraint in Early America*. New York: Oxford University Press, 2011.

Howard, June. "What Is Sentimentality?" *American Literary History* 11, no. 1 (1999): 63–81.

Howard, Leon. "Historical Note." In Melville, *Pierre*, 376.

Howe, Irving. *Politics and the Novel*. New York: Avon, [1957] 1967.

Hulme, T. E. *Speculations: Essays on Humanism and the Philosophy of Art*. London: Routledge & Kegan Paul, 1954.

Humma, John. "Realism and Beyond: The Imagery of Sex and Sexual Oppression in Elizabeth Stoddard's *Lemorne Versus Huell*." *South Atlantic Review* 58, no. 1 (1993): 33–47.

Hutchison, William R. *The Modernist Impulse in American Protestantism*. Durham, NC: Duke University Press, 1992.

Hutner, Gordon. "Reviewing America: John Crowe Ransom's *Kenyon Review.*" *American Quarterly* 44, no. 1 (1992): 101–14.

James, Henry. *The Art of the Novel* (1934). Introduction by Richard P. Blackmur. New York: Charles Scribner's Sons, 1962.

———. *A Small Boy and Others.* New York: Scribner's Sons, 1941.

———. "The Figure in the Carpet." In *The Novels and Tales of Henry James,* 217–77. New York Edition. Vol. 15. New York: Augustus M. Kelley, 1970.

———. *The Golden Bowl* (1904). New York: Penguin, 2001.

———. "Is There a Life after Death?" In *In After Days: Thoughts on the Future Life,* edited by William Dean Howells, 199–233. New York: Harper & Brothers, 1910.

———. *The Portrait of a Lady* (1881). Norton Critical Edition. Edited by Robert Bamberg. New York: W.W. Norton, 1995.

———. *The Spoils of Poynton* (1897). Oxford World's Classics Edition. New York: Oxford University Press, 2008.

Jameson, Fredric. *The Political Unconscious: Narrative as a Socially Symbolic Act.* Ithaca, NY: Cornell University Press, 1981.

Kaufmann, Michael. "The Religious, the Secular, and Literary Studies: Rethinking the Secularization Narrative in Histories of the Profession." *New Literary History* 38, no. 4 (2007): 607–27.

Kearney, Richard. *Dialogues with Contemporary Continental Thinkers: The Phenomenological Heritage.* Manchester: Manchester University Press, 1984.

Kelley, Mary. "Pen and Ink Communion." *New England Quarterly* 84, no. 4 (December 2011): 555–87.

Kete, Mary Louise. *Sentimental Collaborations: Mourning and Middle-Class Identity in Nineteenth-Century America.* Durham, NC: Duke University Press, 2000.

Kierkegaard, Søren. *Philosophical Fragments / Johannes Climacus.* Translated by Howard and Edna Hong. Princeton, NJ: Princeton University Press, 1985.

LaCapra, Dominick. *History, Literature, Critical Theory.* Ithaca, NY: Cornell University Press, 2013.

LaPorte, Charles, and Sebastian Lecourt, "Introduction: Nineteenth-Century Literature, New Religious Movements, and Secularization." *Nineteenth-Century Literature* 73, no. 2 (2018): 147–60.

Landy, Joshua. *How to Do Things with Fictions.* New York: Oxford University Press, 2012.

Lauter, Paul. "Melville Climbs the Canon." *American Literature* 66, no. 1 (1994): 1–24.

Leach, William. "Strategists of Display and the Production of Desire." In *Consuming Visions: Accumulation and Display of Goods in America, 1880–1920,* edited by Simon J. Bronner, 99–132. New York: W. W. Norton, 1989.

Lears, Jackson. "Beyond Veblen: Rethinking Consumer Culture in America." In *Consuming Visions: Accumulation and Display of Goods in America, 1880–1920*, edited by Simon J. Bronner, 73–97. New York: W. W. Norton, 1989.

———. *No Place of Grace: Antimodernism and the Transformation of American Culture, 1880–1920*. New York: Pantheon, 1981.

Lessing, Gotthold Ephraim. *Laocoon: An Essay on The Limits of Painting and Poetry*. Translated by E. C. Beasley. London: Longman, Brown, Green & Longmans, 1853.

Lester, C. Edwards. *The Artists of America: A Series of Biographical Sketches of American Artists; with Portraits and Designs on Steel*. New York: Baker & Scribner, 1846.

Levinas, Emmanuel. "Substitution." In *Basic Philosophical Writings*, edited by Adriaan Peperzak, Simon Critchley, and Robert Bernasconi, 80–95. Bloomington: Indiana University Press, 1996.

Levine, Caroline. *Forms: Whole, Rhythm, Hierarchy, Network*. Princeton, NJ: Princeton University Press, 2015.

Levinson, Marjorie. "What Is New Formalism?" *PMLA* 122, no. 2 (2007): 558–69.

Liebowitz, Karen. "Legible Reticence: Unspoken Dialogues." *Henry James Review* 29 (2008): 16–35.

Liu, Alan. "The Power of Formalism: The New Historicism." *ELH* 56, no. 4 (Winter 1989): 721–71.

Love, Heather. "Close but Not Deep: Literary Ethics and the Descriptive Turn." *New Literary History* 41 (2010): 371–91.

Lukasik, Christopher. *Discerning Characters: The Culture of Appearance in Early America*. Philadelphia: University of Pennsylvania Press, 2011.

Luria, Sarah. "The Architecture of Manners: Henry James, Edith Wharton, and the Mount." In *Domestic Space: Reading the Nineteenth-Century Interior*, edited by Inga Bryden and Janet Floyd, 186–209. Manchester: Manchester University Press, 1999.

Lynch, Deirdre. *The Economy of Character*. Chicago: University of Chicago Press, 1998.

———. *Loving Literature*. Chicago: University of Chicago Press, 2018.

Marsden, George. *Fundamentalism and American Culture*. 2nd ed. New York: Oxford University Press, 2006.

Martin, Michael S. "'I saw a concourse of strange figures': The Masque, Voyeurism, and Hawthorne's Self-Consciousness in *The Blithedale Romance*." *Nathaniel Hawthorne Review* 40, no. 2 (2014): 85–102.

Marty, Martin. "America's Iconic Book." In *Humanizing America's Iconic Book: Society of Biblical Literature Centennial Addresses 1980*, edited by Gene Tucker and Douglas Knight, 1–23. Chico, CA: Scholars, 1982.

Massa, Mark. "'Mediating Modernism': Charles Briggs, Catholic Modernism, and an Ecumenical 'Plot.'" *Harvard Theological Review* 81, no. 4 (October 1988): 413–30.

Massachusetts Sabbath School Society. *The Interpretation of the Bible.* Boston: Massachusetts Sabbath School Society, 1844.

Matthiessen, F. O. *American Renaissance.* New York: Oxford University Press, [1941] 1957.

McDannell, Colleen. *The Christian Home in Victorian America, 1840–1900.* Bloomington: Indiana University Press, 1986.

McWhirter, David. *Desire and Love in Henry James: A Study of the Late Novels.* New York: Cambridge University Press, 1989.

"A Meditation by Paul Potiphar, Esq." *Putnam's,* June 1853, 653–61.

Melville, Herman. "Hawthorne and His Mosses" (1850). In *The Norton Anthology of American Literature,* edited by Robert S. Levine and Arnold Krupat, 2308–20. Vol. B., 7th ed. New York: W. W. Norton, 2007.

———. Letter to Hawthorne, November [17?], 1851. In *Herman Melville: Tales, Poems, and Other Writings,* edited by John Bryant, 42–44. New York: Modern Library, 2001.

———. *Pierre* (1852). Northwestern-Newberry Edition. Evanston, IL: Northwestern University Press, 1999.

Merish, Lori. *Sentimental Materialism: Gender, Commodity Culture, and Nineteenth-Century American Literature.* Durham, NC: Duke University Press, 2000.

Miller, J. Hillis. *Literature as Conduct: Speech Acts in Henry James.* New York: Fordham University Press, 2005.

Miller, Perry. *Jonathan Edwards.* Westport, CT: Greenwood, 1973.

Mitchell, Thomas. *Hawthorne's Fuller Mystery.* Amherst: University of Massachusetts Press, 1998.

———. "In the Whale's Wake: Melville and *The Blithedale Romance.*" In *Hawthorne and Melville: Writing a Relationship,* edited by Jana Argersinger and Leland S. Person, 249–67. Athens: University of Georgia Press, 2008.

———. "Julian Hawthorne and the 'Scandal' of Margaret Fuller." *American Literary History* 7, no. 2 (July 1995): 210–33.

Möhler , John Adam. *Symbolism: Or, Exposition of the Doctrinal Differences Between Catholics and Protestants, as Evidenced by Their Symbolical Writings.* Translated by James Burton Robertson. New York: Edward Dunigan, 1844.

Moore-Jumonville, Robert. *The Hermeneutics of Historical Distance: Mapping the Terrain of American Biblical Criticism, 1880–1914.* Lanham, MD: University Press of America, 2002.

Moretti, Franco. *Distant Reading.* New York: Verso, 2013.

Morgan, Jo-Ann. Uncle Tom's Cabin *as Visual Culture.* Columbia: University of Missouri Press, 2007.

Myerson, Joel, ed. *Selected Letters of Nathaniel Hawthorne.* Columbus: Ohio State University Press, 2002.

———. *Transcendentalism: A Reader.* New York: Oxford University Press, 2000.

Newton, Adam Zachary. *Narrative Ethics.* Cambridge, MA: Harvard University Press, 1995.

Noble, Marianne. "The Ecstasies of Sentimental Wounding in *Uncle Tom's Cabin.*" *Yale Journal of Criticism* 10, no. 2 (1997): 295–320.

Noll, Mark. *America's God: From Jonathan Edwards to Abraham Lincoln.* New York: Oxford University Press, 2002.

———. "Nineteenth-Century American Biblical Interpretation." In Paul C. Gutjahr, ed., *Oxford Handbook of the Bible in America,* edited by Paul C. Gutjahr, 115–28. New York: Oxford University Press, 2017.

Nord, David Paul. *Faith in Reading: Religious Publishing and the Birth of Mass Media in America.* New York: Oxford University Press, 2004.

Novak, Barbara. *American Painting of the Nineteenth Century: Realism, Idealism, and the American Experience.* New York: Praeger, 1969.

Nussbaum, Martha. *Love's Knowledge: Essays on Philosophy and Literature.* New York: Oxford University Press, 1990.

———. *Upheavals of Thought: The Intelligence of Emotions.* New York: Cambridge University Press, 2001.

O'Loughlin, Jim. "Articulating Uncle Tom's Cabin." *New Literary History* 31, no. 3 (2000): 573–97.

"Original Portraits of Washington." *Putnam's Monthly* 6, no. 34 (October 1855): 337–49.

Osgood, Howard. "Real Higher Criticism." *Independent,* July 30, 1891.

Otten, Thomas. *A Superficial Reading of Henry James: Preoccupations with the Material World.* Columbus: Ohio State University Press, 2006.

Otter, Samuel. "Frank Webb's Still Life: Rethinking Literature and Politics Through *The Garies and Their Friends.*" *American Literary History* 20, no. 4 (2008): 728–52.

———. *Melville's Anatomies.* Berkeley: University of California Press, 1999.

———. *Philadelphia Stories: America's Literature of Race and Freedom.* New York: Oxford University Press, 2010.

"Our Artists.—No. IX. Benjamin West." *Godey's Magazine and Lady's Book* 35 (August 1847): 64.

"Our Friend the Collector." *Curio* 1, no. 1 (September 1887): 1–4.

Parker, Hershel. "Historical Note." In Melville, *Pierre*, 380.

Parker, Theodore. "A Discourse of the Transient and Permanent in Christianity" (1841). In *Transcendentalism: A Reader*, edited by Joel Myerson, 340–66. New York: Oxford University Press, 2000.

Pasquesi, Carina. "*The Morgesons*: Elizabeth Stoddard's *Ars Erotica*." *Legacy* 31, no. 2 (2014): 183–206.

Percival, M. O. *A Reading of* Moby-Dick. New York: Octagon, [1950] 1967.

Phelps, Elizabeth Stuart. *Beyond the Gates*. In *Three Spiritualist Novels*, edited by Nina Baym, 139–232. Urbana: University of Illinois Press, 2000.

———. *Chapters from a Life*. Boston: Houghton Mifflin, 1900.

———. *The Gates Ajar*. Boston: Fields, Osgood, [1868] 1869.

———. "The Great Hope." In *In After Days: Thoughts on the Future Life*, edited by William Dean Howells, 19–41. New York: Harper & Brothers, 1910.

"Pierre." *Literary World*, August 21, 1852.

Pierson, Arthur T. *The Bible and Spiritual Criticism*. New York: Baker & Taylor, 1905.

Pippin, Robert. *Henry James and Modern Moral Life*. New York: Cambridge University Press, 2000.

Poland, Lynn. "The New Criticism, Neoorthodoxy, and the New Testament." *Journal of Religion* 65, no. 4 (1985): 459–77.

Porter, Carolyn. "After the New Historicism." *New Literary History* (1990): 253–72.

———. *Seeing and Being: The Plight of the Participant Observer in Emerson, James, Adams, and Faulkner*. Middletown, CT: Wesleyan University Press, 1981.

"Portraiture of Washington: Being an Appendix to the Custis Recollections and Private Memoirs." *Crayon* 2, no. 25 (1855): 389.

Posnock, Ross. "Innocents at Home: Ross Posnock on the Legacy of Leslie Fiedler." *Bookforum* Summer 2003, n.p.

Prickett, Stephen. *Words and The Word: Language, Poetics, and Biblical Interpretation*. New York: Cambridge University Press, 1986.

"Protestantism versus the Church." *Catholic World*, October 1883, 1–13.

Prothero, Stephen. *American Jesus: How the Son of God Became a National Icon*. New York: Farrar, Straus & Giroux, 2003.

"Radical Higher Criticism in the Confessional." *Christian Observer* 90, no. 17 (April 23 1902): 1.

Ransom, John Crowe. "Criticism, Inc." *Virginia Quarterly Review* 13, no. 4 (1937): 586–602.

———. *God without Thunder: An Unorthodox Defense of Orthodoxy*. Hamden, CT: Archon, [1930] 1965.

Reed, Amy Louise. "Self-Portraiture in the Work of Nathaniel Hawthorne." *Studies in Philology* 23, no. 1 (1926): 40–54.

Reed, Ashley. "'I Have No Disbelief': Spiritualism and Secular Agency in Elizabeth Stoddard's *The Morgesons*." *J19* 5, no. 1 (Spring 2017): 151–77.

"Review 1—No Title." *Catholic World*, May 1902, 248.

"Reviews and Literary Notices." Rev. of *Rowse's Portrait of Emerson, Durand's Portrait of Bryant, Barry's Portrait of Whittier. Atlantic Monthly* 3 (May 1859): 653–54.

Rivett, Sarah. "Early American Religion in a Postsecular Age." *PMLA* 128, no. 4 (2013): 989–96.

Robbins, Bruce. "Not So Well Attached." *PMLA* 132, no. 2 (2017): 371–76.

Robie, Virginia. *By-Paths in Collecting.* New York: Century, 1912.

Rogin, Michael Paul. *Subversive Genealogy: The Politics and Art of Herman Melville.* New York: Alfred A. Knopf, 1983.

Rossi, Joseph. "Uncle Tom's Cabin and Protestantism in Italy." *American Quarterly* 11, no. 3 (1959): 416–24.

Schweitzer, Albert. *The Quest of the Historical Jesus: A Critical Study of Its Progress from Reimarus to Wrede.* Baltimore, MD: Johns Hopkins University Press, [1910] 1998.

Sedgwick, Eve Kosofsky. *Epistemology of the Closet.* Berkeley: University of California Press, 1990.

———. *Touching Feeling.* Durham, NC: Duke University Press, 2003.

Serpell, C. Namwali. "Mutual Exclusion, Oscillation, and Ethical Projection in *The Crying of Lot 49* and *The Turn of the Screw*." *Narrative* 16, no. 3 (2008): 223–55.

———. *Seven Modes of Uncertainty.* Cambridge, MA: Harvard University Press, 2014.

Silverman, Gillian. *Bodies and Books: Reading and the Fantasy of Communion in Nineteenth-Century America.* Philadelphia: University of Pennsylvania Press, 2012.

Siogvolk, Paul. "Nathaniel Hawthorne: *The Blithedale Romance*." In "Schediasms," *Knickerbocker; or New York Monthly Magazine* 40, no. 5 (November 1852): 381–85.

Siskin, Clifford, and William Warner. "Stopping Cultural Studies." *PMLA Profession* (2008): 94–107.

Smith, Gail. "From the Seminary to the Parlor: The Popularization of Hermeneutics in *The Gates Ajar*." *Arizona Quarterly* 54, no. 2 (1998): 99–133.

Smith, Shawn Michelle. *American Archives: Gender, Race, and Class in Visual Culture.* Princeton, NJ: Princeton University Press, 1999.

Sontag, Susan. *Against Interpretation.* New York: Farrar, Straus & Giroux, 1966.

Spillers, Hortense. "Changing the Letter: The Yokes, the Jokes of Discourse, or, Mrs. Stowe, Mr. Reed." In *Black, White, and in Color*, 176–202. Chicago: University of Chicago Press, 2003.

Spivak, Gayatri. "Ethics and Politics in Tagore, Coetzee, and Certain Scenes of Teaching." *diacritics* 32, nos. 3–4 (2002): 17–31.

Stein, Jordan Alexander. "*The Blithedale Romance*'s Queer Style." *ESQ* 55 (2009): 211–36.

Stoddard, Elizabeth. *The Morgesons and Other Writings, Published and Unpublished.* Edited by Lawrence Buell and Sandra Zagarell. Philadelphia: University of Pennsylvania Press, 1984.

———. "The Prescription." *Harper's New Monthly Magazine* 28 (December 1863–May 1864): 794–800.

———. Letter dated June 5, 1857, in the *Daily Alta*, July 12, 1857, 1.

Stokes, Claudia. *The Altar at Home.* Philadelphia: University of Pennsylvania Press, 2015.

Stowe, Harriet Beecher. *Agnes of Sorrento* (1862). Reprint of 23rd ed. (1890). St. Clair Shores, MI: Scholarly Press, 1970.

———. Letter to Gamaliel Bailey, March 9, 1851. Reprinted in *The Oxford Harriet Beecher Stowe Reader,* edited by Joan Hedrick, 65–66. New York: Oxford University Press, 1999.

———. Preface to Charles Beecher, *The Incarnation; Or, Pictures of the Virgin and Her Son.* New York: Harper & Brothers, 1849.

———. *Uncle Tom's Cabin* (1852). New York: Oxford University Press, 1998.

———. *Uncle Tom's Cabin.* Norton Critical Edition. Edited by Elizabeth Ammons. New York: W. W. Norton, 1993.

Szczesiul, Anthony E. "The Canonization of Tom and Eva: Catholic Hagiography and *Uncle Tom's Cabin.*" *American Transcendental Quarterly* 10, no. 1 (1996): 59–72.

Tanner, Tony. *Adultery in the Novel: Contract and Transgression.* Baltimore, MD: Johns Hopkins University Press, 1979.

Taves, Ann. "Context and Meaning: Roman Catholic Devotion to the Blessed Sacrament in Mid-Nineteenth-Century America." *Church History* 54, no. 4 (1989): 482–45.

Taylor, Charles. *A Secular Age.* Cambridge, MA: Belknap Press of Harvard University Press, 2007.

Terry, Milton. *Biblical Hermeneutics. A Treatise on the Interpretation of the Old and New Testaments.* 2nd ed. New York: Phillips & Hunt, 1885.

Thoreau, Henry David. *Walden.* 150th ed. Edited by J. Lyndon Shanley. Princeton, NJ: Princeton University Press, [1971] 2004.

———. *A Week on the Concord and Merrimack Rivers.* Princeton, NJ: Princeton University Press, [1980] 2004.

Tillich, Paul. *Dynamics of Faith.* New York: Harper Torchbooks, 1957.

Tomlinson, H. M. Preface to Melville, *Pierre*. New York: Dutton, 1929.

Tompkins, Jane. The Other American Renaissance." In *The American Renaissance Reconsidered*, edited by Walter Benn Michaels and Donald Pease, 34–57. Baltimore, MD: Johns Hopkins University Press, 1985.

———. *Sensational Designs: The Cultural Work of American Fiction, 1790–1860*. New York: Oxford University Press, 1985.

"*Uncle Tom's Cabin*." *Littell's Living Age*, October 16, 1852.

"*Uncle Tom's Cabin*." *Mercersburg Review* (Lancaster, PA), July 1852, http://utc.iath .virginia.edu/reviews/rere116at.html (accessed October 14, 2019).

Veeser, H. Aram, ed. *The New Historicism Reader*. New York: Routledge, 1994.

Verheyen, Egon. "'The most exact representation of the Original': Remarks on Portraits of George Washington by Gilbert Stuart and Rembrandt Peale." In *Retaining the Original: Multiple Originals, Copies, and Reproductions, Studies in the History of Art*, 127–39. Vol. 20. Washington, DC: National Gallery of Art, 1989.

Warhol, Robyn. *Having a Good Cry: Effeminate Feelings and Pop-Culture Forms*. Columbus: Ohio State University Press, 2003.

Warner, Susan. *The Wide, Wide World*. New York: Feminist Press at the City University of New York, 1987.

Watson, Thomas, and Samuel Lee. *The Bible and the Closet and Secret Prayer Successfully Managed*. Edited by John Overton Choules. Boston: Gould, Kendall & Lincoln, 1842.

Weber, Timothy. "The Two-Edged Sword: The Fundamentalist Use of the Bible." In Hatch and Noll, eds., *The Bible in America*, 101–20.

Weinstein, Cindy. "Heaven's Tense: Narration in *The Gates Ajar*." *Novel* 45, no. 1 (2012): 56–70.

Wells, Herbert George. *Boon, The Mind of the Race, The Wild Asses of the Devil, and The Last Trump*. London: T. Fisher Unwin, 1915.

Wheeler, Charlotte Bickersteth. *Our Master's Footsteps; Or, Bible Class Notes for Thoughtful Girls*. London: Elliot Stock, 1883.

Wickman, Matthew. "Theology Still?" *PMLA* 132.3 (2017): 674–80.

Wiegman, Robyn. "Fiedler and Sons." In *Race and the Subject of Masculinities*, edited by Harry Stecopolous and Michael Uebel, 45–68. Durham, NC: Duke University Press, 1997.

Williams, Susan S. *Confounding Images: Photography and Portraiture in Antebellum American Fiction*. Philadelphia: University of Pennsylvania Press, 1997.

Wineapple, Brenda. "Hawthorne and Melville; or, The Ambiguities." In *Hawthorne and Melville: Writing a Relationship*, edited by Jana Argersinger and Leland S. Person, 51–69. Athens: University of Georgia Press, 2008.

Yarmolinsky, Avrahm. *Picturesque United States, 1811, 1812, 1813: Being a Memoir on Paul Svinin.* New York: William Edwin Rudge, 1930.

Yoxall, Y. H. *The ABC about Collecting.* London: London Opinion Curio Club, 1908.

Zboray, Ronald J., and Mary Saracino Zboray. *Everyday Ideas: Socioliterary Experience among Antebellum New Englanders.* Knoxville: University of Tennessee Press, 2006.

INDEX

Abbott, Lyman, 56
aesthetics: antisentimental, 23; of collage, 132–41, 151, 153–56, 159, 167; ethics and, 166; Protestant, 48; restraint in, 30. *See also* beauty; sublime
affect theory, 25
Agnes of Sorrento (Stowe), 71, 195n5
Ahlstrom, Sydney, 33–34
Allston, Washington, 95
American Renaissance (Matthiessen), 16, 19
American Tract Society, 31
American Woman's Home, The (Catherine Beecher), 131
Angus, Joseph, *Bible Hand-Book*, 63–64, 66
anti-Catholicism, 12, 18–19, 23, 28–30, 35, 42, 44, 48–52, 60, 61, 71, 91–96, 103, 128, 130, 162–67, 188; conservative, 28–30, 51; love story of, 32; rationale of, 116; in reviews of *Uncle Tom's Cabin*, 72. *See also* Catholicism; Protestantism
antihistoricism: in literary studies, 48, 176, 187; in reading, 41; theological, 23, 28. *See also* historicism
antisentimentalism: in aesthetics, 23; in literary studies, 28, 46, 48–52, 163. *See also* sentimentalism

Approach to Literature, An (Brooks et al.), 48–49
Arabian Nights, The, 148
Armstrong, Nancy, 17, 182, 183; *Desire and Domestic Fiction*, 17
Arnold, Matthew, 28
Art of Beauty, The (Haweis), 139
Art of Decoration, The (Haweis), 139, 146
Art of Dress, The (Haweis), 139
Athenaeum portrait, 100, 102, 103. *See also* portraiture; Stuart, Gilbert
Atlantic, 123
Attridge, Derek, 25, 169–75, 181–83
Auden, W. H., 46
Augustine, 49
Austen, Jane, *Pride and Prejudice*, 17
Awkward Age, The (James), 171

Bakhtin, Mikhail, 15, 186, 192n24
Barnes, Elizabeth, 70–71
Barth, Karl, 28, 43–44, 46
Barthes, Roland, 76, 184
Bayley, John, 152
Beam, Dorri, 142
Beautiful Houses (Haweis), 139
beauty, 109, 142; erotic, 159. *See also* aesthetics

Beecher, Catherine, 184; *The American Woman's Home*, 131; *Domestic Treatise*, 131
Beecher, Charles, *The Incarnation; or, Pictures of the Virgin and Her Son*, 96
Beecher, Henry Ward, 33, 56, 97, 98
Beecher, Lyman, 56
Beers, Henry, 123, 124
Beloved (Morrison), 167
Berlant, Lauren, 158
Bermingham, Ann, 132
Bersani, Leo, 17, 137
Best, Stephen, 8, 175, 176, 188, 193n2
Beyond the Gates (Phelps), 78
Bible, 4, 6, 24, 32–40, 85, 116, 148, 190; authority of, 43; characters of, 96; interest in, 75; invisibility of God in, 30, 95; language of, 30, 63; mysteries of, 81; readings of, 33, 40, 42, 48, 53–57, 62–67, 70–73, 76–80, 84; revelation from, 28–30, 32–40, 42, 50, 63–67; and theology, 89. *See also* Protestantism; revelation
"Bible and the Closet, The" (Watson), 65
Bible Hand-Book (Angus), 63, 64, 66
Billings, Hammatt, 77
Billy Budd (Melville), 44, 48–52
Blithedale Romance, The (Hawthorne), 5, 58, 59, 89–122, 124, 141; review of, 105
Bodies and Books (Silverman), 19
Booth, Wayne, 6, 25, 169–76, 181; *The Company We Keep*, 6
Bozovic, Marijeta, 178
Brady, Mathew, 104
Briggs, Charles, 39, 194n46
Brinkman, Bartholomew, 132

Britain: domestic novel in, 183; Gothic Revival in, 130; Oxford Movement in, 130; travels in, 97
Brodhead, Richard, 9
Brookes, James Hall, 28, 39
Brooks, Peter, 81, 118, 149
Brown, Bill, 137, 160
Brown, Gillian, 61, 74, 139, 183, 184
Browning, Robert, 49
Brownson, Orestes, 82
Buber, Martin, 160; *I and Thou*, 127
Buell, Lawrence, 6
Bushnell, Horace, 33, 35, 43, 193n30
Butler, Judith, 6, 169

Calvinism: austerity of, 142; baggage of, 70; theology of, 44, 91. *See also* Protestantism; theology
Campbell, Alexander, 33, 34
capitalism, 61, 175; dehumanizing effects of, 139, 152; literary works as expressions of, 183
Cardinal, Roger, 140
Carroll, John, 36
Catholicism: anti-Protestant, 66–67; conversion to, 47, 129; devotional writers of, 30; ecclesiology of, 65; fetishism in, 51, 52; hagiography in, 54; imagery of, 91, 92, 96, 195n5; neo-Thomist, 45; practices of, 10, 27, 86, 91, 96, 129, 130, 148, 160, 188; revelation in, 3–5, 23, 27, 29; rituals of, 4, 8, 29, 30, 37, 62, 65, 81, 91, 195n5; sacraments of, 29–31, 48, 63, 65, 66, 72; Saint Cecilia in, 148; salvation in, 53; sensuality of, 106, 128; sentimentalism and, 71; traditional, 48; transcendence in, 12, 29, 65, 73; worship in, 56, 62, 66, 71, 86, 91, 92, 98, 131. *See also* anti-Catholicism;

Christianity; religion; sacrament; transubstantiation

Catholic World, 47, 56, 66, 113

Chalmers, Thomas, 84, 85; "On the New Heavens and the New Earth," 85

Channing, William Emery, 34, 35

Chesebro, Caroline, *Victoria, or the World Overcome,* 125

Christ Healing the Sick (West), 95

Christianity: deconstruction of privacy in, 51; doctrine of, 80; performative, 118. *See also* Jesus Christ; religion

Christian Union, 27, 48, 49, 79

Civil War, 13, 54, 79, 82, 123, 124, 179

Clarke, William Newton, 39

Coetzee, J. M., 7, 181–82

Coleridge, Samuel Taylor, 28, 35, 43, 175

"Come Back to the Raft Ag'in, Huck Honey" (Fiedler), 17

communion, 2, 3, 5, 12, 19, 22, 66, 75, 79–81, 87, 121, 130; adaptation of, 117; intimacy of, 22–24, 29, 58–63, 67, 82, 91, 93, 118, 129, 149, 152, 165–90; inward, 63; logic of, 75; love and, 13, 16, 22–25, 29, 57–60, 65–67, 73, 78, 87–91, 121–37, 146, 149, 162–90; model of, 73, 86, 135, 176, 177, 184, 185, 188; practice of, 10, 80; reading and, 8, 9, 19, 54–57, 60, 104, 111, 114; and revelation, 61, 62, 79, 87, 124, 154; sacrament of, 29–31, 35, 48, 72; sentimental, 53–87, 90, 113; social understanding of, 140; of spectators, 120; structure of, 61, 66, 131, 132; theatricality of, 150; transcendence and, 25, 29,

59, 62, 80. *See also* intimacy; love; revelation

communitarianism, 61

Company We Keep, The (Booth), 6

Comte, Auguste, 37, 38

consumer culture: historicist lens of, 144; modern, 161; popular, 134; as Protestant counterreformation, 129–40; Victorian, 160. *See also* material culture

Cook, Clarence, 137, 139

Coviello, Peter, 16, 20

Creech, James, 113

Criterion, 45, 46

Crystal Palace Exhibition (1851), 128

cultural politics, 8; power relations in, 163

Cumming, John, 96, 97; *Lectures on Romanism,* 96

daguerreotype, 103, 104

Daily Alta, 129

Dante, 115, 156

Darwin, Charles, 37

da Vinci, Leonardo, 97

Davis, Rebecca Harding, 125

Deleuze, Gilles, 175

Demant, V. A., 46

depth drive, Protestant, 4, 5, 9, 16, 20, 24, 56, 82, 89, 90, 93. *See also* Protestantism

Derrida, Jacques, 170, 174

desire: disturbed, 67; endless, 98; incestuous, 85; as production, 175; unsatisfiable, 96; white for black Americans, 18, 67. *See also* emotions

Desire and Domestic Fiction (Armstrong), 17

Dickens, Charles, 15; characters of, 186

Dillon, Elizabeth, 61, 180–81
Domestico, Anthony, 45, 46
Domestic Treatise (Catherine Beecher), 131
Douglas, Ann, 21, 28, 44, 49–52, 61, 80
Dynamics of Faith (Tillich), 44

Eaglestone, Robert, 168
Eagleton, Terry, 174
Eastern Orthodoxy, 47. *See also* Christianity
Edwards, Jonathan, 44, 45
Eliot, George, 15
Eliot, T. S., 42, 45–47; *The Waste Land,* 45
Elliott, Emory, 116, 118, 199n52
Emerson, Ralph Waldo, 16, 34, 35, 43, 45, 55
emotions: and aesthetics, 95; materialization of, 180; paradox of, 94; ritualization of, 180. *See also* desire
Empson, William, 45
ethicism. *See* literary ethics
Evans, Dorinda, 102

Faber, Frederick William, 30
Feldman, Jessica, 134, 137, 142
Felski, Rita, 6, 7, 10, 21, 175–79, 188
feminist literary criticism, 48, 49, 70, 174
Feminization of American Culture, The (Douglas), 49, 50
Fenton, Elizabeth, 19, 29, 33
Fessenden, Tracy, 12, 15, 19, 29, 31, 163
fetishism: commodity, 127; consumer, 129
fiction: gothic, 18; readings of, 55–57; realist, 137. *See also* literature

Fiedler, Leslie, 192n35; "Come Back to the Raft Ag'in, Huck Honey," 17; *Love and Death in the American Novel,* 5, 17–19
Fisher, Philip, 74
formalism, 7, 25, 45
Forms (Levine), 178
Franchot, Jenny, 14, 15, 19, 29, 34, 79, 92, 106, 113, 197n37
Frank, Lucy, 61, 62, 87
Fugitive Slave Act, 73
Fuller, Margaret, 142, 199n43
fundamentalism, 41
Fussell, Edwin Sill, 125, 128, 149

Gallagher, Catherine, 46, 184, 186; *Practicing New Historicism,* 184
Gates Ajar, The (Phelps), 5, 27, 29, 48, 49, 54–63, 78–81, 87, 89, 163, 189; merchandizing of, 60; review of, 78, 92; sequels to, 60, 78
Gates Between, The (Phelps), 78
General Washington Receiving His Mother's Last Blessing (Powell), 98
genius: awakening of, 18; romantic, 116; work of, 115
Germany, 39
Gilmore, Michael, 70, 72
Girard, René, 57
Godey's, 95, 131, 200n18
God without Thunder: An Unorthodox Defense of Orthodoxy (Ransom), 46–47
Goffman, Erving, 167
Golden Bowl, The (James), 5, 149–61, 164–67, 182, 189
Gordon, Beverly, 132, 200nn17–19
Graff, Gerald, 41
Gray, James, 40–41, 63; *How to Master the English Bible,* 40, 63

"Great Hope, The" (Phelps), 1
Greenblatt, Stephen, 175, 183–86;
    Practicing New Historicism, 184
Greenhalgh, Adam, 103, 198n27
Greenough, Horatio, 95, 98, 198n18;
    Head of Christ, 95
Griffin, Susan, 29, 32
Guattari, Felix, 175
Gutjahr, Paul C., 30, 37–38
Guy Domville (James), 128, 149

Hale, Dorothy, 7, 16, 162, 168, 169, 185, 186
Hall, Herbert Byng, 139, 151
Halttunen, Karen, 58
Haney, David, 174
Hatch, Nathan, 32
Haweis, H. R., 150; *The Art of Beauty,*
    139; *The Art of Decoration,* 139,
    146; *The Art of Dress,* 139; *Beautiful
    Houses,* 139
Hawthorne, Nathaniel, 2, 5, 9, 24, 28,
    52, 58–59, 88–124, 126, 128, 142,
    185, 190; *The House of the Seven
    Gables,* 103; *The Marble Faun,*
    105–7; "The Minister's Black Veil,"
    90; *Mosses from the Old Manse,*
    88, 104; *The Scarlet Letter,* 104, 106;
    "Sights from a Steeple," 106. See also
    Blithedale Romance, The
"Hawthorne and His Mosses" (Mel-
    ville), 88–91, 111
Head of Christ (Greenough), 95
Head of Christ (Sallman), 103
Hecker, Isaac, 113
Hendler, Glenn, 61, 184
Herder, Johann Gottfried, 185, 194n34
higher criticism, 37, 38, 50. *See also*
    historicism
historicism, 3, 7, 9–11, 14–15,
    20–21, 24–25, 28–29, 42–43, 162;

aggressive, 183; biblical, 14, 38, 40–43,
    185; and literary ethics, 48,
    62, 162–90; reductive, 184. *See also*
    antihistoricism; higher criticism;
    New Historicism
history: American literary, 9, 16; art and,
    178; cultural, 3, 12, 20; determinism
    of, 43; intellectual, 12; model of, 187,
    188; political, 20; religious, 14, 39,
    62–63; suspension of, 32, 177; theo-
    logical, 3; and transcendence, 11, 42,
    44; views of, 49, 177, 178
Holden's Dollar Magazine, 104
Holland, David, 32
homophobia, 51, 52
Hopkins, Pauline, 142
House and Home Papers (Stowe), 183
House of the Seven Gables, The (Haw-
    thorne), 103
Howard, June, 180, 184
Howard, Leon, 112
Howe, Irving, 105
Howells, William Dean, *In After Days,*
    1–2, 25, 81
How to Master the English Bible (Gray),
    40, 63
Hulme, T. E., 42–43
Hutchinson, Anne, 32
Hutner, Gordon, 46

I and Thou (Buber), 127
ideology: evils of, 21; market, 21; Prot-
    estant, 31; of transcendence, 11. *See
    also* ideology critique
ideology critique, 9, 52, 162, 176, 183.
    See also ideology; symptomatic
    reading
*Illustrated Self-Instructor in Phrenology
    and Physiology* (Fowler brothers),
    102

In After Days (Howells), 1–2, 25, 81
Incarnation, The; or, Pictures of the Virgin and Her Son (Charles Beecher), 96
Independent, 97
individualism, 61, 83
interpretation: boundaries for, 91; collaboration in, 59, 67, 79; ethical, 168; good, 22; immediacy in, 44; intimacy in, 28, 29, 57, 62, 163, 176, 180, 188; model for, 22, 176; and performance, 127; representation and, 93; work of, 24, 56–59, 89, 94. *See also* representation
intimacy: of communion, 22–24, 29, 58–63, 67, 82, 91, 93, 118, 129, 149, 152, 165–90; erotic, 114; family, 145, 146; feelings of, 100, 140, 143, 145; happily mediated, 129; and humor, 115; and identification, 74; in interpretation, 28, 29, 57, 62, 163, 176, 180, 188; Jamesian, 150; and love, 6, 29, 53, 57; model of, 24, 67; nonrevelatory, 90, 109; public, 61; and reading, 56, 57, 60, 63–67, 105, 181–82; real, 103, 129, 160; revelatory, 27, 34, 37, 38, 42, 44, 58, 62–67, 88–91, 97, 103, 127, 165, 189; renegotiation of, 145; scapegoating, 70; and spectatorship, 135, 140, 149; transcendence and, 37, 62, 80, 162, 167; unconventional, 141. *See also* communion; revelation
Italy: improvisatores of, 120; travels in, 106

James, Henry, 1–10, 13, 20–25, 28, 47, 48, 52, 58–59, 73, 109, 120, 123–29, 132–36, 139, 149–61, 164–69, 174, 179, 182, 201n40; account of novel form of, 185, 186; *The Awkward Age*, 171; characters of, 182; *The Golden Bowl*, 5, 149–61, 164–67, 182, 189; *Guy Domville*, 128, 149; love in, 188, 189; *The Portrait of a Lady*, 174, 182; *Washington Square*, 169
Jameson, Frederic, 174, 176
Jesus Christ, 87, 91, 94–98, 103. *See also* Christianity
Judaism, 47. *See also* religion

Kant, Immanuel, 28
Kaufmann, Michael, 13
Kelley, Mary, 31
Kenyon Review, 46
Kete, Mary Louise, 61
Kierkegaard, Søren, 43, 45
Knickerbocker, 105
Kristeva, Julia, 67

Lacan, Jacques, 67
LaCapra, Dominick, 165
Ladies' Repository, 78
Landy, Joshua, 165
language: of Bible, 30, 63; difficult, 173; of friendship, 170; of love, 90; and performance, 118; pictorial, 94; poetic, 94; as representation of social, 186; and revelation, 28, 42, 76
LaPorte, Charles, 11
Latour, Bruno, 177, 178
Lauter, Paul, 47, 48
Leach, William, 129, 130
Lears, Jackson, 56, 130
Lecourt, Sebastian, 11
Lectures on Romanism (Cumming), 96
Lee, Samuel, "Secret Prayer Successfully Managed," 65
Lee, Roland F., 45

Levinas, Emmanuel, 90, 165, 166, 171
Levine, Caroline, 178, 179, 202n19;
    Forms, 178
Levinson, Marjorie, 7, 191n9
literary ethics, 3–9, 11, 15, 16, 20–25,
    28, 29, 52, 62, 90, 127; ahistorical,
    162–90; on emotions, 49, 169, 170;
    feminist, 48, 49, 70, 174; historicist,
    11, 21, 162–90; humanist, 168–72;
    Marxist, 174, 186; poststructuralist,
    168–72, 174, 182; revelatory ideal
    in, 163–90
literary historicism. *See* historicism
literary history, 9, 22–23, 132
Literary World, 95, 112
literature: American, 21, 42, 44–46, 50,
    52, 62, 126, 162, 181, 192n34; Aris-
    totelian view of, 168; British, 17–20,
    130, 183; demystification of, 11, 13;
    love of, 3, 8, 14, 67–78; modernist,
    43, 45, 181. *See also* fiction; novel;
    poetry; romance
Literature as Conduct (J. H. Miller), 166
Littell's Living Age, 72
Liu, Alan, 187
Long, Lisa, 80
love: Christian, 121; and communion,
    13, 16, 22–25, 29, 57–60, 65–67,
    78, 87–91, 121, 124, 126, 129, 132,
    134–37, 146, 149, 162–90; definition
    of, 31; emotions of, 173; erotic,
    126, 145; eternity of, 1; experience
    of, 29, 56, 57, 117; false, 11; of God,
    3, 5, 45, 63–65, 72, 87, 97; and inter-
    pretation, 17, 22; and intimacy, 6;
    language of, 90; portrayal of, 20,
    56, 57, 126; reading as a story of,
    67–78, 68, 69, 127, 128; revelatory,
    2–3, 22, 23, 63, 78, 88, 126, 144–45,
    159, 162–90; sentimental, 117;

sisterly, 145–49; social actors in, 62;
    transcendent, 2, 4, 14, 29, 57; trans-
    formative, 97; true, 11, 56; universal-
    ization of, 83; unrequited, 170, 171,
    182. *See also* communion; marriage;
    revelation
Love, Heather, 13, 14, 25, 167, 175–77,
    201n2
Love and Death in the American Novel
    (Fiedler), 5, 17–19
Love's Knowledge (Nussbaum), 6, 15,
    164
Loving Literature (Lynch), 19
Lukacs, Georg, 17
Lukasik, Christopher, 102
Lynch, Deidre, 7, 13, 17, 19, 20; *Loving
    Literature*, 19

Mandrillon, Joseph, 101
Marble Faun, The (Hawthorne), 105–7
Marcus, Sharon, 8, 175, 176, 188,
    193n2
marriage: in British novel, 18; of com-
    munion, 168; conventions of, 182;
    false, 115; happy, 156, 160, 165, 168;
    relations of, 140, 153–56; success in,
    127, 155. *See also* love
Marshall, John, 101
Marty, Martin, 30
Marxism, 46
masculinity: authority of, 92, 93, 98;
    and authorship, 23, 92, 103; depth
    drive of, 90, 93; and power, 24, 103;
    of Protestantism, 197n37
Massachusetts Sabbath School
    Society, 64
material culture, 128–30, 140. *See also*
    consumer culture
Matthiessen, F. O., 9; *American
    Renaissance*, 16, 19

McDannell, Colleen, 130–31, 200n14
Melville, Herman, 2, 9, 21, 24, 28,
   45, 48, 50–52, 58, 59, 75, 88–128,
   151, 185, 190; revival of, 4, 44, 47,
   48; *Billy Budd*, 44, 48–52; "Hawthorne and His Mosses," 88–91, 111;
   Moby-Dick, 111, 121; *Pierre*, 5, 45,
   50, 58, 59, 111–22, 124, 141; "The
   Tartarus of Maids," 92
Mercersburg Review, 72
Merish, Lori, 183, 184
mesmerism, 107
Miller, J. Hillis, 6, 154, 166–74, 182,
   183; *Literature as Conduct*, 166
Miller, Perry, 9, 12, 45
Milton, John, 94, 116
"Minister's Black Veil, The" (Haw-
   thorne), 90
Moby-Dick (Melville), 111, 121
modernism: grounds of, 42; literary,
   43, 45, 48, 134, 141–42, 181; virtues
   of, 21
modernity, 12; religion and, 13
Möhler, Johann Adam, 36–37, 65, 66
Moody Bible Institute, 40, 41
Moore, Marianne, 45, 132
Moore-Jumonville, Robert, 38
Moretti, Franco, 13, 14, 177, 201n2
Morgan, Jo Ann, 77
Morgesons, The (Stoddard), 5,
   140–49
Morrison, Toni, 7; *Beloved*, 167
Mosses from the Old Manse (Haw-
   thorne), 88, 104

National Era, 58
neo-orthodoxy, 23, 28, 41–48, 90, 165.
   See also Protestantism
Nevins, William, 34–35

New Criticism, 23, 28, 40–48, 52
New Historicism, 162, 176, 183–87,
   202n15. *See also* historicism
Newton, Adam Zachary, 180
New York Observer, 132, 133
New York Review of Books, 51
Niebuhr, H. Richard, 44, 45
Niebuhr, Reinhold, 44, 46
Noble, Marianne, 57, 67, 70, 71
Noll, Mark, 34, 37
North American Review, 94, 95
Novak, Barbara, 94
novel: American, 18, 19, 48; autobi-
   ographical, 117; ethical value of,
   15; genre of, 16; gothic, 18; history
   of, 17, 18; love stories of, 16, 17;
   realist, 17; sentimental, 7, 54, 56, 57,
   61, 66, 89, 134, 141, 185; Victorian,
   15. *See also* literature; romance;
   sentimentalism
Nussbaum, Martha, 6, 15, 25, 154,
   164–66, 169–76, 201n39; *Love's
   Knowledge*, 6, 15, 164

"On the New Heavens and the New
   Earth" (Chalmers), 85
Osgood, Charles, 104
Osmond, Gilbert, 182
Otter, Samuel, 113, 184, 202n31

painting: and depth, 100; of God,
   94, 95; and landscape, 94. *See also*
   portraiture
Pan-American Exposition (1901), 128
paper doll house, 132–37, 133, 135, 136,
   141, 150, 160, 163, 166, 167, 200n18
paper dolls, 138, 150
Pasquesi, Carina, 141, 144
patriarchy, 21, 61; invisible, 70, 92, 103

Peale, Rembrandt, 98, 100–102; *Patriae Pater,* 101, 198n18
Pease, Donald, 9
Percival, M. O., 45
performance: of author, 190; interpretation and, 59, 127; mutual, 156, 158, 167; spectatorship and, 149, 167. *See also* spectatorship
Phelps, Elizabeth Stuart, 1–3, 5, 9, 10, 13, 24–27, 31, 49, 50, 54–62, 66, 67, 79–87, 90, 91, 118, 125–30, 179, 183; *Beyond the Gates,* 78; *The Gates Between,* 78; "The Great Hope," 1; pictorialism of, 92. See also *Gates Ajar, The*
philosophy: German, 28; Scottish Common Sense, 183
Pierre (Melville), 5, 45, 50, 58, 59, 111–22, 124, 141
Pierson, A. T., 39
Poe, Edgar Allan, 114
poetry: Bible as, 94; of Browning, 49; of Whitman, 16. *See also* literature
Poland, Lynn, 42, 43
politics: of interpretation, 176–78; of reader, 172
Porter, Carolyn, 11, 16, 187, 188
Portrait of a Lady, The (James), 174, 182
portraiture, 93–95, 98–100, 116, 117; great, 99; power of, 100, 119. *See also* painting
Posnock, Ross, 17, 18
Pound, Ezra, 45
Powell, William, *General Washington Receiving His Mother's Last Blessing,* 98
Practicing New Historicism (Greenblatt and Gallagher), 184

"Prescription, The" (Stoddard), 140–41
Pride and Prejudice (Austen), 17
Protestantism: antihistoricist, 28, 29, 41; Catholic-friendly, 31, 56, 167, 188; conservative, 32, 38, 41, 42, 48, 51, 81, 128, 162, 163, 167; cult of invisibility of, 24; fundamentalist, 41; Gilded Age, 130; hermeneutics of, 87; iconophobia in, 91, 93–99, 102, 104, 106, 121; intimacy in, 30, 31, 36, 98; invisibility of God in, 24, 62, 95, 103, 117; liberal, 38, 43, 71, 97, 128; and literacy, 60; literalism in, 79; materialism in, 130, 131; orthodoxy of, 45, 47, 55, 61, 125, 167; propriety of, 27; resurgence of, 44; revelation in, 3–5, 10–14, 23, 27, 30, 42, 48, 62–67, 71, 76, 91, 124, 132; revivalist, 66; songs of, 51; theology of, 8, 27–29, 66, 71, 91; transcendence in, 12, 42, 66, 70; worship in, 86, 91. *See also* anti-Catholicism; Bible; Calvinism; Christianity; depth drive, Protestant; neo-orthodoxy; Reformation; religion; theology
"Protestantism versus the Church," 66
psychology, nineteenth-century, 102
publishing: economy of, 104; in New York, 123; of a pamphlet, 100
Putnam's, 131

Quest of the Historical Jesus, The (Schweitzer), 41

Rancière, Jacques, 180
Ransom, John Crowe, *God without Thunder: An Unorthodox Defense of Orthodoxy,* 46, 47

realism, 5, 18, 57, 146; psychological, 5, 16, 24, 60; romance and, 123, 124

Reed, Amy Louise, 89, 105

Reed, Ashley, 12, 125

Reformation, 130. *See also* Protestantism

religion: American civil, 103; American Protestant, 167; authority in, 30; demographics of, 4; explanations of, 15; hybrids of, 55, 56; idea of, 11, 12; intimacy and, 22–24, 27, 29, 30, 60–63, 67; and literary studies, 1–16; and modernity, 13; natural, 130; orthodoxy in, 45; promises of, 107; and race, 71; and reading, 201n2; and romance, 131; tension in, 70, 71, 81. *See also* Catholicism; Christianity; Protestantism; revelation; theology; transcendence

Reni, Guido, 97

representation: forms of, 51; and interpretation, 93; literary, 3; proper, 91; and Protestantism, 23; of self, 24; space of, 77; taboo, 92; unmediated, 96. *See also* interpretation; painting

revelation, 19, 22, 42–44, 79, 124, 189; Catholic ideal of, 23, 27; communion and, 61, 62, 79, 87, 124, 154; critique of, 89, 126; erotic, 126; failure of, 165; ideal of, 142; intimacy of, 27, 34, 37, 38, 42, 44, 58, 62–67, 88–91, 97, 103, 127, 165, 189; invisible, 88; knowledge and, 140; language of, 28, 42; love and, 2–3, 22, 23, 63, 78, 88, 126, 144–45, 159, 162–90; moments of, 144; mutual, 121; one-to-one, 119; overvaluing of, 122; promising of, 67, 90, 113; Protestant ideal of, 3–5, 10–14, 23, 27,

30, 42, 48, 62–67, 71, 76, 91, 132; reading and, 22, 30, 32–37, 55, 63–67, 164, 165, 168, 171; romantic, 89, 96, 126; sensation of, 49; transformative, 168; transparency of, 141, 154–55, 158–59, 173; of truth, 180; wish for, 94; withholding of, 7, 23–27, 45, 48–52, 58, 67, 76, 89, 113, 114, 162, 170, 179, 180, 190. *See also* Bible; communion; religion

Richardson, Samuel, 17

Rivett, Sarah, 12

Robbins, Bruce, 178, 187

Rogin, Michael Paul, 89, 113

romance: gothic, 5, 16; and realism, 123, 124; of self-invention, 18; value of, 110. *See also* novel

romanticism, 28, 43, 57; American, 44, 89; conventions of, 144; German, 84; gothic, 60; pastoral, 40; Protestant, 45; and sentimentalism, 90, 119

Rosier, Ned, 139

Ruskin, John, 130

Ruth Hall (Fern), 184

sacrament: aesthetic of, 70, 72; in Catholicism, 29–31, 48, 63; participation in, 121; presence of Christ in, 66; revelatory reading as, 64. *See also* Catholicism; religion

Sallman, Warner, *Head of Christ,* 103

Sánchez-Eppler, Karen, 61

Sand, George, 67

Scarlet Letter, The (Hawthorne), 104, 106

Schleiermacher, Friedrich, 28

Schweitzer, Albert, *The Quest of the Historical Jesus,* 41, 194n51

"Secret Prayer Successfully Managed" (S. Lee), 65

Secular Age, A (C. Taylor), 125
secularization, 11–13, 129
Sedgwick, Eve, 8, 10, 21, 28, 50–52, 57, 162, 175, 176, 191n10
sentimentalism, 27, 28, 32, 44, 49, 51, 57, 70, 113, 125, 179; accounts of, 21; and alienation, 115; and Catholicism, 71, 130; debate over, 28, 49; definition of, 61; evangelical, 98; false emotion of, 61, 91; flat characters of, 142; literary defenses of, 60, 162, 181, 184; middlebrow, 134; Protestant, 5, 13, 16, 54; romanticism and, 90, 119; scenes of, 20; typology of, 58. *See also* antisentimentalism
Serpell, C. Namwali, 7, 15, 127, 160, 168; *Seven Modes of Uncertainty,* 15
Shakespeare, William, 115, 173, 174
"Sights from a Steeple" (Hawthorne), 106
Silverman, Gillian, *Bodies and Books,* 19
Skinner, Otis, 67, 69
Smith, Gail, 79–80
Smith, Joseph, 32
social change, 62; in culture of display, 128–30, 139, 140, 142
social formalism, 186
spectatorship, 90, 93, 104, 135, 140, 167, 168; public, 180. *See also* performance; vicariousness
Spillers, Hortense, 67, 71, 85
Spiritualism, 55
Spivak, Gayatri, 6, 181
Spoffard, Harriet Prescott, 142
Stein, Jordan, 108
Stoddard, Elizabeth, 5, 24, 58, 59, 73, 109, 123–29, 132–49, 154, 161; *The*

Morgesons, 5, 140–49; "The Prescription," 140–41
Stoicism, 164
Stokes, Claudia, 33
Stowe, Harriet Beecher, 5, 20–24, 53–56, 60–62, 66, 67, 70–79, 83–87, 90, 91, 96, 118, 121, 125–30, 149, 179–85, 195nn4–5; *Agnes of Sorrento,* 71, 195n5; Calvinist baggage of, 70; domestic economy of, 74, 139; fiction of, 96; *House and Home Papers,* 183. *See also Uncle Tom's Cabin*
Stuart, Gilbert, 98–103, 111; Athenaeum portrait of, 100, 102, 103, 112, 198n27
Stuart, Moses, 37
subjectivity, 20, 73–74
sublime, 28, 39, 43, 48, 51, 59, 76; Protestant, 76; transparency and, 143. *See also* aesthetics
Swedenborg, Emanuel, 84
Swift, Jonathan, 172, 174
symptomatic reading, 52, 71, 182, 193n2. *See also* ideology critique

Tanner, Tony, 17
"Tartarus of Maids, The" (Melville), 92
Taves, Ann, 31
Taylor, Charles, 12, 125, 191n13; *A Secular Age,* 125
Taylor, Isaac, 84
Terry, Milton, 39, 40
theater: artifice of, 150; pleasures in, 149
theology, 1, 10, 24, 87; anti-Catholic, 47; Bible and, 89; Calvinist, 44, 91; Catholic, 66; conservative, 31; crucifixion in, 70; heterodox, 16; liberal, 28, 31, 38, 39, 41, 44;

theology (*continued*)
modernist, 45; Protestant, 8, 27–29, 66, 167, 168. *See also* Catholicism; neo-orthodoxy; Protestantism; religion

Thoreau, Henry David, 16, 30

Tillich, Paul, *Dynamics of Faith*, 44

Tolstoy, Leo, 180

Tomlinson, H. M., 45, 112, 113

Tompkins, Jane, 21, 28, 52, 61, 162, 163, 181, 185

transcendence: artistic, 23; Catholic, 12, 62, 81, 128; communion and, 25, 29, 59; disembodied, 70; ethical, 10; of God, 42, 91; hidden, 49, 91; idea of, 11; immaterial, 35; intimacy and, 37, 62, 80, 162; literary, 10, 162, 187; multiple forms of, 12, 15, 125, 168; and otherness, 126; Protestant, 12, 128; seaside, 142–44. *See also* religion

Transcendentalism, 28, 34, 35, 41, 44

transubstantiation, 30, 87. *See also* Catholicism

Turner, Nat, 32

Two Marys at the Tomb (Weir), 95

Uncle Tom's Cabin (Stowe), 5, 55–61, 63, 67–78, 68, 69, 81, 89, 139, 149, 150, 179–80, 184; cultural portability of, 200n33; feminist account of, 70; theatrical versions of, 60, 69

Van Vechten, Carl, 47, 151

Veeser, H. Aram, 183, 186

Verheyen, Egon, 101, 102

vicariousness, 51, 52, 57, 70, 156. *See also* spectatorship

Victoria, or the World Overcome (Chesebro), 125

violence: racist, 70; redemption in view of, 70; revelation and, 140

Warfield, B. B., 39

Warner, Susan, 57; *The Wide, Wide World*, 57, 185

Washington, George, 98–100, 102, 103

Washington Square (James), 169

Waste Land, The (T. S. Eliot), 45

Watson, Thomas, "The Bible and the Closet," 65

Watt, Ian, 17

Weaver, Raymond, 47

Weber, Timothy, 41

Weinstein, Cindy, 80, 81

Weir, Robert, *Two Marys at the Tomb*, 95

Wells, H. G., 151

West, Benjamin, *Christ Healing the Sick*, 95

Wheeler, Charlotte Bickersteth, 65

Whipple, John Adams, 104

Whitman, Walt, 16

Wide, Wide World, The (Warner), 57, 185

Wiegman, Robyn, 18

Williams, Raymond, 174, 184

women: creativity of, 92; gender of, 72; Protestant, 131; sexuality of, 67, 92; suffering bodies of, 73

writing: life of, 89; of women, 92

Zboray, Mary, 54

Zboray, Ronald, 54

CPSIA information can be obtained
at www.ICGtesting.com
Printed in the USA
LVHW021406250620
658982LV00002B/577